"AL NEUHARTH IS A PLOTTER—AND PROUD OF IT."
—*The New York Times*

Al Neuharth, America's premier media tycoon and founder of *USA Today,* takes you inside newsrooms and boardrooms to tell you the plot of his amazing success story. A story that illustrates in delightfully devastating detail:

— How to be ready always to rock the boat

— How to best the boss

— How to beat backbiting with backbone

— How to write your own rules and form your own club

— How to wear a bull's-eye on your chest and shake off the darts and arrows that hit you

— How to scuttle the S.O.B.'s trying to get you

— How to use the right mix of niceness and nastiness

— How to stop critics from wrecking your plans

— Above all, how to have fun playing the game

"Al Neuharth brought new meaning to the word 'opportunity'."
—Rosalynn Carter

"Al Neuharth is the only man I know who would go after Moby Dick with a harpoon and a jar of tartar sauce."
—James Head,
former editor, *Parade Magazine*

Al Neuharth is the author of these other books:

 ▷ Plain Talk Across the USA

 ▷ Profiles of Power

 ▷ Truly One Nation

 ▷ Window on the World

 ▷ World Power Up Close

 ▷ Nearly One World

CONFESSIONS OF AN
S.O.B.

AL NEUHARTH

Ⓟ
A PLUME BOOK

PLUME
Published by the Penguin Group
Penguin Books USA Inc., 375 Hudson Street, New York, New York 10014, U.S.A.
Penguin Books Ltd, 27 Wrights Lane, London W8 5TZ, England
Penguin Books Australia Ltd, Ringwood, Victoria, Australia
Penguin Books Canada Ltd, 2801 John Street, Markham, Ontario, Canada L3R 1B4
Penguin Books (N.Z.) Ltd, 182-190 Wairau Road, Auckland 10, New Zealand

Penguin Books Ltd, Registered Offices: Harmondsworth, Middlesex, England

Published by Plume, an imprint of New American Library, a division of Penguin Books
USA Inc. Reprinted with permission of Doubleday, a division of Bantam Doubleday
Dell Publishing Group, Inc.

First Plume Printing, October, 1990
10 9 8 7 6 5 4 3 2 1

REGISTERED TRADEMARK—MARCA REGISTRADA

Printed in the United States of America

To my dear departed Mom, Christina:
May she relish these remembrances.

———————

To son Dan and daughter Jan:
Let them see the light of this legacy.

Contents

CONFESSIONS
OF AN
S.O.B.

I

WHEN YOU CALL ME THAT, SMILE

How dare I call me an S.O.B.?

What will my dear, deceased mother and father think?

I think they'll laugh and love it. Especially my mom.

She was a widowed maverick mother who brought up two boys by herself by grit and wit.

She wrestled with the ruthless realities of life her way. And she let me make my rules, my way.

As a kid, I was a playful prankster. As a grown-up, a mix of monkeyshines and Machiavellianism.

As founder of *USA TODAY* and CEO of Gannett, I became a much-discussed and cussed media mogul.

People often called me an S.O.B. Some to my face, with a smile. Others behind my back, with a smirk.

They meant either that:

▷ I was a thorn in their side or a pain in the ass.
▷ I had won their admiration, affection, even envy.

The nice thing about calling someone an S.O.B. in today's world is that it means whatever you want it to mean. Dictionary definitions are vague or varied, or don't appear at all.

S.O.B.'s forerunner, son of a bitch, was defined in England in 1712. That's a vulgar term, reflecting unfavorably on one's mother.

But S.O.B. is no relation to son of a bitch.

In my book, an S.O.B. is someone who uses whatever tactics it takes to get the job done—to rise to the top. As nicely as possible. A little nastiness when necessary.

It takes all kinds of S.O.B.s to make the world work. Most are lovable. Many are borderline. Some are bad.

As you read *Confessions of an S.O.B.*, you'll be able to judge how the epithet fits me. And how it applies to your friends, your foes—maybe even to yourself.

As long as you smile, you can call anyone an S.O.B.

CREAM AND S.O.B.s RISE TO THE TOP

"Al's a lovable little S.O.B."

BOTH MY EX-WIVES

It was the Christmas season. A time of good cheer.

Also a time of strife and struggle for my three-month-old national newspaper, *USA TODAY*. December 1982.

I spread season's greetings in my own way.

Tender, loving notes and calls to family and friends. Warm words of thanks and holiday good wishes to close coworkers.

And this distinctive touch to my two key associates, John Curley and John Quinn . . .

Whoinhell is in charge around here?

Do I have to do everything myself?

Page One of this morning's *USA TODAY* was a damn disaster.

Dull stories. Dumb editing.

▷ No headlines really grab the reader.

▷ No stories that help the reader.

▷ No good pix of women or minorities—just the usual white males.

▷ And the blue sky came out purple. Furchrissakes!

Maybe you guys should put in your applications at *The Washington Post*. At this rate, *USA TODAY* will never see the New Year.

Bah! Humbug! Please fix by Monday.

—AN

P.S. The week wasn't a total waste. Go back and look at yesterday's paper. That Page One was full of good examples of how to do it. If you could follow that formula every day, it would be a piece of cake to sell this new baby to readers and advertisers. Merry Christmas.

I confess that was an S.O.B.'s note. But I call it a "Love Letter." I call all of my notes that, and I've written thousands of them through the years.

Sometimes they're tough. Sometimes tender. Sometimes a mix of the two. But I never mince words.

My two closest colleagues, Curley and Quinn—then the two top news executives at *USA TODAY*—understood what every word in that note meant. And they knew what I expected them to do about it.

Love Letters like this are one of the reasons that within five years *USA TODAY* went from scratch to the most widely read newspaper in the nation.

And they're one of the reasons I became a successful S.O.B. who rose to the top.

One of the ruthless realities of life is that nobody gets to the top by standing quietly or patiently in line. Unless you are born there.

If you were born a blue blood and the road to the top is paved for you with family gold, my story may not do you much good. Unless you want to beat your boredom and have some fun.

If you were born middle class or poor and have to make your own way, these confessions should help you climb the ladder to success.

I was born poor. And by the law of averages, probably destined to be bored most of my life.

But I'm poor no more. And certainly not bored.

Inside Boardrooms and Bedrooms

These *Confessions of an S.O.B.* share with you what my maverick means and often wayward ways have meant to me, my family, my friends, my coworkers, my enemies.

In my professional life, we'll go inside boardrooms and newsrooms to share the fascination and exhilaration of successes and the devastation of failures.

In my personal life, we'll share love and laughter, sadness and sorrow—from the family room, living room, bedroom.

Examples:

▷ From a dollar-a-week butcher boy in South Dakota, to a fifty-dollar-a-week Associated Press reporter, to a corporate CEO with annual pay of $1.5 million-plus.

▷ From a fatherless home since I was two, to two long-term marriages—that both ended in divorce. And two children now grown-ups who are my best friends.

▷ From a failure as the creator of a sports weekly tabloid, to founder of *USA TODAY*, the most widely read and the most imitated newspaper in the USA.

▷ From success with dozens of media acquisitions and new ventures, to a failure in the biggest deal I tried to pull off— a merger between my Gannett and CBS.

▷ From frivolous schoolboy schemes to insidious corporate conspiracies.

▷ From a cub reporter writing about Little League baseball to interviewing governors and presidents, prime ministers and kings across the USA and around the world.

To play such a variety of games and win most of them, you really should have a Jekyll-and-Hyde personality, or at least pretend you do.

Sometimes that means being pleasant and playful.

Sometimes passionate and pig-headed.

Sometimes cool and controlled.

Sometimes irritating and intimidating.

Sometimes belligerent and blasphemous.

Sometimes a little bullshit helps, too.

You cannot always be polite or proper about things. The more you rock the boat, especially if you go on to win the race, the more people will try to put you in your place—or what they think should be your place.

Pay no attention to the nay-sayers.

When you succeed, their jeers will turn to cheers. Those who laughed at you will laugh with you. And your last laugh will be the best laugh of all.

While I laugh and kid a lot in telling my story, these *Confessions of an S.O.B.* have a very serious side. They are meant to be taken to heart.

I hope after you read them you will:

▷ Take the world more seriously.

▷ Take yourself less seriously.

Any successful S.O.B. must remember that life is a marvelous mix of ruthless realities, remarkable opportunities, overwhelming victories, frustrating failures. The key is to deal with them all and never forget that life should be a helluva lot of fun.

No Dues, No Blackballing

If you do that, I shall welcome you to my S.O.B. club. No applications to fill out. No dues to pay. No blackballing by the establishment.

All it takes is a self-pledge that you have the drive and dedication and determination to get to the top. With a little baffle and bullshit thrown in when necessary.

After you succeed, you must step aside while you're still on top. Then, your farewell will be as fulfilling as mine was.

At my sixty-fifth birthday party, when I retired as chairman of *USA TODAY* and Gannett, my son Dan, thirty-five, and daughter Jan, thirty-four, were two of two hundred special guests.

All their lives they had watched me play any role that would help me rise to the top. From nice to nasty. Sometimes they approved. Sometimes they didn't.

But on this special night of toasts and tributes, these two grown-up kids gave me the most meaningful gift of all. A fancy black silk warm-up jacket. Embroidered on the back in white silk letters:

Only Cream and S.O.B.s Rise to the Top.

PLAIN TALK:

There's a little S.O.B. in all of us.

II

THE MAKING OF AN S.O.B.

"I have never let my schooling interfere with my education."

MARK TWAIN
USA author

Fate made me an S.O.B.

I'd like to take full credit for it, but I really can't.

Fate—and others—had much more to do with it than I did.

Fate made me fatherless at age two. I had to go to work as a kid to earn my keep and make my way.

I learned much more on the streets than I did in school.

Some of my early bosses made me a mischievous boy. That led to a grown-up scheming S.O.B.

My mother—and my grandparents—helped a lot, too.

These teachings of theirs transformed me from a kid struggling to survive to an adult sitting on top of the world:

▷ I picked up on my grandmother's pleasantness. Because of her, I outcharmed many a friend.

▷ I grasped my German grandfather's pragmatism. Because of him, I outfoxed many an enemy.

▷ I soaked up my widowed mother's winning ways: You have to struggle to survive. Then strive to succeed. And live to enjoy. Because of her, I often outdid myself.

It was all written on the wall when I was born in the bedroom of my parents' home on the wrong side of the tracks in Eureka, S.D.

Fate wrote: "Thou shalt be an S.O.B."

Sure, I could have erased the handwriting. But I'm glad I didn't. Instead, I engraved it. My tombstone could carry this epitaph:

Here lies an S.O.B.

"There are two lasting bequests we can give our children. One is roots. The other is wings."

HODDING CARTER, JR.
Pulitzer Prize—winning
editor-publisher, Greenville, Mississippi

DAKOTA DREAMS AND SCHEMES

*"Usually, first you want money out of life.
Then power. Then glory. Al didn't have any
of these at first, but he ended up with
them all."*

DERICK DANIELS
former president,
Playboy Enterprises

I got my first job promotion when I was nine years old. Not a raise, but a big promotion.

I was promoted from harvesting cow chips by hand—that's manure to city folks—to herding cattle on horseback on the parched prairies of my grandfather's farm in South Dakota.

That was like going from garbage collector to grand marshal.

The pay was the same. No money. Just board and room for the summer.

It was 1933. Depth of the Depression and the Dust Bowl days.

My grandmother, Katharina, leaked the good news about my promotion. She came to pick me up in Grandpa's Model A Ford on my last day of school in the fourth grade.

"Allen, Grandpa's gonna give you the new job you want. You'll have your own horse to herd cattle. It's because you did such a good job picking up cow chips last summer," Grandma gushed. "But don't let on I told you."

I could tell she was proud of me. Grandma liked me a lot. She also felt sorry for me.

My father, Daniel, who died when I was twenty-two months old, was her first child. A wiry, soft-hearted woman who never weighed over a hundred pounds except when she was pregnant, Grandma had fifteen more children.

She lived to be ninety. But she always had a special soft spot in her heart for the two offspring of her firstborn.

After my Dad died, my brother, Walter, who was seven years older, and I often got special favors from Grandma.

But not from Grandpa John.

He was a gritty German who figured everyone should be treated alike and made to earn their way. I had been lobbying him all winter to give me a bigger job the next summer. But I lobbied Grandma to lobby for me, too. And that's what got me my promotion.

When we got to the farm and Grandpa made my new job official, he just said, "You did a good job with the cow chips last summer. Now, let's go pick out a horse so you can get to herding the cows."

My promotion as a kid taught me:

▷ If you have a lousy job, you're more likely to get promoted out of it if you buckle down and do your best, rather than be a wimp and do your worst.

▷ It works to cultivate friends in high places who will help get you promoted—even your grandmother.

The Art of Collecting Cow Chips

If you don't think my promotion was a big deal, let me explain.

Cow chips are dung droppings left to dry in the sun. My job was to push a wheelbarrow across the prairie, pick up the chips, bring them back and stack them neatly inside a fuel shed. There they'd stay dry for use in the cook stove all winter.

Chips that have thoroughly dried in the sun don't smell or mess up your hands or your overalls. Those that haven't, do. Even an eight-year-old kid learned the difference in a hurry.

Most farmers burned cow chips because they didn't have firewood. Not many trees grew in South Dakota until President Franklin Delano Roosevelt put in his "shelter belt" in 1935.

Many farmers didn't make it in those Dust Bowl days. But Grandpa did because he hedged his bets.

Grandpa farmed over a thousand acres. Raised wheat, a little corn, and lots of cattle. But he also was the county tax assessor and sold Farmers' Insurance. So he had some money coming in when crops failed.

He inherited the family homestead in 1904, when his father died. At age thirty-one, Grandpa started an expansion program.

He borrowed money to buy more land and build a second floor on the old sod house.

Grandpa had a special inheritance plan. Instead of making his children wait until his death, he gave all the boys their inheritances when they got married. He and Grandma had eleven boys. The five girls were not included in his inheritance plan because in those days girls were supposed to get married and their husbands were supposed to take care of them.

A Farmer's Family Jewels

One of my most treasured documents is a handwritten note in German dated 1916. In it, my grandfather gave my father these family jewels:

▷ Four horses, two harness sets.
▷ One wagon, one plow, one drag (rake).
▷ Eighty acres of land.

Grandpa's inheritance note estimated the value at $3,000.

With his eighty acres of land and tools, my father, Daniel, then twenty-one, took his new bride, Christina, twenty-three, and set out to make his way. But a horse and a plow did him in.

Dad's leg was mangled as he was tilling his soil. Unable to work the land any longer, he and Mom moved to Eureka, a town of 1,228.

Dad sold what he had inherited and started a small creamery. He bought milk in big cans from farmers, and sold milk, cream and butter to the townsfolk.

The rest of his inheritance went to buy a small house on the wrong side of the tracks in Eureka. That's where I was born.

The creamery business was healthy, but my dad was not. Despite repeated trips to the Mayo Clinic in neighboring Minnesota, his injured leg wouldn't heal. Complications led to tuberculosis of the bone. He died two months before my second birthday.

I never knew my dad and have no memories of him except those passed on by my mother and brother.

Because I didn't remember having a dad, I was sure I didn't need one.

My mother considered marrying again. I despised every man who came to visit her.

When I was in the first grade, she called a family powwow

to ask my brother and me how we felt about her marrying a widower farmer who had proposed. She explained it would mean moving to his farm. But she emphasized we would have a bigger house, lots of land to play on, and we wouldn't have to worry about food or clothes.

My brother, seven years more grown-up, said it was up to Mom. I threw a tantrum.

"I don't want a dad. I don't need one. We've got all the family we need," I screamed. "If you marry him, I'll run away."

I was bluffing, of course. I didn't yet have the guts to run away. I was just being a brat to get my way. It worked.

My Debut As an S.O.B.

My mother rejected her suitor's proposal. I don't think she ever dated again. I've often wondered whether I did the right thing for Mother. I know it turned out to be the best thing for me. If she had married the guy, my name would be Schmidt and I might still be down on the farm.

That tantrum was probably my debut as a self-centered S.O.B. A six-year-old kid had overruled his mother and big brother. From that day on, I was the family policymaker.

Mom did her best to hold things together. She had a few hundred dollars from the sale of the creamery. She earned a little money by cleaning people's houses on the better side of the tracks.

But the winter after my promotion from cow chip collector to a young cowboy herding cattle, Mom called another family meeting.

"We're almost out of money," she said. "Unless we sell the house, I don't know how we'll pay the bills."

Mom's parents and all her brothers and sisters lived around Alpena, a town of 499 about 125 miles south of Eureka. Since my father's death, they had been urging her to come home.

"We could probably buy a house for a little less money in Alpena. I think it would be easier for me to find work there," Mom said.

Were we willing to move?

This time I jumped at the idea.

We might be more important in a town of 500 than we were

in a city of 1,200. Maybe we could even buy a house on the right side of the tracks.

"Let's go!" I said. The vote was 3–0.

When my mom sold our Eureka house for $1,700, I thought we had all the money in the world. She let Walter and me hold the check a minute before depositing it. At age ten, I knew what it was like to feel really rich!

Mom bought a house in Alpena for $1,000 from the publisher of the weekly *Alpena Journal*, Allen Brigham. He had become so rich as a newspaper owner that he could afford a bigger house. That's the first time I realized you could make a lot of money in newspapers.

But even his hand-me-down house was on the right side of the tracks. In fact, in Alpena all the houses were on the same side of the railroad tracks, which ran along the very eastern edge of town. Living where poor and rich were integrated made the poorer people feel better psychologically, I think.

I didn't know anything about the poverty level. But since Mom had $700 left after buying the house, I felt sure we would never be poor again. Mom knew better.

"I'll find any kind of work I can. But unless you both get paying jobs, our savings will be gone in a few years," she told Walter and me.

The three family breadwinners got these jobs:

▷ Mom went to work at the U and I cafe washing dishes for a dollar a day. She took in laundry and did ironing at night. Some weeks she made more than $10.

▷ Walter was seventeen. After school and on Saturdays he weighed and crated chickens that farmers brought in to Lundborg's grocery store. He made $2.50 per week.

▷ I was only ten, so my choices were limited. The paper route to deliver the *Minneapolis Tribune* was open. It had two customers who each paid 15 cents a week. I got to keep 6 cents; the newspaper got 9. My first paying job earned me 12 cents a week.

Within a year, I built my two-newspaper route up to eleven subscribers. Most of the new subscribers were relatives who bought the paper because of my persistence or because they felt sorry for me.

Now I was making 66 cents a week. I bragged years later to

circulation sales executives of my 450 percent business increase in one year.

I loved delivering—and reading—newspapers. But being a paper boy was a risky business. Every Friday when I went to collect my 15 cents, some customers couldn't be found or couldn't pay.

I had to send my 9 cents per paper per week to the *Tribune* at the end of each month, whether I collected or not. Some weeks my 66-cent income went down to 51 cents, or 36 cents, or even 21 cents.

Putting Meat on the Table

When I was thirteen, I decided I'd look for a steady job with a guaranteed wage. The man who owned the butcher shop, Tom Rosser, was one of my *Tribune* customers. He liked my prompt deliveries and my personality.

When I asked him for a job as a butcher boy, he said, "I'll pay you a dollar a week and all the cheese and salami you can eat. You'll sweep out before school each morning, sell meat after school each afternoon and on Saturdays, and help me slaughter cows and pigs."

Being a butcher boy sure beat delivering papers. I never went hungry because I could snack on the job. Mom, Walter, and I were eating better at home, too. Rosser often gave me hamburger or liver or other cheap cuts that were about to spoil. We had more meat on the table than most poor people.

Rosser was a nice guy to work for. But he was also an S.O.B. when it came to business.

A few days after I started work, he instructed me, "You put your thumb on the scales when you weigh the meat and charge the customers a few pennies extra. Not the poor widows. Just those who can afford it. That will pay for your weekly salary."

When I told Mom about that, she said it wasn't nice, "but you have to do what the boss says." I did it, but I was very selective in who I cheated. A selective S.O.B. in the making.

One of my best customers was the wife of the owner of the drugstore. After a while, I thought it might be more fun selling ice cream sodas than salami, so I gave Mrs. Bentsen special treatment. I saved the best cuts of meat for her and always took time to chat with her and kid her.

Since Grandma had lobbied Grandpa to give me a promotion, I thought Mrs. Bentsen might get her husband to hire me at the drugstore. It worked. For the second time in my early career, I charmed a woman into lobbying for me.

Three years after I became a butcher boy, Bentsen offered me a job as a soda jerk and general clerk in his drug store for $3 a week, after school and on weekends.

My new job taught me about the lifestyles of people around town. Bentsen's was an all-purpose drugstore. From ice cream to toilet articles to packaged liquor and condoms.

As a sixteen-year-old kid, I learned who all the drinkers or drunks in town were. And the marrieds and singles who practiced birth control with condoms (which everybody then called rubbers). I figured most of the married men who bought rubbers were cheating on their wives. Back then very few married couples worried about how many kids they had.

The Making of a Media Minimogul

When I was a senior in high school, I realized that power was more important to me than money.

The power of the press hooked me when I became editor of the *Echo*, our Alpena High School paper. It wasn't really a newspaper, just a quarter page in the weekly *Alpena Journal*. But everybody in town read it.

I wasn't good enough in sports to be a star. But as editor of the *Echo*, I finally was a big shot on campus.

I decided whose name went in the paper and what was said about them. My pals got most of the ink. Their achievements in sports, drama, and other extracurricular activities were exaggerated. The kids I didn't like didn't get much publicity. I felt like the most powerful kid in Alpena High.

If having control of a newspaper could do that for me, I liked it. I was a media minimogul in the making.

PLAIN TALK:

Street learning is the best learning.

CLEANING UP DIRTY TRICKS

"Neuharth only deserved a C-plus in classes but an A-plus for campus shenanigans."

GORDON AADLAND
former columnist,
Volante, University of South Dakota

I met my first S.O.B. role model at a crossroads near Heidelberg, Germany, in the final weeks of World War II. He threatened to lock me up behind barbed wire.

General George S. Patton, Jr. The sometimes bad guy, all-time big winner for the Allied forces.

Our 86th Infantry Division was part of Patton's Third Army. I had made staff sergeant, heading an intelligence and reconnaissance platoon.

Corporal Fran Devine of Wisconsin and I were marching two dozen captured German soldiers to a prison encampment for interrogation. We had stopped to rest at a crossroads.

Patton and his driver pulled up in his star-studded jeep. Patton was a nonstop guy. Didn't believe in slowing down or resting. And a master at staging temper tantrums.

The general jumped from his jeep and growled at us:

"Get those fucking Krauts on their feet and moving, or I'll put you behind the same barbed wire they're headed for!"

We snapped to, saluted, and moved on.

Devine grumbled about what an S.O.B. Patton was. I laughed. Of course, he was a borderline S.O.B. But he was a winner. He knew how to move men and win wars. I would have followed him nonstop all the way to Berlin on foot. I hoped I would develop a little of his S.O.B. quality in me someday.

He's still a hero of mine. I've seen the movie *Patton* eleven times.

Army service is what took this eighteen-year-old boy out of the country and the country out of the boy:

▷ Training in Minnesota, Texas, Louisiana, California, New Jersey.

▷ Service in both Europe and the Pacific.

▷ Furloughs and fun in Paris, London, Manila, New York, Los Angeles.

After V-E Day, our 86th Division and the 84th were the first two to return from Europe. We were hailed in a victory parade down Fifth Avenue in New York. After thirty-day furloughs at home for "rest and recuperation," we were the first to be redeployed to the Pacific, where the war was still on.

We were lucky. We were on board troopships en route to the Philippines when the atomic bomb was dropped on Hiroshima. For the Japanese it was a disaster. For us it was a blessing.

The Business of Bluffing

On my trip back from the Philippines to California, our troopship looked like a gambling casino. Everybody wanted to score a big hit before being discharged from the Army.

Tom Rosser had taught me to play poker when things were slow in the butcher shop in Alpena. It became one of my favorite pastimes. Poker pays off for the business of bluffing. A game with a practical purpose. When to hold, when to fold. How big a risk to take.

I had saved nearly $200 from my sergeant's salary. I decided I'd go home either broke or with a nice bundle. A thousand dollars was my magic goal.

In nine days and nights of poker playing, I parlayed the $200 into $1,100. It was my first big gamble and I won. The poker winnings paid for the used eighteen-foot house trailer that became home for my bride, Loretta, and me after we were married in June 1946.

That summer we hitched my house trailer to her old 1937 Ford V-8 and got a job with a traveling carnival. We made two-

or three-night stands at county fairs in small towns across South Dakota, northwestern Iowa, and southwestern Minnesota.

As carnies, we learned how to flimflam the public in an innocent way. The owner assigned us to a string-pulling stand. It bothered Loretta that the major prizes on display were not really attached to the strings that the customers could pull. Strings on the good prizes only went to the overhead loop.

I felt a little like I did about the thumb on the scales at the butcher shop. The boss made me be an S.O.B.

When I enrolled at the University of South Dakota in the fall, Loretta got a job teaching in a one-room schoolhouse near the campus at Vermillion. Her $1,200-a-year salary supplemented my $90-a-month GI Bill allowance.

I wanted to get a degree in journalism. But after nearly four years in the Army, classrooms seemed pretty dull. Besides, I cared much more about being a big man on campus than getting good grades.

As I had learned at Alpena High School, the power of the press was the way to become a big shot. During my freshman and sophomore years, I wrote sports for the university student newspaper, the *Volante*. In my junior year, I was named editor.

I became friends with the paper's business manager, Bill Porter. We were opposites, so we made a good team.

He had money and belonged to a fraternity, the Phi Delta Thetas. I rejected fraternities as part of the establishment. They were packed with privileged kids. And I never ran with the privileged pack—then or thereafter.

Fraternities and sororities controlled most of the campus activities. I thought nonaffiliates, or independents, who were in the majority, should rule. Actually I wanted to be the power behind the ruler.

Taking On the Establishment

I figured out how Porter and I could outsmart the establishment, using one of their own—Porter—to beat them.

Each year, in a rotating system, one fraternity would nominate a male for president of the student body and the rest of the Greek organizations would fall in line. Under the rotation system, it was not the Phi Delts' turn that year. So Porter couldn't run as the Greek candidate. Independent candidates didn't stand a chance. Neither did women.

Although a popular member of the Phi Delt fraternity, Porter was more ambitious than fraternal. We built a ragtag new political party of this unlikely coalition:

▷ War veterans.

▷ Independent students.

▷ One fraternity—Porter's Phi Delts.

We unveiled our new "grassroots" Liberal Party in a *Volante* scoop. You couldn't tell from my news stories, but this big new political party was launched by a small roomful of people. It nominated Porter for president.

The fraternities and sororities were enraged. Porter's nickname became "Scab."

I had no qualms about using the power of the press to put my pal in office.

When the *Volante* ran feature stories on the two candidates, I asked the Greek candidate, Alpha Tau Omega's Hank Haugan, to come in for his photo session dressed in a coat and tie. Porter was pictured with a sport shirt and a big smile. Clearly a common man.

The *Volante*, the only paper on campus, was supposed to serve all the students. Yet I strongly endorsed my pal Porter editorially. I called on independent students to beat the minority rule of the Greeks.

Despite the voice of the *Volante*, I figured the election was going to be close. The Greeks always turned out in big numbers and voted as a bloc. We needed to do something dramatic to break that bloc.

Many of the sorority girls knew and liked the handsome and personable Porter. They weren't happy with the "scab" label the fraternities had pinned on him. How could we tip them in our direction?

I formed a two-person political dirty tricks team.

The night before the election, Porter and I armed ourselves with several buckets of whitewash and paintbrushes.

I stood watch at my 1937 V-8 getaway car. Between 2 A.M. and 4 A.M., Porter himself painted dozens of signs attacking him on the sidewalks of the administration building and the student union, where the voting was to take place. I told him it was important for his peace of mind that he wield the paintbrush himself.

The self-deprecating signs read: *Beat Scab Porter.*

The next morning the signs were the talk of the campus. Some sorority girls were moved to tears. They deplored the dirty campaigning. Of course, they blamed the fraternities.

"Scab" Porter won in a walk, 867 to 693.

Shame on Me

The next morning Professor Bill Farber, head of the government department, stopped me on the sidewalk.

"Well, how do you feel?" he asked.

"Pretty good," I bragged. "Democracy is finally ruling on this campus."

He scolded me, "You've got the only voice on campus, which is supposed to belong to all the students. Do you really feel proud that you used it to elect your buddy student body president? Don't you think you encouraged a dirty campaign?"

I had a hunch he also had a hunch who painted the signs. He was saying "shame on you," and he was right.

I shrugged him off. But he made me think. And to realize I really had bent the rules.

The self-inflicted "scab" signs were shameful. But I justified those as retaliation for the scab label the political opponents had put on my pal.

But managing the news columns for my cause and my candidate was censurable and inexcusable.

Later I vowed never again to practice or to tolerate the kind of unfair and irresponsible journalism I was guilty of in high school and college. That's why:

▷ *USA TODAY* refuses to run anything attributed to anonymous sources and does not endorse any candidate in presidential elections.

▷ I raise hell with newspapers which not only slant news but think their role is to crown or dethrone political friends or foes.

It took me a while to clean up my act. But I'm glad I got my irresponsible kid journalism out of my system before I began practicing grown-up newspapering.

PLAIN TALK:

Developing S.O.B.s should develop some responsibility.

III

LEAPFROGGING THE CAREER LADDER

"Only those who dare to fail greatly can ever achieve greatly."

ROBERT F. KENNEDY

I learned my career leapfrogging lessons the hard way. I fell off the ladder, early and hard.

But I was lucky. I was only twenty-nine. Young enough to pick myself up and try again.

Since I fell off a weak little ladder I had built in South Dakota, my next climbs were on bigger and stronger ones—Miami, Detroit, Rochester, and beyond.

I learned to leapfrog the ladder with these career lessons:

▷ Don't run with the pack—until or unless you can lead it.

▷ Be your own pitchman. Sell yourself. Attention does not come quickly to the humble.

▷ Plan or plot your own promotions. Show your boss how you can do more work so that he/she can have more fun.

As the career climb gets higher, it gets tougher. So do the career lessons, especially about bosses.

If the boss thinks you can make him look good, he will pull you up the ladder with him.

If the boss worries that you are making yourself look too good, he may try to push you off the ladder.

If the boss cannot see beyond tomorrow, you should find a new boss.

Either way, set your sights on your own visions and keep reaching—even for the moon.

"Ah, but a man's reach should exceed his grasp, or what's a heaven for?"

ROBERT BROWNING
English poet

BLOODIED
AND BROKE
AT TWENTY-NINE

"Neuharth went from a Horatio Alger in his casserole and salad days to a William Randolph Hearst in his champagne and caviar days."

DAN GREANEY
former editor, *Harvard Lampoon*

If you're over thirty and haven't had a major failure in your business or professional career, time is running out on you.

In pursuing my dream for money and power, I succeeded in scoring my first big failure when I was twenty-nine.

A friend and I lost nearly fifty thousand dollars—all raised from small stockholders—in my first business venture. I wound up broke, in debt, and bloodied, but not bowed.

Everyone should fail in a big way at least once before they're forty. I don't mean little disappointments, like screwing up an important assignment or quitting a good job or even getting fired from a normal job. It needs to be a big failure. You can only fail big if you take a big risk. The bigger you fail, the bigger you're likely to succeed later.

You need to fail when you're old enough to really learn something from it, but still young enough to pick yourself up, dust yourself off, and start over.

Some parents worry that their kids might fail. I'm concerned because mine are in their mid-thirties and haven't failed yet. If they don't hurry, it will be too late for them to fail and learn anything from it.

None of the big league games I played and won as a grown-up would have been possible without the lessons I learned from losing my most important little league game as an overgrown kid in my late twenties.

My scheme to get rich and famous failed because of mismanagement. I was the one who mismanaged it.

Chicken Little Was Wrong

I learned more from that failure than from any of my successes in later life. The most important thing I learned is that the sky doesn't fall when you fail. Chicken Little was wrong. The moon and stars are still there. And the next time you reach for them, you're more likely to get them in your grasp.

Of course, that's true only if you learn from your failures. To do so, you have to analyze them. And take the blame.

The venture that was to become my first big failure was dreamed up during my senior year at the University of South Dakota in 1949–50. Your last months in college are a good time for dreaming and scheming. Beats studying for tests.

My friend Bill Porter and I were feeling heady from our college successes. We ran the campus—just the way we planned it.

Now we were ready for fame and fortune in the real world.

Porter was more interested in fortune, probably because his father owned a furniture store in Madison, S.D., and he grew up on the right side of the tracks. He already felt important.

Fame meant more to me than fortune, probably because we were nobodies when I grew up on the wrong side of the tracks in Eureka, S.D. I wanted to become important.

I was not interested in a nine-to-five newspaper job that I would stay in the rest of my life. I saw the future clearly— starting a newspaper that I would ultimately own or control. I wanted to leapfrog the normal, dull career ladder.

The plan I presented to Porter:

▷ We would start a weekly statewide sports tabloid for all of South Dakota. I had the name for it: *SoDak Sports*. It would be patterned a little after the national *Sporting News*, only more interesting.

▷ I would be the editor and publisher. He would be business manager.

▷ We'd raise the money needed to start it through the sale of stock. I jokingly called it begging, borrowing, and stealing.

▷ From our founders' fees and salaries for the first two

years, Bill and I would end up with at least 51 percent of the outstanding stock. I'd own 51 percent, Bill 49 percent of our share. We shook hands on the deal.

At least 51 percent is important in any deal—50-50 is no way to run any business. Even among friends. A tie vote means you do nothing. Do-nothing businesses don't work.

Since we didn't have any money, neither of us would put any money into it. No personal borrowing. Our personal risks would be our time, our energy, and our reputations.

At the time Bill had two years to go in law school. He wanted his law degree as a hedge. I figured we needed a couple years to raise the money and to refine our plan for *SoDak Sports*. In the meantime I'd try to get a South Dakota newspaper job that would help in the *SoDak Sports* venture.

I had spent the summer after my sophomore year as a reporter on the *Mitchell* (South Dakota) *Daily Republic* and after my junior year on the *Rapid City* (South Dakota) *Journal*. Each offered me a job on graduation.

But they each covered only a small area of the state. Since *SoDak Sports* was to be statewide, I wanted to work where my byline on stories would be seen across the state. Only the Associated Press and United Press offered that possibility. Neither had an opening.

I pitched the state bureau chief for the AP, Harl Andersen, to expand his two-person staff and especially his statewide sports coverage by hiring me. He made the request of his superiors at the AP in Minneapolis. Lucky for me, they approved it a week before my graduation.

Opportunity Beats Money

Andersen offered me $50 a week as a reporter for the AP in 1950. The Mitchell paper had offered me $60. I took the lower-paying job because it would help pave the way for *SoDak Sports*.

In fact, in the next two years, I turned down two AP promotions—one to Minneapolis for $70 a week, the other to New York for $85. I was using the Sioux Falls job to build my South Dakota power base. A little more money doesn't matter as much as the right opportunity when you're in your twenties.

For two years, Bill and I used our evenings, weekends, holidays to plan and plot for *SoDak Sports*. Bill practiced law before he had a license to do so by drawing up our incorporation papers.

Once incorporated, we began peddling *SoDak Sports* stock, mostly in blocks of $100. At first it was really tough going. We had no sophisticated prospectus, mostly a vision and a lot of enthusiasm.

We did develop a bush-league business plan, but it was by guess and by golly. It projected profitability after two years of publication. And we guessed we needed $50,000 for start-up costs and to cover our losses during the first two years.

Bill was a better stock salesman than I was. I could open the doors and talk enthusiastically about the idea. But I had trouble closing the deal, asking for the order. Bill sold more than twice as much stock as I did.

I'm not a good salesman on a specific small order. I'm better at showmanship than salesmanship. That's why I can sell multimillion-dollar ideas easier than I can sell a $5 item.

My sports writing for the AP helped spread the word about *SoDak Sports*. Everywhere I went to cover major sports events, I talked about it. From locker rooms to barrooms.

Most people who invested with us were betting with their glands, for sports sentiment or enthusiasm. They liked the idea and hoped it would work, but nobody expected to get rich from it. Except Bill and me.

Most investors anted up $100. The biggest bettor was in for $700. The average was under $200.

By late summer, 1952, we were ready. We announced a starting date of November 21, 1952, near the end of the football season and the start of basketball. Basketball was the biggest spectator sport in South Dakota. Many high schools were too small to field a real eleven-man football team. Six-man and eight-man football substituted in some towns.

Because we were starting *SoDak Sports* on a shoestring, we could only afford to spend peanuts on promotion. Most of our cash reserve was earmarked to pay the printer's bill, postage for mailing the papers, rent for a one-room office behind Sid's Liquor Store in Sioux Falls.

Most of our two salaries was to be in stock. We each drew

only $100 cash per month, just enough to cover food and gin. Bill and I both loved martinis. We often had a hamburger or macaroni-and-cheese for dinner, so that we could afford a martini beforehand. Martinis are good for dreamers, if you limit them to one or two.

One of our *SoDak Sports* policies was a pledge Bill and I made that we would have at least one martini a day for the rest of our lives. I haven't missed many. Although in my sixties I switched from gin to vodka.

I was a slow learner about that. Vodka is almost tasteless, so good and bad vodka taste about the same. Good gin tastes like a combination of gasoline and onion juice and you get used to it. Bad gin tastes even worse and gives you headaches and hangovers.

One of the schemes Bill and I hatched over one of our martini hours was how to get free publicity for *SoDak Sports*. The key was the state's sportswriters and sportscasters, since they already had the audience we were after.

I had gotten to know them all as an AP sportswriter. So I named each a contributing editor of *SoDak Sports*. They loved it. No pay, but their name was listed on the masthead of this new statewide sports paper. They gave us lots of ink and airtime before and after our first edition. And tips for features and story ideas.

Most publishers of South Dakota's daily newspapers didn't object to their sports editors helping us. They knew that what we were trying to do couldn't be done anyway, so they weren't worried about us as possible competitors.

Disarming the Enemy

I helped convince publishers we were no competition by saying we would be just a "second read" for their sports fans.

I used the same "second read" approach in trying to disarm the nation's newspaper publishers about the introduction of *USA TODAY* thirty years later. But most of them were a little more sophisticated and eyed us warily from the beginning.

When we started *SoDak Sports*, the entire staff was three full-time staffers and one part-time volunteer. Bill, a secretary, my wife Loretta, and me.

These are the hats I wore:
▷ The boss, as editor and publisher.
▷ The only news staffer, as reporter and photographer.
▷ The head huckster, as promotion director.

I wrote every story and every headline in what was usually a twelve- to sixteen-page tabloid. Still, I met every deadline. Later, the only deadline I missed was the one at the bank.

Much of what went into our weekly *SoDak Sports* was stolen and rewritten from daily newspapers around the state. But I also created lots of polls and reader participation features.

We had contests for everything from the state's prettiest cheerleader to the best waterboy.

We printed *SoDak Sports* on peach-colored newsprint. We stole that idea from the *Minneapolis Tribune* and the *Des Moines Register*. Both had peach sports sections on Sunday.

We even stole their promotional slogan "Reach for the Peach." To this day I've never hesitated stealing a good idea from another publication and adapting it to my own use. Most so-called new ideas really aren't new. Usually they're old ideas brought up to date.

The Page One cover of our first issue was a story and picture spread about the first All-SoDak high school football team. And second team. Third team. Honorable mentions.

Dozens of athletes from small towns who never had their names in any paper except their local weekly became heroes. We made them statewide stars under the All-SoDak banner to promote the name of the paper.

We printed seven thousand copies of the first issue. It was a sellout.

The Bible According to Brokaw

NBC anchorman Tom Brokaw was then a 135-pound quarterback on a six-man football team in Pickstown, S.D., population 2,217.

"*SoDak Sports* became our bible," Brokaw recalls. He also recalls how he used the paper to embarrass a classmate who was his rival for big shot in Pickstown.

"Running back George Hall was better than I was. He also was more popular with the girls. I decided to take him down a notch, so I started the rumor that he would be on the *SoDak Sports* all-state team in its next issue.

"George and his admirers were hanging around the post office waiting for that issue of *SoDak Sports* to arrive. When it did, he was not on the team. They were crushed. I was hanging around the edges of the group, watching with delight," Brokaw remembers.

Clearly Brokaw had the making back then of another lovable South Dakota S.O.B.

We also staged a number of promotions that paid off in fun, if not always in more circulation or advertising.

The two biggest circulation contests awarded these prizes:

▷ An all-expense-paid trip for two readers to the 1953 World Series, won by my beloved Yankees over the then Brooklyn Dodgers, four games to two.

▷ A trip for one (our cost cutting had begun) to the 1954 Rose Bowl game, won by Michigan State over UCLA, 28–20.

The contests were designed to boost our circulation. Of course, the most important thing was that I got to go along to see my first two big-time sports events.

I wasn't able to get advance tickets for either. So I learned something about scalpers.

At the Commodore Hotel in Manhattan, I landed three $7 left-field seats for $15 each from a scalper. Then I found another scalper with three box seats for the same price. When I tried to hustle the first three, a big plainclothes cop spotted me as an amateur and grabbed me. "You sell those to me at the price on the ticket or you're going to jail for scalping," he threatened. I lost $24. Welcome to New York.

Later I learned that by game time at the stadium scalpers were happy to sell their tickets at or near face value.

I never again hesitated going to a major sports event without tickets. I've even bought some for less than face value by waiting until after the game was underway, when scalpers start to panic.

Promotion contests like these were fun and got us attention. What more could we ask for? Profits, that's what.

By the end of our first year, *SoDak Sports* had:

▷ 12,000 paid weekly circulation. Our target was 10,000.

▷ Two pages of advertising a week. Our target was five.

▷ Losses of $40,000. Our projection was only $25,000.

Meeting just one out of three goals wasn't good enough. We were one year old and in deep financial trouble.

In fact, our circulation success was a problem, not a blessing. *SoDak Sports* sold for 10 cents a copy. That did not cover production and distribution costs. Like most newspapers, we expected advertising to pay the bulk of the bill and take us to profitability. But our advertising bombed. And because our circulation kept growing, the more papers we sold, the more money we lost.

Twenty-two months after we started our venture, we ran out of time and money. On September 24, 1954, we published our last edition.

Porter's law degree came in handy again. In the beginning we had been able to incorporate without paying a legal fee. Now, we could go into receivership the same way. We did.

Stock Certificates: Worthless Wallpaper

When we opened our doors for a sale of desks, typewriters, and other office equipment, I braced for the worst. I expected angry shareholders to come in and call us thieves or scoundrels.

The opposite happened. Quite a few shareholders dropped by. Some actually bought some of the equipment, even though they already owned a piece of it as a stockholder. All were gracious and grateful for having been along on the ride. No one lost any big money and they thought our joint venture was worth the price.

After we sold all our assets, our creditors received less than 35 cents on the dollar.

SoDak Sports stock was worthless. I had enough of it so that I later papered one wall of my study with the stock certificates as a reminder of my failed venture.

I always like to keep reminders of failures around. That's why my memos are still on peach paper—the same color we used to print *SoDak Sports*.

Such mementos may not keep me humble. But they are meaningful reminders that nobody's perfect. And that the next failure could be just around the corner, so keep your guard up.

The night of our "fire sale," after we walked out of the *SoDak Sports* office for the last time, Bill and I shared our usual martinis. We shed some tears over our second and third and fourth.

Since then, I've laughed often about how lucky I was to fail as I did.

If I'd succeeded, I might have gone through life satisfied with such joys as gin, gin rummy, and golf at the Minnehaha Country Club in Sioux Falls.

Instead I ran away from home.

There was a monkey on my back. But I was young enough so that I vowed to run far enough and hard enough to shake it off. And I did.

PLAIN TALK:

Little League failures lead to Big League successes.

PROMOTE THYSELF

*"That failure [SoDak Sports] sealed
Neuharth's future. He began to think of
himself less as a writer than as an editor
and publisher involved in commerce, and he
learned to hedge his bets."*

PEOPLE MAGAZINE
September 28, 1987

Failure shouldn't stop your drive to succeed. How you
respond to failure makes all the difference.

I had two options:

▷ Hang around South Dakota, wallow in my wounds, and
let people sympathize with me.

▷ Pick myself up, dust myself off, and head out for new
adventures.

I didn't want to just survive. I wanted to thrive. So I ran
away from home. At age thirty.

My target: Florida, a state of opportunity. I hoped I could
make it big there and have fun in the sun, too.

I took direct aim at the *Miami Herald*, considered one of
the best major papers in the South.

A pretty big jump. *SoDak Sports* was unknown outside
South Dakota and at its peak reached a once-a-week circulation
of 18,000. The *Miami Herald* had a circulation of over 200,000
daily and nearly 300,000 on Sundays.

I did some research on the newsroom bosses at the *Miami
Herald*. Managing editor George Beebe had worked in Billings,
Montana, and his wife, Helen, was from Montana. I figured with
that background, he'd at least know where South Dakota was
and that might help me.

My letter of application to Beebe was better than any news
story I'd ever written.

I didn't try to hide my *SoDak Sports* experiences. I wrote
Beebe that I was probably his first chance to hire a "self-
confessed failure."

Then I attached copies of *SoDak Sports* and a letter of recommendation from South Dakota Governor Sigurd Anderson. The governor, an avid sports fan, boasted about how great *SoDak Sports* had been for the state and dismissed its financial failure as just one of those things.

Beebe bit. He called and offered me a reporter's job, sight unseen, at $90 a week.

Even though I was broke and out of work, I stalled him. "This will be a big move for me and my family," I said. "I'd like to come down and look around first."

Beebe explained their policy was not to pay expenses for job interviews. I later found out why. He had a desk drawer full of applications from Yankee reporters, all wanting to work in Miami.

I decided to make the trip at my expense. I borrowed $200 from my brother-in-law, rode the train sitting up in a coach for two days and two nights.

Look Cool, Even If You're Not

When I walked into the *Miami Herald* newsroom, I was scared stiff and trying not to show it. Wall-to-wall journalists, more than two hundred.

I needed a job desperately. Yet I was casually looking things over. Beebe had many more applicants than he could consider. Yet he was trying to sell me on taking the job.

That gave me the upper hand.

From that day on, I've never sweat a decision, large or small. Appearing cool and in control is the key, even when you aren't.

That night I looked around town. Miami and Miami Beach night life reminded me of the World War II scenes in Paris and Manila. The next day I came back and accepted. We agreed I'd report to work ten days later on December 30.

I rode the train back to South Dakota, borrowed another $300 from my brother-in-law, loaded everything we owned in a U-Haul rental trailer and headed off to our new adventure. Loretta, six months pregnant, and year-old son Dan came by air two weeks later.

After a month at the *Miami Herald*, I knew this would be a piece of cake. Here's why:

▷ At *SoDak Sports*, I wrote and edited thirty to forty stories on deadline days.

▷ At the *Herald*, most reporters averaged one or two stories a day. Often they worked on one story for days.

I kept up my *SoDak Sports* pace. When I took a story on the phone for rewrite from a reporter on the street, I'd bang it out in ten or fifteen minutes and be ready for more.

Old-style and long-time reporters didn't like the pace I was setting. Behind my back they called me the "Wheatfield Kid."

But soon acting city editor Merlin Test put me out on the street as a real reporter, my first promotion in Miami.

In a few months, with luck and perseverance, I scored front-page scoops on police scandals, religious mail-order scams, stories that freed a mentally retarded drifter who had been jailed on a drummed-up murder charge.

I worked hard, but I played hard too. The combination paid off on my first big international story. I was assigned to join President Eisenhower's "Operation Amigo" trip to Latin America to cover for the *Miami Herald* and its sister *Chicago Daily News* wire.

Don't Run with the Pack

I wrote pretty routine stories, as did the White House press corps, until we arrived in Rio de Janeiro. The first night there was a carnival of celebrations.

The next day, when the press plane took off from Rio to São Paulo to be with Eisenhower, I wasn't aboard. I decided to spend the day on the Copacabana beach, relaxing, thinking, planning, plotting—and girl watching.

Basking in the sun, I heard excited conversation and spotted several people huddled around a radio.

"Americanos! Americanos!"

A tourist from the USA translated a fragmented report: A Brazilian airliner and a DC-6 military transport plane had collided in the air near the Rio airport.

On the military plane: nineteen members of the United States Navy band. All were killed. They had been scheduled to play for Eisenhower and Brazil's President Juscelino Kubitschek that night.

I rushed to the crash site, interviewed witnesses, and called the *Herald* to dictate my account with dramatic first-person sidebar stories from eyewitnesses.

After I finished, my boss Beebe came on the phone.

"Good copy," he said. "By the way, why aren't you in São Paulo with Ike and the rest of the press today?"

"George, I just had this feeling that the biggest news today was going to be in Rio," I quipped.

Beebe laughed. He was an understanding boss, who cared more about results than rules.

Beebe gave me one more big test—a three-month assignment in the Herald's Washington bureau.

Then he gave me this option:

"You can either become our Washington bureau chief when Ed Lahey retires, or you can run the city desk here. Think about it and let me know which appeals to you most."

Not bad choices for a Dakota kid who had been belly-up and broke three years earlier.

Where Will the Promotion Lead?

Running a Washington bureau for a newspaper like the *Herald* or a group like Knight Newspapers was heady stuff. Prestige. Pretty good money for a reporter. But my research showed most bureau chiefs make that a lifetime job. They're in the Washington mainstream, but only on the fringe of their newspaper's heart or hierarchy.

With every promotion, I tried to figure out in advance where that job would lead. Some people view promotions as a measure of arrival. I saw them as points of departure to the next, bigger job.

The city editor's job would make me the quarterback of the local news staff. In the middle of every major newsroom decision. Constantly in touch with the top bosses.

This could be the first big step on the ladder to top management, with money to match.

I picked it as the better long-term opportunity. But I wanted to move into it my way.

"Make me an assistant on the desk for a few months. Then let me move around the newsroom on the business desk, state desk, sports. That way I'll learn how the whole thing works—and I'll find out who is working and who isn't."

Beebe bought the idea. For three months I hovered here and there. People unloaded their frustrations and their ambitions on me. They weren't sure what I was up to, but they felt they were talking to a peer, not a superior.

Then I told Beebe I was ready. He told acting city editor Merlin Test that he was being replaced the next day but didn't reveal the identity of the successor.

That night after work, Test invited a group of his city desk friends to a booze bash so they could sympathize with him and speculate about his successor. I joined the drinking but didn't do much talking.

The next day when Beebe made the announcement, everybody figured I'd been a sneaky S.O.B. and a spy for three months.

I may have been a borderline S.O.B. But I turned out to be a helluva lot better city editor than I would have been without that experience. Eventually, the staff realized that, too. As good as the *Herald* was, we learned together to do better for the reader.

Surround Yourself with Stars

During my flotsam-and-jetsam period, one of the people who leveled with me was Derick Daniels, of the Raleigh newspaper family. He sat on the *Herald* news desk editing copy and writing headlines.

"This place has a few good writers, but a really shitty city desk," he told me. And he told me how he'd fix it.

One of my first moves was to make him my top assistant on the city desk. He made me look good there, and later as my city editor on the *Detroit Free Press*.

I had never taken a management course in college. My textbooks on how to get ahead were Horatio Alger stories. But I knew it took more than just hard work—the more first-class help I surrounded myself with, the better I'd look.

Finding and training good assistants is essential to moving up. You can't do everything yourself. And if you try, you'll probably focus so narrowly that you will limit your advancement.

I always attempted to surround myself with people who are:

▷ Smart enough to get the job done well.

▷ Loyal enough to do things my way and make me look good.

▷ Good enough to take my job when I am ready to move up.

This always allowed me to be pushed up from below as well as to be pulled up from above.

I also believe that if you can't beat 'em, join 'em. Or better yet, have them join you. That opportunity presented itself quickly.

We learned that the city editor of the competing but smaller *Miami News*, John McMullan, was disgruntled there. The fact is, McMullan was always disgruntled everywhere. He couldn't get along with people—subordinates, superiors, or the public.

But he had unequaled instincts for news. He had beaten us regularly on local stories. I told Beebe I had just the spot for McMullan.

"Promote me to executive city editor. Let's hire Mac as city editor. He can deal with the news. I'll handle the people and the ideas."

Some of the newsroom people were shocked that I'd "give up" my job to the opposition. They didn't realize that I considered my new role as executive city editor just another stopping-off place. I already had my eyes on the next promotion.

Beebe's number two man was night assistant managing editor Bill Townes. Nice guy. Good story ideas. But no manager. Beebe's frustrations with Townes were apparent.

After a few months as executive city editor, I planted the seed with Beebe: "You know, George, our city desk is in great shape now. It really doesn't need both McMullan and me. If you named me assistant managing editor, Mac could run the city desk nicely and I could help you run the whole newsroom."

When Townes found out what was happening, he found work in Baltimore. When the office wags realized what had happened, they changed my nickname to the "Black Knight."

Learning from a Mix of Mentors

After Beebe named me assistant managing editor, he busied himself more and more with community affairs. He liked that better than the pressure of newsroom deadlines. I loved the pressure—and the fact the top three guys in the Knight organization were now keeping a close eye on me.

They were:

▷ Jack Knight, then sixty-four.

He inherited the *Akron Beacon-Journal* from his father. Leveraged it into a chain that then included the *Herald, Chicago Daily News, Detroit Free Press*, and *Charlotte Observer*.

He spent his winters in Miami and was in the newsroom nearly every day. A blustery battler. Loved gambling, horse racing, risk-taking, fun. Great news instincts. A keen eye for the bottom line. The best all-around newspaperperson I've ever known. My kind of guy. Loose and lovable.

▷ Jim Knight, then forty-nine.

The money man. Always braced for battles with newsroom people because he didn't think they understood the value of a dollar. During an economic turndown, he put in a 5 percent reduction in the newshole and expected me to resist it.

I didn't. "Jim, no problem," I said. "We'll write a little tighter and get as much news in the paper as we do now." From that day on, Jim took a shine to me. He put me on newspaper-wide committees and included me in management meetings that opened the door for me outside the newsroom. But not my kind of guy. Too straight and strict.

▷ Lee Hills, then fifty-two.

His main job was executive editor of the *Detroit Free Press*. He was really resident publisher there, although Jack Knight held that title. But Hills also kept the executive editor's title in Miami and held an umbrella over Beebe.

A smart North Dakota native. Creative thinker. Great planner. Ambitious, but more insecure than his ability and achievement should have made him.

All three became my mentors. They offered a multiplicity of management styles and philosophies. They were in their prime, practicing all they had learned. I was in my thirties, a time for learning. And I was learning, fast.

PLAIN TALK:

Help your boss help you to your next job.

FROM SOFTBALL
TO HARDBALL

"When Neuharth walks into a room unannounced, heads turn as if tugged by a magnet. He is the kind of enormously driven and focused individual who is able to set whole teams of grown people into motion with one mere cock of an eyebrow."

DETROIT MONTHLY MAGAZINE
August 1987

The fast track in Miami led me to a larger and much tougher arena—the hardball league of Detroit.

Hardball competition consumed Motown:

▷ The auto industry's Big Three fought each other for dominance and profits.

▷ The UAW and Teamsters led labor unions in winning the highest wages in the country.

▷ Three major newspapers had fought one of the nation's fiercest wars for circulation and advertising superiority.

Two of Detroit's leaders—a friend and a foe—helped me learn about street smarts and toughness:

▷ Jack Knight, my mentor, explained a valuable lesson to me at Woolworth's lunch counter.

Knight was the strongest personality in the newspaper business in the 1950s and '60s. He knew how to charm his friends and intimidate his foes. His tough, no-nonsense style commanded universal attention and respect.

▷ Jimmy Hoffa, tough guy for the Teamsters, gave me a lasting lesson at the negotiating table.

His roughneck image was backed up by unrelenting attention to what he wanted. He used whatever it took—mainly threats and fear—to gain respect from the Teamsters and with management.

Both men showed me it's not enough just to be smart. Or just tough. You have to be both. Street smarts mixed with toughness were their long suits.

When my Miami mentors decided I was ready to help them at Knight's largest newspaper, the *Detroit Free Press*, I didn't hesitate.

"I'll go anywhere you want me to. When?"

"Tomorrow morning," said Lee Hills, executive editor of the *Free Press* and the *Miami Herald*.

Hills explained what was happening in Detroit that weekend. The *Detroit Times*, a Hearst newspaper and number three in town, was closing its doors.

The *Detroit News*, number two and in the Scripps-Booth family, had bought all the assets of the *Times*, including its subscription lists and circulation team.

Losers in a Crapshoot

"We've been number one in Detroit with the *Free Press* in a three-paper market. Now we're going to be number two in a two-paper market. But I've got some plans on how to win the lead back. I want you to come help me as my assistant," Hills said.

I jumped at the chance. No questions about salary, title. I'd seen other people wring their hands and sweat over decisions like this. Not I.

I recognized an opportunity and was eager to go for it. The *Free Press* was the biggest in the Knight chain—circulation 501,115 compared to the *Herald*'s 305,065.

After my meeting with Hills, he said Jack Knight wanted to talk to me to give me a little of the feel about the Detroit situation.

"I was in a crapshoot in Detroit and lost," Knight said. "I thought Hearst would sell to me. But the bastards at the *News* outbid me. Now we'll have to beat them both."

Then he put my role in perspective: "Kid, you've done all right in the softball league in Miami. Now we'll see how you can do in the hardball league in Detroit."

Hardball, indeed. Everything was faster, more intense. The stakes were bigger. Everybody was looking for an edge.

Miami had thrived on newcomers and loose structure. Detroit was ruled by an entrenched establishment.

Twenty-four hours later I sat in on a crucial Sunday-morning meeting of *Free Press* executives. Hills outlined to the newspaper's top management his creative and detailed plan to win over former *Times* readers.

As the meeting ended, almost incidentally, Hills announced to the group that he had brought me from Miami to be his assistant to help in the battle.

He was more explicit with me: "I'll draw up the ideas. I'll do the planning. Your job is to implement those plans. Mainly in the newsroom. But I also want you to be my eyes and ears in the business office."

A dream job. More responsibility. Higher visibility. The chance to learn about the business side without giving up my first love, the newsroom.

Many at the *Free Press* resented my being there and labeled me the "Miami Mafia." But I was the boss's boy and that helped me get the job done.

The *Free Press* likely would never be number one in Detroit again. But thanks to Hills's plan and our plots, we remained a close and competitive number two.

Learning from Good, Bad S.O.B.s

A few weeks after I arrived on the scene, Knight asked me to lunch. I looked forward to our visits because he was a good teacher. He was gruff and tough, but he knew how to bring out the best in products and people. He was a lovable S.O.B.

We walked around the corner from the *Free Press* to the staid and stuffy Detroit Club.

He ordered a martini, straight up. I ordered mine on the rocks. We talked about his Sunday "Editor's Notebook" column, for which he won the Pulitzer Prize. Then he put down his glass and said, "Let's go."

"Aren't we going to have lunch?" I asked.

"Yeah. Let's go."

We walked six blocks to the old Woolworth five-and-dime. He led me down the stairs to the basement lunch counter.

"What would you like, kid?" he asked.

"You're buying lunch. What are you having?"

He ordered a hot dog, with mustard and catsup, and a Coke. I had the same.

This immaculately dressed multimillionaire glanced around the counter where Detroit's underprivileged were having a cheap stand-up lunch.

He pointed to a heavyset black woman.

"What do you think she read in the paper this morning?" he asked me.

"Damned if I know," I replied.

Then he pointed to a shabbily dressed, elderly white man leaning on a cane.

"What do you think he read?"

"Is this a quiz?" I asked. I thought I was being cute. He didn't.

"Why don't you go ask them?" he suggested firmly. I did. Of course, neither of them had read the paper. Both said they were too busy rushing off to work trying to eke out a living. The paper didn't help them do that.

Knight smiled. "Well, now I hope you've got it. Hills is going to give you a membership in the Detroit Club and the Detroit Athletic Club. But damn it, don't eat lunch there every day. That's what Lee does. He talks to the same people about the same damn things every day. Don't fall into that trap."

Pretty good advice for anybody trying to sell any consumer products:

▷ Keep your feet on the street.

▷ Don't become a captive of your own comfort.

My second-most important lesson came from Jimmy Hoffa. He ran the Teamsters then. The Teamsters and the UAW ran Detroit.

Hoffa was the smartest tough man I ever met. I've met smarter. A few tougher. But none as smart and as tough. He was a bad S.O.B.

The test came when the Teamsters struck the Free Press over a new wage settlement. During a twenty-nine-day shutdown, we agreed to mediation. I sat in with the three-member newspaper negotiation committee. Our leader was business manager Henry Weidler, then a tired sixty-four.

Hoffa was a tough and spritely forty-seven. He looked like a boxer. Short. Muscular. A neck as thick as a bull. A head as hard as a bull's. And a body just as strong. A hairy chest displayed with an open-collared shirt.

A Jimmy Hoffa Pee Break

We met nearly nonstop for thirty-six hours. Hoffa's signal for a break was always the same: "I have to go take a piss."

Then he'd lead his Teamster mates from the table, pee, splash some water on his face, sometimes drink a beer, and dash back in the room, ready to fight again.

Weidler would go to the john, check his zipper carefully, wash and wipe his hands neatly, straighten his tie, drink a cup of coffee, and drag slowly back into the negotiation room.

He was no match for Jimmy.

I learned from that: physical stamina, coupled with smarts, is a winning combination.

When it was over, the Teamsters had gotten nearly everything they demanded before the strike began.

Since I was the new man and low man on the totem pole, I was unable to make any real contributions at negotiations. But when we resumed publication, the news pages were mine, and I used them.

During the strike, Hoffa and his Teamsters had been parading as underpaid truck drivers. For our first poststrike edition we prepared a story listing each Teamster's wages the previous year. It showed they made more money than most of the motor city's automobile workers—or the newspaper reporters and ad salespeople.

Hoffa called me in a rage, after printers tipped the Teamsters that the story had been set in type.

"You print that story and you've had it. You let the wives of my men know how much money they're making and I'll get your ass," Hoffa threatened.

We ran the story. He didn't get me. His enemies got him first.

I was learning a lot in the hardball league. But I wasn't having as much fun as I had in Miami. Beebe was loose and relaxed and appreciated some of my practical jokes. Hills was a better journalist but he was uptight and thought laughing was rude.

Many times he would admonish me: "You just don't realize how often people misinterpret the jokes that you play on them. You don't realize how that hurts you." When I cracked a joke, he would be the one person not to even smile.

If It's No Fun, Run

For me it's easier to work effectively if I'm having fun. I always looked for a work environment that:

▷ Attracts and holds people who are amusing, entertaining, even frivolous when events allow it.

▷ Encourages people to take themselves less seriously.

▷ Rewards people who know how to have fun while taking their jobs very seriously.

Also, it had been over two years since my last promotion. A pretty slow pace after my Miami experience. That added to my restlessness.

And I was beginning to have doubts about the future leadership of the Knight organization. It was the number one newspaper chain in the country. Jack Knight and Lee Hills made it that. But it was clear Jim Knight would take over soon and the business side would dominate. That bothered me.

The business side doesn't understand the heart and soul of a newspaper: news. Most business-side newspaper executives would be as comfortable selling shoes as news.

Jim Knight had picked as his alter ego Alvah Chapman, who later became CEO. A bright guy who knew the business side well. But not my type. He was so straight he made the very proper Hills look like a comedian. Working with Chapman would have made me climb the walls.

Like a lot of career people in their late thirties, I was ripe for the right offer.

PLAIN TALK:

No-fun bosses make even good jobs dull.

BREAKING OUT OF
THE BOX

A phone call out of the blue gave me the break I was looking for as I approached my thirty-ninth birthday. The executive editor of Gannett Newspapers, Vin Jones, invited me to breakfast at an editors' convention in Minneapolis.

When we met, Jones told me he represented Paul Miller, the president and CEO of the Rochester, N.Y.-based company. Would I be interested in moving to Gannett?

I told Jones I was very happy where I was, but I wouldn't close the door on anything without listening. He told me Miller would be in touch.

The conversation left me with mixed emotions. I was flattered to be pursued, but would I really want to work for a little company like Gannett?

This was a relatively small regional outfit with sixteen newspapers, average circulation under 50,000. Not only was it a smaller company, but its reputation was several notches below Knight. The papers were profitable, but bland.

The opportunities would have to be pretty special to pull me to Gannett. But something else was pushing me again: boredom.

All my life boredom has pushed me to new adventures. I'm bored easily. Boredom is like a twitch or a trick knee with me. I can only cure it by moving around or moving on. A new job. A new venture. A new setting.

Lots of people are bored. But most don't know what to do about it.

Author Theodore H. White described it this way: "Most ordinary people lived their lives in boxes, as bees did in cells."

I was never content to be contained in a box. Boredom in Detroit paved the way to Rochester.

Miller invited me to Rochester to see the city and meet with some of his top people. They were pleasant gentlemen, but clearly small-time managers running a small-town company.

I was making $25,000 a year in Detroit. Miller offered me $30,000 to become general manager of the company's two newspapers in Rochester. I told him I would think about it.

Tell-Tale Knee-Jerks

Miller called a few days later. And a few days after that.

"I really want you to join us," he said. "Do you remember that offer I made you? Whatever it was, add $5,000 to it."

That told me something about Miller.

I always look for tell-tale signals of what people are really like:

▷ An off-hand comment after drinks.

▷ A change in facial expression.

▷ Unusual traits, like a shaky hand or sweaty palms or armpits.

▷ Premature comments—talking before thinking.

Learning to read people gives you an edge.

Miller was easy to read. His $5,000 hike in my salary offer was a knee jerk. He knee-jerked easily, and I often took advantage of that after I went to work for him.

Miller told me I had first come to his attention through Monty Curtis, director of the New York-based American Press Institute at Columbia University, where I had conducted several lectures.

I asked Curtis for advice on my job-changing decision. "Make a list of the ten things that are most important to you professionally or personally," Curtis suggested. "And then rate the two companies."

I did.

The two report cards were weighted heavily toward future company growth. Adventures and new ventures. Personal promotional possibilities. Present salary or job title were not as important.

I gave Knight a ten-point "loyalty" bonus. Even so, Gannett won, 94 to 92. More importantly, my gut told me:

▷ There were no Gannetts in the Gannett Company. A professional manager could take that company as far as he wished.

▷ If I was as good as I thought I was, I could be that guy. This company could be mine to run.

The clincher really had come when Miller talked with me of his hopes to expand Gannett outside the Northeast. He was a year-round golfer who loved Florida. He had tried unsuccessfully to buy several small papers there. He was impressed that I knew Florida as well as I did. I harbored dreams of returning to Florida to do new and exciting things. Miller could help me realize those dreams.

Stage-Managing the Job-Switch

When I called Miller to say I'd take the job, I conditioned it on his making a phone call that I would orchestrate. He was to call his friend Jack Knight and emphasize that Gannett had sought me out. And I wanted to witness the call. I was taking no chances on keeping the record straight that I had not been job hunting.

I trumped up a reason to meet with Knight in his office exactly at 1 P.M., the appointed time for Miller's call.

The phone rang.

"Oh, hi, Paul." Knight began.

I could only hear Knight's end of the call, but Miller later filled me in on the rest of the conversation.

"I just want you to know that you've got a young fellow we're interested in," Miller said. "We've approached him and made him an offer and I think he's going to accept. His name is Al Neuharth."

"He's sitting across the desk from me," Knight said.

"Well, I just wanted you to know . . ." Miller said.

Knight suddenly turned gruff.

"I don't understand the purpose of this phone call!" he barked.

Miller said again that it was a courtesy call.

"I don't understand the purpose of this call! I'll see you around on the golf course."

Knight hung up.

He turned to me.

"Well, kid, are you going to take it?"

"Yes, I am."

"If I thought you were making a damn fool mistake, I'd try to talk you out of it," he said. "But Paul's little company sure as hell can use you. We'll miss you, but good luck."

A cool professional reaction from a cool, confident guy. We remained friends until his death eighteen years later.

Most of my friends thought I was loony to leave Detroit for the boonies of Rochester.

I figured it differently. I was ready for a new adventure. I didn't care what other people thought. Too many people pass up good career opportunities because they're afraid of what other people will think.

I had done all right as a hardball player in the major leagues. Now I'd find out if I was ready to manage a minor league team and lead it into the majors.

Understanding Corporate Culture

Before I moved to Rochester, I read two books:

▷ The biography of Frank Gannett, founder of the chain. His personality and vision had dominated Gannett, and I wanted to understand this corporate culture I was entering. It gave me an early line on the key players then still at Gannett.

▷ *Smugtown, U.S.A.*, a book with some fact, some fiction about Rochester published two years earlier by area weekly newspaper editor Curt Gerling. Understanding the Rochester community was as important as understanding Gannett.

Gerling described "Smugtown" this way:

"To start out with you'll need a few clean shirts, well-kept nails, and a Hickey-Freeman suit.

"Of course, you'll enroll Republican and open an account at the Lincoln-Rochester Bank.

"You'll pledge allegiance to the flag at Rotary, hold hands and sing 'God Bless America' at the Lions . . . All this is essential to a fellow on his way to recognition as a [Rochester] 'go-getter' and 'young man worth watching.' "

I don't believe in decision-making journalists joining clubs—or aligning themselves with any special interest group. So in Rochester I did not enroll Republican—or Democrat. I didn't join the Rotary or Lions either. I was friendly without being affiliated.

I did buy two Hickey-Freeman suits (they were manufactured there), but I didn't wear them much. I preferred more casual garb.

I never became a card-carrying member of the coat-and-tie club. Too establishment for me. Over the years my preference for informal but distinctive clothes became an integral part of my style.

Dressing casually and in the same colors—mostly black and white and gray—was a deliberate decision to draw attention to myself. Distinctive style gives a human dimension to bosses. It's also the stuff of which legends are born.

When I wore a black-and-white ascot to a fancy restaurant in New York, I created a story that would be retold in national publications for years to come. All because I wanted to get past the *maître d'* without wearing a necktie.

"A tie is required here, sir," he said in typical haughty New York *maître d'* tones.

I whispered, "I'm sorry, but I have throat cancer. I'm under strict orders from my doctor not to wear anything tight around my neck."

It was the first time I'd seen a New York *maître d'* apologize. He ushered me and my properly dressed guests to our table with care and concern.

In Rochester it was clear to me I was moving into a cautious, conservative, comfortable, cozy crowd and that I'd have to cool it—for a while. I wanted to understand this establishment, even though I had no desire to really become part of it.

Snooping Among the Troops

Miller and I agreed I would be general manager and operating head of the *Rochester Times-Union* and *Democrat and Chronicle*, combined circulation 263,665. But borrowing a page from my *Miami Herald* book, I suggested I snoop around first and ease into the job.

We announced my vague title as a general executive of Gannett. For a month I moved about without any apparent duties. I mixed with executives, editors, reporters, ad salesmen, circulation managers—on the job, in bars and restaurants, and in their homes.

The advantage was they didn't consider me their boss. They saw me as a coworker and poured their hearts out.

Few employees will tell their bosses what they really think. Especially not in a formal office setting.

In later years I took pulses of my people by playing poker with them, inviting them to sports events or barrooms. In those environments, if you keep your reporter's eyes and ears open, you learn a lot.

Most at Gannett were intensely loyal to Miller. He had been the Associated Press Washington bureau chief when Frank Gannett brought him to Rochester as his assistant sixteen years earlier. When Gannett died in 1957, Miller became the boss.

He took a keen interest in the newsroom operations. But he left business matters to others.

My predecessor as general manager, Donald Ulysses Bridge, sixty-nine, had been a strictly hands-off manager. My style was/is either totally hands-on or totally hands-off, whichever is needed at a given time. Never half-and-half.

When I'm involved in something, I want to touch it, hold it, massage it. When the boss puts his hands on something, everyone knows it's important. So they get more involved, too.

Then, when I'm convinced something is working and a successful pattern is set, I step away and let others do the job.

This alternating hands-on and hands-off style gives people examples when they need them. Then the ultimate freedom and satisfaction to perform on their own at the right time.

Not everyone welcomed the change to hands-on when my GM role in Rochester was announced a month after my arrival. I rewrote headlines in the newsroom. Made sales calls with advertising staffers. Rode circulation trucks. Showed up in the pressroom at midnight to check the printing quality.

Most of my attention was on the newspaper product. We increased the amount of news space. Organized both papers into four specific sections every day. Moved all ads off section fronts for better news and picture display.

"A place for everything and everything in its place" became our motto—a direct steal from Lee Hills in Detroit and Miami.

Putting a New Spin on Old Ideas

In fact, nothing we did was really new. As always, the best ideas were those we stole from elsewhere. Then we modified them, and multiplied or divided.

It didn't matter whether they were little ideas from *SoDak Sports* or big ideas from Detroit and Miami. The trick was adapting them for size and scope. If you remember your arithmetic well enough to multiply and divide, you can effectively adapt from small ponds to big ponds and vice versa.

After two years I had the Rochester newspaper operation rolling. Results:

▷ Combined circulation had increased from 263,665 to 277,567.

▷ Annual operating earnings went up by one third, from $2.7 million to $3.6 million.

Nearly everyone there thought I was on a sure track to ultimately take over Gannett. All I had to do was coast.

The long-time managing editor of the *Rochester Times-Union*, Vernon Croop, told me how to get to be the boss of Gannett: "Come to work on time, go home on time, keep your nose clean, and don't rock the boat."

But that wasn't my style. Coasting is boring. At forty-one, I wanted to keep peddling uphill.

My dreams kept focusing on a return to Florida and a new adventure to avenge my *SoDak Sports* failure.

PLAIN TALK:

Coasting is for kids on bicycles.

VULTURES VS. VISIONARIES

"Optimism has always been a chief tenet of Neuharth."

COLUMBIA JOURNALISM REVIEW
May-June 1985

Vultures come in all forms. Birds. Beasts. Humans.

They prey on the dead. Or the young. Or the new. Human vultures feast on visions. They love to destroy new ideas.

I've often used vultures to motivate myself and others. Vultures, unwittingly, helped me realize my dream in Florida.

The stage was the Space Coast, where there is more vision per square mile than anywhere in the world.

Paul Miller and I both had designs on Florida. He wanted to buy newspapers and play golf there. I wanted to launch a new newspaper, take it to the moon, and make a name for myself.

My failure with *SoDak Sports* didn't extinguish my itch to start a newspaper from scratch. It encouraged me all the more.

And I had learned how *not* to do it.

Miller's interest in my project contrasted sharply with the rebuff I got at the *Miami Herald* six years earlier.

In late 1959 I traveled up the Atlantic Coast to Cape Canaveral to open a news bureau for the *Herald*. It was a trip that would change my life.

I was there, watching through binoculars from the balcony of the Vanguard Motel, when a Redstone missile blasted off. This unmanned seven-story rocket was to pave the way for manned space travel.

It didn't take an MBA or a genius to figure out the future was here. The population of the area had been 23,000 in 1950. It was projected at 70,000 by 1960 and 250,000 by 1965.

The Soviets had been spinning Sputnik around the globe. We were just beginning to play catch up with them. The space race was on and sure to accelerate. And so was my imagination.

I went back to the *Herald* and asked to see Jim Knight, the money man.

"I've just come back from the Canaveral area," I told him. "People are pouring in from everywhere. Mostly well educated. They're getting really good-paying jobs on the space program. There'll be a quarter million of them in five or six years. And no local daily newspaper in the area! There's a vacuum we can fill if we act before anybody else does."

"What do you have in mind?" he asked, pokerfaced.

"I think we should start a new daily up there. I don't have any facts or figures for you yet, but my gut instinct says it could work."

His expression didn't change. "We're doing pretty well already. Let's concentrate on the *Herald*." He dismissed the idea with a wave of the hand.

That was my introduction to the reality that most money men and big corporations aren't interested in new ideas. The comfortable status quo drives most corporations. It drives me crazy.

Four years later, when I was negotiating with Paul Miller to join Gannett, he told me that he was interested in expanding, particularly into Florida. I gave him a brief account of my idea of starting a daily newspaper on the Space Coast.

When he expressed interest, that helped me decide to leave Knight and join Gannett. I wanted to work for a company that was willing to try new things. And one based in blustery Rochester, N.Y., should have special designs on Florida.

Newspapers That Deserved to Die

The newspaper industry wasn't known for births in the 1950s and '60s. Daily newspapers were dying by the dozens. Four in New York. Three in Boston. Three in Los Angeles. Three in Montreal. A total of 365 throughout the USA and Canada.

These widespread deaths had a lot of doomsayers predicting the expiration of the fourth estate. My reaction was different. I thought that most of these vanishing dailies deserved to die.

That was not a popular position for me to take with my friends in the press, especially in management.

They blamed the deaths on the unions or rising newsprint costs. I thought the culprit was mismanagement. Bosses of these newspapers had screwed up the way I had at *SoDak Sports*, only on a bigger scale.

Newspapers could not only survive but thrive, if they figured out how to appeal to the television generation, how to modernize their equipment to produce higher-quality newspapers at lower cost, and how to reach out for new audiences in mushrooming growth areas.

Publishers and editors needed to take their blinders off. They needed some new blood and new ideas. Maybe a kick in the ass. I heard opportunity calling.

My goal: Wiping out the *SoDak Sports* memory with a successful sequel on the Space Coast.

Besides fulfilling my dream of starting a successful new newspaper, the Florida plan was fundamental to my vision of making Gannett the biggest newspaper chain in the USA.

We had to break out of our box as a small regional New York-based company. A Florida newspaper would give us an important southern anchor. And the purchase of the *San Bernardino* (California) *Sun and Telegram* was to give us the western anchor four years later.

After two years in Rochester, I presented my detailed Florida plan to Miller. We had talked about the idea from time to time and he was almost as eager as I was. But he also liked the way things were going in Rochester and he was nervous about my attention being diverted elsewhere.

"Paul," I said, "I'll keep one eye on Rochester, the other on Florida. You'll get two for the price of one." He liked that.

Highlights of my big-picture scenario:

▷ I would become president of Gannett Florida, a new subsidiary, while retaining my Rochester general manager title.

▷ We would launch a new seven-day morning newspaper for the Space Coast in the spring of 1966.

▷ We would try to buy two small papers in the area to give us a base for our new venture—the *Cocoa Tribune* and *Titusville Star-Advocate*. Estimated cost $3 million.

▷ We'd commit $2 million for building expansion and presses.

▷ The Gannett Board would have to commit to supporting an investment in operating losses of $3 million to $5 million over a three- to five-year period.

I had learned my lesson about start-ups.

My $50,000 at *SoDak Sports* hadn't lasted long enough to give that venture a fair test in the marketplace. I was determined to have deep pockets to dip into this time. I projected profitability for the new paper in the fifth year.

Miller loved the whole plan. He wasn't particularly interested in the financial details. This was his ticket to Florida, sunny winters, and year-round golf.

But when we presented the plan to chief financial officer Cyril Williams and corporate general manager Lynn Bitner, they thought we were crazy. Gannett had only about $7 million in annual earnings. They were sure we'd take the company down the tube.

Gannett was a private company then and Miller had firm control. He told the rest of the board members what we were going to do and they agreed—some readily, some reluctantly.

Bitner was the most reluctant. A hard-headed German (like myself), he was nicknamed "the Baron" by others at Gannett. He considered himself number two in the company, although Miller had been careful not to make that designation.

Because Bitner was the point man Miller used on acquisitions, he was sent to Florida to try to buy the 9,000-circulation *Cocoa Tribune* as the first step in our plan. The owner was Marie Holderman, a spritely widow in her early eighties.

How Not to Make a Deal

I had known her from my days at the *Miami Herald*. I knew she had rejected dozens of offers, so I tried to coach Bitner on how to approach her.

But Bitner did it his way. He went to Florida with his golf-playing buddy Bill Stretch, also a Gannett board member from whom Miller had bought the *Camden* (N.J.) *Courier-Post*.

The two walked in on Mrs. Holderman unannounced. Bitner introduced himself and Stretch and said, "We're from Gannett and we want to buy your newspaper." She showed them the door.

Bitner returned to Rochester, reported what had happened, and said the paper couldn't be bought. Of course, before coming home, he and Stretch lingered to play three days of golf in Florida at company expense.

Bitner was trying to torpedo my Florida plan. So I convinced Miller to let me go see Mrs. Holderman.

I called her and told her I was going to be in the area and would like to have lunch with her and her manager, John Pound. Pound, in his sixties, was a former printer at the paper and also Mrs. Holderman's live-in lover. I had dined with them before, when I was with the *Herald*.

Her favorite restaurant was the Surf, a popular seafood place on Cocoa Beach. I remembered her favorite dishes—crab bisque and broiled pompano. I called ahead to make sure the Surf had both available on the day of our date.

I pay attention to what people eat and drink, as well as what they say. My follow-up notes after meeting people frequently mention such specific details that serve as reminders in the future. Part of that is the reporter's curiosity in me. Part is the chairman's goal of control.

Over lunch, Holderman, Pound, and I reminisced about the old days. She was as salty and outspoken as always. Her husband had died many years earlier and left her with a weak weekly paper. Now she and Pound ran it as a profitable little daily. But she longed for the Florida she used to know.

"Al, remember the first time you came here in 1959?" she asked. "It was so pleasant here then. All we've had since is progress. I'm so fucking tired of progress."

I laughed and sympathized with her.

"Marie, I know how you feel. But you can't fight it. This place is going to the moon. I think you can make this progress pay off for you, rather than piss you off."

Then I added, gently, "Gannett is going to start a new daily for this area. We're going to put a lot of money into it. I want you to know our plans in advance because I don't want what we do to hurt you. If you join us, we'll pay you a fancy price for your paper, and you and Johnny and others can go on our payroll and help us with our venture." An acquisition attempt combining affection and fear.

I told her we would pay a million and a half dollars or more for her paper. She didn't say no. She said she'd think about it.

I went back and told Miller I thought we could make a deal. Two weeks later Pound called me.

"If you will pay $2 million, I think Mrs. Holderman would sell to you."

I said that was a little higher than what we had in mind.

"But why don't we send the Gannett plane down to bring y'all up here and talk about it?" He liked the idea.

Derby Day Payoffs: $20 and $1.9 Million

They arrived on Saturday, May 1, the day of the 1965 Kentucky Derby. I met them at the airport. I knew Mrs. Holderman loved horse racing and gambling, so I bet her $20 that Lucky Debonair would win the Kentucky Derby. He did.

I've found that making small bets is a fun way to relate to people. It humanizes a relationship. Anytime two people exchange money, it increases the bond.

I'll bet with anybody on anything: who is going to sing the National Anthem before the World Series game; the number of pickoff pitches to first base; the time my corporate jet will touch down on the runway.

Employees especially like to brag that they have bet the boss—win or lose. I always pay promptly if I lose. And I send quick dunning notes when I win.

For Mrs. Holderman, losing $20 to me didn't matter. She went home a millionaire.

When we gathered in Miller's office, Pound was more nervous than I had been the day I walked into the *Miami Herald* newsroom.

Pound opened the conversation: "We appreciate your sending the plane for us. We just wanted to come up and tell you that Mrs. Holderman has decided not to sell her newspaper."

Mrs. Holderman, shocked, yelled across the room, "Dammit, Johnny, that's wrong. We came up here because we want to sell!"

Everybody laughed and that broke the ice.

"I think the *Cocoa Tribune* is worth $1,900,000," said Mrs. Holderman assertively. "Cash. All cash."

Paul and I were prepared to go higher. We looked at each other and nodded. Paul said in his wonderful casual manner, "That seems like a fair price to me. Can we shake hands and agree on it?"

It took the lawyers about three weeks to close the deal. It was so simple it should have taken them about three hours.

Miller, Bitner, Williams, and I went to Florida to announce the deal and deliver Mrs. Holderman's check. When we left our newest newspaper, I was driving, Miller beside me in the front seat. Both of us were happy. Bitner and Williams were in the back seat, unhappy.

"Well, we bought you the fuckin' thing. Now what are you gonna do with it?" Williams asked sarcastically.

"We're going to use it to help take us to the moon," I responded, with a smirk.

Bitner shot back, "Just make damned sure you don't take us down the drain instead."

PLAIN TALK:

Don't let vultures cloud your visions.

BUILDING MOLEHILLS INTO MOUNTAINS

"Neuharth's most impressive early accomplishment was the daily paper he started from scratch in Florida. Within a year, TODAY had a reputation as perhaps the best paper of its size in the country."

ESQUIRE MAGAZINE
September 1979

Worrying about problems is a pretty sure way never to find solutions.

I never worry. Ever.

Of course I think about problems. But I don't waste my time worrying about them. That's counterproductive. The key is to focus on solutions.

That doesn't mean wearing rose-colored glasses. It means looking clearly at the pros and cons. Trying to turn every weakness into a strength, building beautiful mountains out of bothersome little molehills.

Every new idea or new product poses potential problems. Trying to capture a market like Florida's Space Coast where newspapers from Miami, Orlando, Daytona Beach, and Tampa all had a piece of the pie was a problem.

That's why one of my first moves was to call in pollster Lou Harris to help me find the solution.

I first met Lou in Detroit, thanks to Jack Knight's imagination. Jack called me there one day and said, "I've just read the book *The Making of a President* by Teddy White. He gives Lou Harris credit for Jack Kennedy winning crucial primaries in West Virginia and Wisconsin. If Lou's that good at getting votes, why can't he help us get more readers for the Free Press?"

Harris had never done newspaper-reader research. But his work for us in Detroit identified targets and helped boost our circulation in the suburban markets. From that point on, Lou dealt heavily in newspaper research and quit private polling for politicians. He knew his newspaper clients would pay their bills. Politicians sometimes did not.

The Harris name and reputation gave my Space Coast project credibility. But I made it clear his job was to tell us "how" to start our new newspaper, not "whether" to do so. My gut instincts had already answered the latter.

How to Find Out What Will Fly

Bosses need to know how to use outside consultants. Too many use them simply to confirm their own judgments. I didn't need someone to tell me whether to start a paper in Florida. I needed information on what kind of newspaper would fly.

Key Harris findings:

▷ Space Coast residents, who were mostly newcomers, loved new ideas, new frontiers.

▷ They had no loyalty to local institutions. Their loyalties were still back in Ohio or Michigan or Massachusetts.

▷ Their interests were global, not local.

Those findings helped me when Gannett's money men made one more effort to torpedo my new project.

Bitner and Williams lobbied Miller to abandon the new newspaper idea. "We can expand the *Cocoa Tribune* to seven days a week without all that huge cost. Gradually it will grow and make more money," Williams argued.

I gave Miller three reasons why the new newspaper was the way to go:

1. Space Coast residents could be grabbed by something new, but not by a warmed-over old product.

2. A successful new newspaper would get Gannett the attention of the industry.

3. All involved in the new venture would have fun.

Then I added this veiled threat to quit:

"If you just want to do something small and build on the little old *Cocoa Tribune*, put Bitner in charge. If you want to do something big, put me in charge." Miller stuck with me. A few years later Bitner took early retirement.

Those watching thought I was taking the biggest risk of my

career. To me it was not that big a deal. I expected to succeed.
But I had failed before and survived, so I wasn't afraid.

Coworkers at Gannett were betting that I'd either be the
next president of the company or a copy boy, depending on the
success or failure of the new newspaper.

One of those who resented my being there because he had
hopes of succeeding Miller some day was assistant managing
editor John Dougherty of the *Rochester Times-Union*.

Likening me to the early U.S. failures in space, Dougherty
predicted, "Neuharth is like a rocket. He'll go up like a rocket
and come down like a rocket."

For the next year I divided my time between Rochester and
Florida, mostly Florida.

Putting together a staff was the first challenge. Staff emphasis was on youthful enthusiasm, diversity. The average age of
newsroom staffers was twenty-seven. They were on an adventure. They were willing to work hard and make a name for
themselves. They weren't preoccupied with pension plans.

The First TODAY Newspaper

A name for the new newspaper was a key decision. I had
rejected all the traditional newspaper names but couldn't come
up with just the right label myself.

The newspaper's business manager, Maurice "Moe" Hickey,
did. I had brought him in from Gannett's Elmira, N.Y., newspaper. He was a night crawler, a born womanizer. On one of his
nocturnal adventures it hit him: "TODAY."

When he proposed it to me the next day, I knew that was
it. I thought he had stolen it from NBC's "Today," the morning
TV show, but he claimed it was original thinking. We added
Saturn rings to the "O" and the slogan "Florida's Space Age
Newspaper."

It was just the modern, far-out touch we needed to get the
attention of the Space Coast crowd.

Reader interests came first in every decision. We knew that
if we got the readers, advertisers ultimately would follow. If we
didn't, they wouldn't. A simple prescription for any new publication, if you have the capital to stay with it until "ultimately"
arrives.

All four sections were wrapped in news—front and back. No ads allowed on those pages. All major features in exactly the same place every day—national news, local news, sports, TV, columns, comics. These were improvements most editors could not make in established newspapers because of advertiser objections or traditions.

But we had a problem with comics. King Features' George Driscoll, the dean of newspaper syndicate salesmen, explained the problem—and the solution.

"I can't sell you any good comics because a few years ago a greedy guy named Neuharth at the *Miami Herald* insisted that they get statewide territorial rights on everything they bought.

"All I have left are the dogs. But why don't you print them in color every day and readers won't notice how bad they are!"

Color Me Red

At that time the only daily color comics in the country were in the *St. Louis Post-Dispatch*. I took Driscoll's advice. Some adults missed popular comics like "Blondie" and "Peanuts." But the kids thought getting "Mickey Mouse" and "Tiger" in red, blue, and yellow every day was great.

We turned that potential weakness into such a strength that the competing *Orlando Sentinel* later mimicked it. A number of others followed with daily color comics.

During eight months of planning, none of our competitors knew exactly what we were up to. I played on the Bitner-Williams wish and spread the word we simply were going to expand the *Cocoa Tribune* and add a Sunday edition. That explained our building addition, new presses, staff hirings.

Then, on January 27, we made it official: *TODAY*, Florida's Space Age Newspaper, would be launched on March 21, 1966.

The planning pace quickened. For the last two weeks before the launch date, we produced complete prototypes of the newspaper every day—printed them, put them on trucks, dropped them at delivery points to pinpoint timing, then picked them up and burned them at the local dump to keep them out of the hands of the competition.

"An unforgivable waste of money," Bitner complained.

"Practice makes perfect," I replied, by then gaining confidence and getting a little cocky.

On March 21 we were ready.

For thirty days we delivered free copies of *TODAY* to every household in Brevard County, more than 52,000. It worked. The new newspaper was its own best promotion vehicle.

After two weeks, Harris went back for a survey on pricing. We had planned, after the thirty-day free period, to sell the paper at half price—a nickel daily, 25 cents a week. Tens of thousands of half-price coupons had been printed.

Harris's survey found readers had become hooked quickly. "You're crazy if you make any half-price offers," he advised. We threw the discount coupons away and went for it.

When Jim Knight, watching from Miami, heard about our pricing decision, he told me, "That's your fatal mistake."

But we found out people will pay for a newspaper what they think it's worth. Our prepublication projection for paid circulation called for 20,000 at the end of the first year. The actual results:

▷ 33,000 after ten weeks.

▷ 40,000 after twelve months.

During the same period the competition took a dive on the Space Coast:

▷ The *Orlando Sentinel* dropped from 27,000 to 19,000.

▷ The *Miami Herald* from 10,000 to 6,000.

Our quick circulation success was costly. Because we started out with low ad rates based on less than 20,000 circulation, we lost money on every paper we sold. The same thing had happened to me at *SoDak Sports*. But this time we had deep enough pockets to absorb those temporary losses.

Bitner and Williams used the losses to keep the pressure on Miller to pull the plug on me.

"Everything at *TODAY* exceeds our expectations," Bitner told one and all. "The circulation. The advertising. The goddamn losses."

I resisted their pressure to jump ad rates dramatically because I thought advertisers might think they were being gouged. Any new franchise is a little fragile for a while. So we adjusted rates gradually, albeit substantially, every six months. Fifteen years later we used the same approach at *USA TODAY*.

By August 1968, in our twenty-ninth month of publication, we broke into the black. Well ahead of schedule. *TODAY* has been profitable ever since.

An investment of less than $10 million has returned profits averaging several million dollars a year for twenty years. And if it were for sale, its market value would be well over $200 million.

A Paperboy on the Moon

When Neil Armstrong became the first human to walk on the moon in 1969, I decided the nation's Space Age newspaper should be the first paper delivered there. So I asked James Webb, then a Gannett director and formerly the head of NASA, "Who do I talk to to get *TODAY* sent on a moon mission?"

Webb was a good friend, but he laughed at the idea. "They can't do that. No commercial products allowed."

I decided to go higher. President Lyndon Johnson was an ardent backer of the space program. When he made a Cape visit, we hosted a community breakfast for him.

"*TODAY* covers the space program like nobody else does. We'd like to send a copy to the moon. Who do I have to talk to?" I asked the President.

"You can't do that. They can't take commercial products," LBJ replied.

I wasn't going to take no for an answer. I never do. There had to be a way.

I turned to Buddy Baker, then managing editor of *TODAY* and the former promotion manager. "Buddy, you've got to figure out how to get one of the astronauts to take *TODAY* to the moon."

In those days the astronauts were very much a part of the Cocoa Beach community. Not exactly the way Tom Wolfe portrayed them in his part-fact, part-fiction book *The Right Stuff.* But they mixed with the local crowd.

That night Baker approached one of his drinking buddies, astronaut Alan B. Shepard, Jr., in Lee Caron's Carnival Club at Cocoa Beach. He told Shepard that I had struck out with LBJ and Webb.

"Do me a favor and make me a big shot with my boss,"

Baker asked of Shepard. Shepard did. Along with his golf club and golf ball, he took a microfilmed *TODAY* on the next moon mission. Shepard has often joked that he was the first paperboy on the moon. Baker often brags about accomplishing what his boss couldn't.

I learned the way to get things done is to deal with the people who actually can do it themselves. For example, now when I need a suite at a crowded Hilton hotel, I don't call my friend Barron Hilton. I cozy up to the desk clerk or the assistant manager.

I had aimed too high with the President of the United States and the former NASA director. But our aim at reaching for the moon was right on target.

TODAY was a winner. The first successful new newspaper of any size since World War II. Dozens of deaths and now a real, live birth.

The *SoDak Sports* monkey was off my back.

PLAIN TALK:

The difference between a mountain and a molehill is your perspective.

IV

POWER: USE
IT OR LOSE IT

"His enemies shall lick the dust."

THE BIBLE
Psalms 72:9

Getting to the top means taking one smart step at a time.

Managing, maneuvering, manipulating your way from one stepping stone to the next.

Most stepping stones are people who offer opportunity or obstruction.

Many are other S.O.B.s playing the same game you are.

Some are challenging S.O.B.s who have what you want.

Others are threatening S.O.B.s who want what you have.

Some are lovable S.O.B.s.

All must be dealt with accordingly.

Some can be stepped around gracefully—as painlessly as possible.

Some must be stepped over briskly—without looking back.

Some must be stepped on.

Some can be danced with and enjoyed.

I confess I have taken all those steps with all kinds of S.O.B.s.

Dancing around with other lovable S.O.B.s is the most fun. Everyone enjoys that game, and usually the best S.O.B.s win.

But when niceness alone doesn't work, a little nastiness must be applied.

The right mix is the only sure way to the top.

"Be vigilant, because your adversary, the Devil, walketh about, seeking whom he may devour."

THE BIBLE
1 Peter 5:8

BESTING THE BOSS

The time had come in my Gannett career to let the boss know that a new generation of leadership was ready to take over.

That's not an easy job. And I didn't relish it.

But that's the price of progress.

Try it only if you're sure to win.

Paul Miller had hired me at Gannett. Initially he had helped me. When I became heir-apparent, he began harassing me. After being pushed into promoting me, he humiliated me. Now he was hounding me.

For the past three years as president, I was really running the company. But as CEO Miller continued to take most of the credit.

It was clear he would hang on by his fingernails as long as the Lord and the board allowed. I was determined not to be around if that happened.

He was approaching sixty-seven. I was nearly forty-nine.

I had been on a fast track:

▷ From reporter to president in sixteen years.

▷ Along the way, a promotion every year or two, or at most three.

Now three years had gone by, and I was still one step away from the top. So I made my move. I did it reluctantly, not precipitously.

Getting along with the boss had always been one of my long suits.

In fact, getting along with the boss is one of the most

important aspects of anyone's job. Even if he or she is an S.O.B. Most bosses are—at least sometimes.

Three tips for getting along with the boss:

▷ Make the boss look good by doing everything so well that the boss's own reputation will be enhanced. At first don't worry about who gets the credit.

▷ Lighten the boss's workload. By offering to do anything you can do almost as well as the boss can, you free up some of his time, for work or play. If you're really good at this, it may encourage the boss to seek a promotion himself, opening the door for you to move up.

▷ Gradually establish the kind of reputation for yourself that would make the boss look bad if he fires you or if you leave. That requires being noticed. Generating publicity, but backed by substance.

That last one worked best when I began pressing Paul Miller. He would have loved to fire me. And he would have been delighted if I had quit. But he knew that, inside and outside the company, his own image would suffer if either happened.

I had made several moves before 1973 to prepare Miller and me for my succeeding him as CEO. I had hoped to do it in an orderly, planned, cooperative way. That would have been better for him, for me, and for the company.

But each time I took a step forward, he dug in his heels and tried to push me back.

It started in the summer of 1966. I had pulled off the successful launch of *TODAY* in Florida. Observers began writing about me as the shining new light at Gannett.

Miller liked what I had done, but he didn't like the attention I was getting.

In the past, Miller and Gannett had been synonymous. Now the new name of Neuharth was part of the equation. He resented it.

I was feeling pretty cocky about the success of the Florida adventure. I wanted to position myself to try more of the same.

I wrote Miller a note, suggesting he spell out my role more clearly as Gannett's number two person. I offered four options:

1. Name me a vice president.
2. Name me executive vice president.
3. Name me president.
4. Fire me.

And I noted:

"I confess, I prefer No. 3 (President). But, being by nature a conservative fellow myself, I suppose if I were making your decision, I might consider No. 2 (Executive Vice President) as an intermediate step. If you don't think I'm good enough for options 1, 2 or 3, you probably should pick No. 4 (fire me)."

Then I added a P.S.:

"If you decide to name me Exec. Veep, what's wrong with adding chairman to your president's title? That would then make it easier to peel off the other one to me, as and when you wish.

"If you need board votes, I'll be glad to round them up for you and I promise never to mention that it would be a nice sixtieth-birthday present for you."

I thought I was pretty clever showing the boss how he could get himself promoted. And reminding him of his age. He thought I was a pushy kid and stonewalled.

Same Stage, Different Actors

A few months later, another unexpected phone call helped me get what I wanted.

Jack Flynn, the sixty-three-year-old publisher of the New York *Daily News*, was looking for someone with news background as a successor. He was part of the *Chicago Tribune* company, which owned the *Orlando Sentinel*. I had gained his attention when *TODAY* successfully stormed the Space Coast and the *Sentinel* suffered.

He invited me to New York for an interview.

I told him the prospect of running the New York *Daily News* interested me, but I wasn't job hunting. At that time the *Daily News* had a circulation of 2.1 million, the largest daily in the USA.

Pretty heady stuff for the Dakota kid. I told Flynn I would consider an offer, but only if he would call Paul Miller and tell him he had sought me out. Shades of Detroit and the Knight-Miller telephone conversation.

As before, I arranged for Flynn to call Miller at an appointed time, when I would be in Miller's office. Paul picked up the phone. He loved getting calls from publishing pals, especially those in the big time.

"Hi, Jack. Good to hear from you," he said enthusiastically.

Then I eyed Miller closely as he listened to what Flynn and I had decided would be the message:

"Paul, I just wanted to let you know we're looking at a young man in your organization. He's not been job hunting. We approached him, and we're going to make him an offer. He told me he wouldn't consider it unless I told you first. His name is Al Neuharth."

Miller didn't bat an eye. He recognized the scenario. But he was, as always, gracious and gentlemanly with Flynn. He thanked him and made some small talk. When he hung up the phone, he turned to me with steely eyes and asked:

"What do you want?"

My response: "You know what I want. I want you to name me the number two guy in this company. If I can be that, I'd like to stay here. If I can't, I have to consider other opportunities."

Miller suggested we go out to his house late that afternoon and talk about it.

Putting the Job on the Line

Over martinis—he always is a gracious host—he asked me again, "What is it you want?"

"I want everybody to know that I'm number two and will become your successor," I reiterated.

"They already know that," he countered.

"You and I may know, but *they* don't. I need a title that spells it out. If you name me executive vice president, I'll be a lot more help to you. If you don't, I'll have to consider other options," repeating my thinly veiled threat to pack up for New York City.

Finally Miller saw the virtue in my wisdom. "You write the press release and I'll put it out," he said.

Paul Miller has great class. He loves to win in style, but he can lose in good style, too, with a smile and a handshake.

So I had promoted myself to executive vice president. I was forty-two and felt I was on top of the world. The boss was nearly sixty, and I figured I had clear sailing to his seat.

It didn't take long to find out Miller had second thoughts. He wanted to slow down the train, not speed it up.

I wasted no time printing up stationery with my new title. I copied Miller on a letter that went to Gannett editors concerning an upcoming project.

He circled the corner bearing my title and penciled this note: "Why the new stationery?"

I fired right back, "Because the old was outdated. I have a new title, remember?"

The battle of the memos between the boss and would-be-boss had begun. It was to go on for seven years, and got nastier as time went on.

Actually the first few years in my new role we tolerated each other pretty well. He liked the improved image we were getting for Gannett nationwide. I loved the action and higher visibility.

But little things bugged him. Usually it involved changes I made, or refused to make, in the newspapers.

Miller was a golf-playing buddy of both President Nixon and Vice President Agnew. He didn't like the press treatment both were getting

He sent this telegram to our Washington bureau chief, Jack Germond: "Please stop writing that Agnew is 'criticizing, assailing, lambasting college officials and young people.' This is inaccurate and unfair. Don't unfairly and erroneously generalize as your bureau has now done for days running."

Germond called about the telegram. I told him to ignore it.

Then I sent Miller this note: "Suggest you stop telling reporters like Germond what to write or what not to write. Or at least you should discuss such things with me in advance, right?!"

Miller sent it back with this pencil-scrawled rebuttal:

"I'm the boss, right?! Please try to remember that."

Really not bad advice. I was getting a little big for my breeches.

Shit-Kicker Newspapers

Germond resigned later to join the *Washington Star* as its political writer. After departing, he called Gannett "a bunch of shit-kicker newspapers."

Miller coveted his title as editor of the *Rochester Times-Union* and really wanted everything in it to reflect his ultraconservative point of view.

He wrote a scathing note about *The New York Times*' Russell Baker's syndicated column, which we carried weekly: "Why do we print such rubbish as many of Baker's columns, including today's? Let's drop."

We didn't drop it. Instead I sent Miller this response:

"One of the reasons the *Times-Union* will show only about 2,000 increase in circulation this year compared to well over 3,000 for the *Democrat and Chronicle* is that editors too often select content for the *T-U* with your interests in mind, rather than the widely diverse interests of over 100,000 reader families."

The note provoked him as I knew it would. He fired back:

"This is silly and utterly beyond proof. Anyway if the way to get circulation is to print crap I don't like . . . I don't care about the circulation."

Despite the increasing tenseness in our relations and my growing testiness, things at Gannett were going well. Miller devoted more and more time to his AP role, including several foreign forays. Even the old-school Gannett business types accepted the fact I was in charge during Miller's absences.

But I overlooked no opportunity to keep urging Miller to promote himself to chairman and name me president. Finally at the annual meeting on May 26, 1970, he relented and made what he called a surprise announcement—the naming of me as president of Gannett.

I got what I wanted, but the reaction was too much for Miller.

The next day he tried desperately to undo it with this memo:

> To All Gannett Publishers, General Managers, Editors:
>
> Some confusion has been manifest in connection with my announcement at our annual meeting yesterday and the election of myself as chairman and chief executive officer and of Al Neuharth as president . . .
>
> Of course, the Associated Press didn't help. As you may know, my favorite wire service reported that Miller "resigned."
>
> I attach a copy of the statement I prepared for use

at the meeting. As I say, the title I have taken is chairman and chief executive officer.

Chairman will henceforth be the top job in Gannett.

Al is my deputy and right-hand bower. His full title is president. The board and I have designated him as chief operating officer. But that is descriptive, not part of the title.

I had gone from chief operating officer to bower in less than twenty-four hours. I was feeling the sting of Miller's resentment over what he had been nudged into doing. From that day on, it was apparent no nudging would dislodge the CEO's title.

As Miller's sixty-fifth birthday approached, his best friend on the Gannett board, Rochester banker John Remington, suggested we throw a big birthday bash for Paul.

We enlisted Miller's wife, Louise, in the planning, and she was enthusiastic. We booked the entire Country Club of Rochester and invited movers and shakers from across New York State.

Boycotting His Own Birthday Party

The day the invitations were mailed Remington told Miller of the nice surprise we had planned for him.

Miller said, "I ain't going!"

Remington thought Paul was kidding. But the reason for his attitude soon was made clear:

"You tell Neuharth I know what he's trying to do. He wants to emphasize to everyone that I'm sixty-five years old. I'm serious. I'm not going."

Remington came to me in a dilemma. The invitations were out. What would we do?

"That's your problem, John," I said. "Frankly I don't give a damn whether he shows up at his own party or not."

In the end Remington finally convinced Paul he had to attend. He sulked most of the night.

After it was over I promised him I would never throw him another birthday party. I kept that promise until his eightieth. By then he had retired and mellowed, and loved every attention

I gave him, even if it meant highlighting his age. And once I had the CEO title, I could afford to mellow, too—at least toward Paul Miller.

Miller's resentment over my impatience became more and more personal. I've never seen him angrier than at an Associated Press Managing Editors Convention at Kansas City in November 1972.

My first marriage had ended in divorce earlier that year. I was dating Lori Wilson, a popular Florida state senator who was getting media attention because she was elected as an independent.

I had arranged for the senator to be on the APME program, on a political panel discussion along with Alabama Governor George Wallace and his then wife, Lurleen, and "Doonesbury" artist Garry Trudeau.

When Senator Lori arrived, I put her up in Paul Miller's suite at the hotel. She was only staying the night and Miller wasn't arriving until the next day. Of course I was trying to impress my date by giving her the boss's fancy suite.

The next afternoon, Miller called me to his suite and raged, "You want to quit, get fired, or start over?"

"What are you talking about?" I asked.

"You don't think I know what happened last night? You had that blonde in my suite. How dare you!" He was livid.

"Do you know who that blonde was?" I asked.

"I don't give a damn who she was. You put her in my suite. People are talking about this blonde staying in my suite!" He was beside himself with anger.

I thought maybe I could calm him down by being cute.

"You weren't here, so nobody thinks you slept with her. And I didn't sleep with her—in your suite." (I added that in the interest of accuracy.) "So what's the problem?"

He sputtered and told me to get the hell out of the place before he threw me out.

Later, after Lori and I married, Paul and she became good friends.

That evening, when Paul and I ran into each other at a convention reception, he was his characteristically friendly self. Not a hint of the nasty encounter. However nasty in private, he is always Mr. Niceness in public.

That was the painful part of fighting with Paul Miller. I enjoy a good fight as much as anyone, especially when the stakes are my boss's job as CEO. But I had to joust with a mentor who is as charming as he is strong-willed.

Even as I write this, I have regrets that things became so unpleasant. But there is no pleasant way to unseat a boss whose time is up. And there is nothing more detrimental to a company than to have most major things on hold while the boss is obsessed with holding on.

The sixty-fifth-birthday incident convinced me that I could never again nudge Miller into changing his role or mine. I figured the next time it would take a sledgehammer. So I began forging the hammer.

In the early seventies, the Gannett board of directors had twelve members. They had some similar characteristics:

▷ All were white males.

▷ All had been brought on board by Miller.

Even so, most had developed a high regard for me. It had been clear to them at board meetings for several years that I was really running the company.

Some—but not all—felt that Gannett's unofficial retirement age of sixty-five should apply to the CEO as well as to others.

The strongest director was James Webb, the man whom President John F. Kennedy had picked to head NASA to take us to the moon. Webb also had been an undersecretary of state and budget director for President Truman.

PP: A Pal and Protector

The weakest director was William P. Rogers. He had been U.S. Attorney General under President Eisenhower and Secretary of State under President Nixon until Henry Kissinger aced him out. Rogers was a long-time golfing buddy of Miller's.

Webb was chairman of the board's management-succession committee. Other members of the committee were Rochester banker Wilmot R. Craig and former Secretary of Commerce Alexander B. Trowbridge.

After the sixty-fifth-birthday incident, Webb and I had frequent informal discussions about what we dubbed the "PP"—the Paul Problem. Webb told me his soundings indicated that nearly all board members favored my becoming CEO. The lone holdout was Rogers. He thought only Paul himself should decide when or whether he wanted to step down.

"If you're willing to let Paul continue as chairman with you becoming CEO and president, I think I can arrange that," Webb offered.

I told him that was exactly what I had in mind. "I have no desire to dump the person who hired me. I just think the time has come to make it clear that I'm the boss, so I can get on with getting Gannett back into gear."

Webb kept meeting resistance from Rogers, the other half of the "PP" problem—Paul's Protector. Webb was both an administrator and a compromiser, who liked unanimous agreement on any issue, so he kept postponing the inevitable.

My own soundings indicated that if it came to a vote, I'd win 10–2. Miller's only votes would have been his own and that of his pal and protector Bill Rogers.

I made my move as we entered 1973.

"Jim, this has to be the year," I told Webb. "Paul will be sixty-seven this year; I'll be forty-nine. If I'm not CEO this year, that's the end of the line for Gannett and me."

It was not a threat; it was a promise. Webb knew I meant it.

He arranged for Paul and me to meet with him privately in April 1973 at his home on Massachusetts Avenue in Washington. That's an avenue of diplomats. But there was nothing diplomatic about Webb's approach with Miller.

Webb's wife Patsy brought us all tea. Then Jim got right to the point:

"We all know the purpose of this meeting. Paul, I'd like you to pick a date when you will give up the chief executive's title to Al. If you don't, the board will have to do it for you."

Miller was sullen and silent.

Webb continued, "I'd like to suggest it be done at the annual shareholders' meeting next month."

"Oh, no!" Miller cried. "Not then!"

"Why not?" Webb asked.

Miller's reply: "That's too soon. There are a lot of things we have to arrange and put in place before we can make such a major move. The annual meeting is just too soon."

He was not only trying to buy more time, but he clearly didn't want it done when there were people around. Our annual meeting always drew several hundred, especially his Rochester friends, and got heavy media attention.

I didn't care if we made the announcement in a telephone booth or in the men's locker room at Paul's country club. I just wanted it done.

"Why don't we agree on the regular board meeting in June?" I suggested.

Webb thought that was a splendid compromise.

Miller tried one more stall.

"I'll have to have some assurances," Miller said.

"Like what?" Webb asked.

"I want a promise that I can stay as chairman another five years."

I surprised him. "Fine with me." Once I had the CEO's title, I didn't care how long he hung around.

"And I want to know how the press announcement will be worded."

I surprised him again.

"Fine, you write it. I'll edit it and put it out," I said.

Webb was relieved. We all shook hands. Miller was glum. But the game was over.

A No-News News Release

Webb advised the other directors. In preparation for the June meeting, Miller drafted the news release about as I expected he would.

ROCHESTER, N.Y.—Paul Miller today announced that he is stepping down as chief executive officer of Gannett but will continue as chairman. Miller, who is also president of the Associated Press, has been the head of Gannett for sixteen years.

Miller said he also will continue as president of the AP and will be very active as chairman of Gannett for at least five more years.

During his reign at Gannett, that company has become one of the largest media companies in the United States . . .

I burst into laughter when I read his proposed release. Three paragraphs and still no mention of the new CEO. The news was being left out of this lifelong newsman's news story.

Finally in the fourth paragraph, he wrote: "Miller is passing on the chief executive's title to Allen H. Neuharth, who has been president for three years."

"Stepping down" and "passing on the title," indeed! Actually the title had been wrestled away from him.

I suggested to Miller that maybe the new boss's name should be a little higher up. So we made some revisions.

The next five years had to be the most miserable of Paul Miller's professional life. Not because I made them so. He did.

In fact, once I had the CEO title, I became friendlier and even solicitous of Paul. I arranged interesting travel assignments for him. Urged him to enjoy more golf outings. Made sure a company plane was available whenever he wanted it.

But he was embittered. At board meetings he listened silently as I, and others of the new generation of leadership, outlined what we were doing and planned to do. He offered no support. He knew it was useless to offer any opposition.

His was the fate of so many bosses, especially corporate CEOs, who don't know enough to quit while they're ahead:

▷ They usually suffer in sadness while what was once their world moves on in its own way at its new pace.

▷ What was once respect and/or admiration from their colleagues turns to coldness and contempt.

After I became CEO, I moved quickly to revamp the makeup of the board, bringing in women, minorities, a diversity of philosophy. As the all-white-male makeup changed, Paul's presence was almost unnoticed.

As the end of his five-year chairmanship approached, he asked if he could stay on another year. It had to be a demeaning move for him. But I agreed. He was no problem for me. The only problem was within himself.

On January 1, 1979, Miller finally retired as chairman. He was seventy-two.

Just one year later, on January 5, 1980, he suffered a massive stroke. He never regained his speech. It became difficult for him to move about. The game of golf, which he loved so much, now provided him only memories. He has suffered through many miserable years, still alive as this is written in 1989.

An unhappy termination of a brilliant career of a many-talented and multifaceted man. Those last years he held on as chairman should have been spent enjoying the fruits of his labor. Instead, they were spent in unhappiness.

I've often blamed myself for not having forced him into retirement at a time when he could enjoy it. To him, it seemed as though I was simply an ungrateful young upstart, interested only in his job.

On reflection, I should have bested this boss sooner. He, the company, and I all would have been much better off for it.

I made a solemn vow then that my departure would be different.

PLAIN TALK:

He who leads should learn when to leave.

COVERING YOUR ASS

"Neuharth: He's done it all, so you can't fool him."

BUSINESS WEEK
September 30, 1985

Now that I was on top, I knew others would want to topple me. Maybe not right away. But somewhere, somebody would be plotting for my job.

It's human nature. Some S.O.B. wants something you've got.

In your personal world it may be something you're perfectly willing to share, like your friendship or your love.

In the business world the target is probably your job.

I should know. I overcame a coup attempt from someone I asked to join my Office of the Chief Executive, with the full knowledge that he wanted my job.

I believe in practicing the S.O.B.'s Golden Rule:

Expect others to do unto you what you would do to them.

The modern translation: *Cover your ass.*

I don't run from my enemies. Most people try to avoid enemies. I believe in keeping an eye on them and keeping the lines of communications open. Adversaries make mistakes. If you're up close when they do, you have a better chance of besting them.

Karl Eller never was a friend, even though we were—and still are—friendly. He was looking for big-time respectability. He dreamed of being a major media mogul. Still does.

He pieced together newspapers, broadcast stations, and

billboard companies to form Combined Communications Corp.

In 1978, when we first discussed his company merging with Gannett, I knew he had more in mind than a merger.

Instinctively I sensed Eller wanted to make the deal primarily because he figured he would end up running the Gannett Company. His ambition made him impatient, one of his weaknesses. Here's how I exploited it:

▷ Because Eller was in heat about the merger, we were able to buy his company for about $100 million less than it was worth.

▷ Because his impatience made him act too quickly on proposed deals, he made himself look foolish.

▷ Because it would become obvious to the Gannett board that I was a broader-based and better CEO than Eller, when/if he made his move to get my job, I figured I'd beat his ass. He did and I did.

After my first meeting with Eller, I invited him to join me for a weekend at Pumpkin Center, my Florida home, so we could really get acquainted. He jumped at the idea.

Pumpkin Center is an overgrown log cabin on seven oceanfront acres in Cocoa Beach, within sight of the launchpads of the Kennedy Space Center. It's where I work and play and hold a variety of business meetings, small and large. It is very private, but the nearby launchpads give it a futuristic air.

Never Forfeit an Advantage

The first day Eller and I swam, sunned, and played tennis. He cheated. He foot-faulted badly on every tennis serve. I called him on it. At first he tried to ignore my calling him. But when he realized I was serious, he toed the line. That told me something about our future relationship.

The next day we talked business. Both of us agreed our two companies merging would be a marriage made in heaven if we could work out the details.

That evening he left my study to go to his guest suite to call his wife, Stevie, in Phoenix. Pumpkin Center has a room-to-room intercom system. Eller had talked to me on it from his suite. He forgot to push the "private" button before calling his wife.

Eller's end of that conversation was broadcast clearly into the speaker in my study. He spilled his scheme.

"Honey, this is gonna work—I know it is," Eller told his wife. "If we put it together, I'll run it all within six months. I promise you. . . . Al's okay, but he's just not as good as I am. We'll get some of our people on the board, and then we'll convince them all I'm a better CEO. I'll have it all. It's an opportunity of a lifetime."

Later he and I had dinner at the Surf restaurant, at my usual corner table where we could talk. He was hyper. I was calm. Hearing his goal of getting my job made me realize how his saliva was running for the deal and that I could get a better price on his company if I kept my cool.

We agreed we'd arrange a meeting to start negotiations the following week in Tucson. Eller had attended the university there, and we owned the *Tucson Citizen* newspaper. We both knew the city well and felt we could bring our financial teams there without them being noticed.

I stayed out of the negotiating room, as I nearly always did at the beginning, so that chief financial officer Doug Mc-Corkindale could stall and say he'd have to check with me. At a midafternoon break, Doug reported, "They really have an inflated idea of what they're worth. They're talking $500 million."

I told him to keep listening but not to appear eager. They broke off talks at the end of the day, far apart.

Eller asked if he and I could have dinner, privately.

Over dinner Eller showed me how eager he was.

"Don't you just feel this deal is right?" he asked. "We'd be the biggest thing in our business."

"The deal may be right, but your price is wrong," I responded, showing no enthusiasm. We parted without any future meeting plans.

A month later Eller called, as I expected he would. He knew I would be in Atlanta for the convention of the American Newspaper Publishers Association. "Can we get together?" he asked.

We agreed to meet in my suite at the Atlanta Hilton. When he walked in, it was clear he was still hot to trot. Doug was with me. Eller's lawyer, Larry Wilson, was with him.

Karl said he'd been thinking a lot and still felt we should get together. On what basis could we make a deal?

I had Doug tell him we'd give him stock worth about $337 million. Eller let his glands make the decision. We bargained a bit; then he accepted a price of $362 million, a bargain for us by about $100 million.

Hold Your Enemies Close

A year later, following the normal protracted FCC hearings, the deal was finalized. Now that Eller was part of Gannett, I knew exactly where I wanted him.

My guideline was a Sicilian motto from the Godfather: "Hold your friends close. But hold your enemies closer."

With confidence, or cockiness, I didn't hesitate offering seats on the Gannett board of directors to Eller and two other representatives of his choice. And I asked him to join my Office of the Chief Executive.

I considered that an appropriate part of the price to make Gannett's biggest deal yet. Eller erroneously figured it was a way for him to dethrone me.

At CCC, Eller had established himself as a first-class deal-maker. There's a big difference in being a deal-maker and a manager. I'm both. Eller isn't. He is interested primarily in going from deal to deal like a dog in heat. He doesn't care to manage what he gets.

After the Gannett-CCC merger, Eller remained based at his company's former headquarters in Phoenix. I suggested he might like that and he bought it enthusiastically. That way he felt included, but I could exclude him anytime I wanted to from the main events in Rochester.

When Eller came to Rochester for our first OCE meeting, I praised him in front of the group and asked him to discuss his hopes for contributing to the company.

He closed with this statement: "I think I can bring some good acquisitions into Gannett. I think I can get us into some areas maybe that we're not even in now, if Al will let me."

The room was so quiet you could hear a pin drop. Eller had telegraphed to all of us his insecurity. He acknowledged that he could only do what I would let him do.

Eller decided the way for him to impress the Gannett board was to make more deals than I'd been making. The first three months he was with us, he proposed deal after deal.

Most of them were not very big or very well thought out and/or didn't fit our overall growth plan. His silliest suggestion was to buy a billboard company in England. The company was too small and in too much trouble for Gannett to be interested. But Eller saw it as a way to show the board that he could expand Gannett abroad.

When we rejected that deal, Eller became increasingly frustrated. His game plan to blitzkrieg our board was not working. I knew it was just a matter of time before he would make a kamikaze attack.

Five months after Eller joined Gannett, I was attending a publishers' convention at the grand old Boca Raton Hotel in Florida. After lunch most of the publishers went off to play golf.

I don't golf. I've watched people play golf and covered it as a sportswriter. The trouble with golf is you can't think about anything important while you're concentrating on a drive, pitch, or putt. I like to think all the time. You can do that while jogging, swimming, or sunning.

I was sunning outside a cabana at the Boca Raton Beach Club when I was paged. I went around the corner to a phone on a wall near the pool. The operator said I had a long-distance call from a Mr. Eller.

"Hi, Karl, how are you?" I said cheerfully, even though I was irritated that Eller was interrupting the little time I had to enjoy the sun.

"I just called to let you know that I am putting out a press release. In fact, it's going out right about now," Eller said.

"Oh, tell me about it."

"It says I'm resigning as an officer of Gannett because you and I have serious differences over philosophy, policy, and style."

"Well, that's interesting. Do you go into details in the release?"

"No. But I mention that I am staying on as a director of Gannett."

"Well, I'm a little surprised, but I understand it. I'm sorry you're leaving, because I thought you could have made a lot of contributions."

"Oh," added Eller, "one other thing. I really think—I don't know quite how to say this—but I really think I should be running the Gannett company."

"Well, that's no surprise to me. You've run a company, and I've run a company. I can understand that you would want to run this company. But as I've told you, the job's not open."

"Well, I'm going to have a try at it," Eller said.

"What do you mean?" I asked calmly.

"I'm going to talk to the directors and tell them that I think I can do a better job of running the company than you can."

Beauties and the Beast

Here I am, in my swimming trunks, standing at a cabana phone, bikini-clad women all around me, and this guy is telling me he is going to try to take my job away from me.

I took a deep breath to stay relaxed.

"Karl, you have every right to do that. Do you have a specific plan or timetable in mind?" I asked.

"I'm going to go see each of them [the directors] individually. I'm going to ask for their vote at the December 18 board meeting in New York." It was now November 12.

Eller loved to talk. By keeping my temper in check and not fighting back, I had baited him into telling me his game plan. After he revealed how he was planning to play his cards, I played my trump card.

"Karl, with our directors scattered all over the country from California to New York, logistics could be a problem. Why don't you take a Gannett company plane and it will be easier for you to go see everybody."

Silence. He was shocked.

"You really mean that?" he finally asked in disbelief.

"Sure. That way you'll be able to see everybody before the next meeting, and then they can decide what they want to do about you and me."

Eller was astonished that I was doing him this favor. I figured I was simply giving him enough rope to hang himself.

Then I left the beach and went to work.

I knew the press would be after me as soon as Eller's news release hit. He was, after all, a director and officer of Gannett, and he was picking a public fight with the CEO.

I banged out this brief statement on my typewriter and told our public relations people to distribute it immediately: "I am sorry to see Karl leave. He is a very able executive. But he was

CEO of his own company for many years and I can understand why he doesn't want to play second fiddle to me."

The press understood it, too. They sensed no sour grapes on my part. I made no further comment. It was a one-day story.

After putting out my statement, I had my two secretaries start calling all Gannett directors. I made notes on exactly what I would say to each one.

My son, Dan, was then living in nearby Fort Lauderdale. We had agreed he'd stop by at 7 P.M. so we could have dinner together. When he walked into the suite, both secretaries were working the phones. Notes were spread here and there.

"What's going on? This looks like campaign central," Dan said.

"It is," I replied. I put him to work on the phones as well. It was 11 P.M. before we had reached all the directors. Then he and I had a midnight dinner at which we planned additional strategy to overcome the coup attempt.

I told each director of Eller's press statement and mine. I also told them to expect a visit from Eller. I joked about giving him a company campaign plane to go after my job.

That hit the right note with nearly all directors. If I had discouraged them from seeing him, it might have encouraged them to think he had something to offer, or that I had something to hide.

Our board had fifteen directors at that time. I figured Eller had four votes going in, his own plus these:

▷ Tom Reynolds, the Chicago attorney who had been Eller's lawyer for CCC and joined our board when we made that deal five months earlier.

▷ John J. Louis, Jr., also a CCC board carryover. A wealthy Chicago businessman who later became ambassador to the Court of St. James.

▷ J. Warren McClure, a malcontent and misfit who had been given his seat by my predecessor and had his eyes on my job from day one.

I figured the longtime loyalty Reynolds and Louis had for Eller was too strong for me to overcome so quickly. And I knew McClure's dislike of me would drive him into the Eller camp, especially if Karl offered Mac some top management post, as I expected he would.

The question mark was Paul Miller. He was still bitter over having the CEO title wrestled away. The bylaws permitted him to stay as a voting director until he was seventy-five. He might be Eller's fifth vote.

Only Two Votes to Spare

My count meant I needed to hold my supporters. I had only two votes to spare.

Eller helped me, as I figured he would. His pitch to the directors was amateurish. He flew into their hometowns unannounced, called from the airport. His brief visits offered no real reasons why he should replace me, except that he thought he could do a better job.

One by one the directors called me to report on his visit. Clearly, those who called were also reaffirming their support for me. Miller didn't call.

The director closest to Miller was Wes Gallagher, who had been Associated Press president when Miller was AP chairman. Gallagher thought Eller would be a disaster as Gannett CEO and volunteered to lobby Miller on my behalf.

His report: "Paul promised me he won't vote against you. He may abstain. But don't do anything else to piss him off between now and the board meeting, or he might change his mind."

On the eve of the board meeting, I was pretty sure of ten votes. Eller didn't know that. He got his pal Louis to invite all directors except me to an informal dinner at which he hoped to make his pitch that would put him over the top.

My supporters told me they would not attend the dinner. I urged one to go as my spy and report back on who attended and what happened. The lovable S.O.B. did. As a result I slept very well that night. I knew I had the votes.

At the next day's board meeting I moved through the agenda routinely. At "other business," I paused, looked at Eller, Reynolds, Louis, and McClure.

I knew their plan had been for Reynolds to move that Eller replace me as CEO and for Louis to second the motion. But there was no motion. Silence.

Again I asked for other business. Paused. Scanned and

smiled at each of the four. Still silence. Then I called for a fifteen-minute recess, during which I said I was convening a special meeting of the management continuity committee.

Gallagher was chairman of that committee. "Wes," I said, "what's the matter? Do you suppose those dumb bastards can count and know they only have four votes?"

"Of course," he said. "Adjourn the meeting."

But I wanted to have some fun. I pulled out a resolution I had had prepared in advance. It read: "RESOLVED: That this board of directors hereby requests the resignation of Allen H. Neuharth as Chief Executive Officer and elects Karl Eller to succeed him."

I told the committee, "I'm going to offer the resolution to fire myself. Doug will second it. Then we'll have a roll-call vote and put those four pricks on record."

Wes turned white. Then red. Then he hit the ceiling. "You goddamned fool! You've won. Quit playing games. Let's go home."

The other two members of the committee, banker Bill Craig and activist Dolores Wharton, agreed strongly with Gallagher. They talked me out of forcing the vote.

"Okay," I laughed. "But you're taking all the fun out of winning."

When we reconvened the board meeting, the other members were on the edge of their seats. Each had his/her speculation of what the committee meeting was about.

I called the board to order, again asked for any other business. Silence.

"I'd like to report on our meeting of the management continuity committee," I said. Long pause. "We agreed unanimously to wish you all a very Merry Christmas. The meeting is adjourned."

Laughter, some nervous.

I learned later that Eller and his cohorts had speculated during the recess that I would come back asking for his resignation. I didn't have to. Humiliated if not humbled, he resigned as a director three months later, as I expected he would.

Two of his supporters provided a satisfying sequel. At the next board meeting in February, both Louis and Reynolds asked to see me privately. They are men of honor and offered to resign. McClure didn't offer anything. I got rid of him three years later by lowering the retirement age for directors who were former company executives. That became known as the "McClure amendment."

The Art of Reforming a Foe

I told both Louis and Reynolds that I understood their loyalty to Eller. "Now that he's gone, I hope I can earn that same kind of loyalty to me. I want you to stay on our board. I think you can make real contributions to this company." They were surprised and grateful.

Even though Reynolds and Louis joined the board with the wrong team, they ultimately became strong supporters and excellent directors, with the right care and feeding.

This demonstrated that adversaries can become your allies if you're willing to invest the time and effort.

There's an art to turning a foe into a friend. Always assume there's no reason for an intelligent person to dislike you. And don't hold grudges yourself.

That philosophy paid off with Reynolds and Louis.

Three years later, as a key member of the executive compensation committee, Reynolds led the move to double my annual base salary from $450,000 a year to $900,000—then, a year later, to $1 million. As I had predicted, Reynolds made a great contribution.

PLAIN TALK:

Give your enemies enough rope to hang themselves.

SKINNING SHARKS

"When Neuharth wears a sharkskin suit, you can't tell where the suit ends and Al begins."

LOS ANGELES TIMES
September 7, 1978

A new kind of robber baron is stalking corporate USA—the raiders and traders who steal public companies from unwary or unprepared CEOs.

I was ready for the guy who tried to steal my company.

Cincinnati billionaire Carl Lindner is a shark in sheep's clothing.

Like all corporate sharks, he required special treatment. I overcame Lindner in a classic behind-the-scenes contest that I made public only after I knew I had beaten the S.O.B.

I say "overcame" instead of "fought off," because you don't fight off sharks in the traditional sense. You must bait and hook them in a calculated way.

Once you spot a shark swimming in the business waters around you, your instinct will be to fight back quickly. If you do, chances are you'll get cut up at best, or killed at worst.

I don't run or try to swim away from sharks. But I carefully size up both the shark and the surroundings. My baiting attracts sharks to my waters, rather than my swimming into theirs. That way you can decide whether to go for a quick hook or a leisurely catch.

When Lindner became Gannett's second-largest shareholder in 1979, I knew he had ulterior motives.

Lindner was on close terms with other Wall Street raiders and always referred to them warmly by first names as his friend Ivan (Boesky), or Carl (Icahn), or Mike (Milken), or Boone (Pickens), or Saul (Steinberg).

His goals were the same as theirs, but his style much different. Lindner is straitlaced, soft-spoken, slow-talking. He doesn't smoke or drink. He shuns publicity. He's a devout churchgoing Baptist. But the dollar is his god almighty.

He buys his way into companies as a substantial shareholder, courts management, then increases his holdings, maneuvers his way on the board, and ultimately takes control. He's done that at Penn Central, United Brands, Circle K, and others.

Lindner got his stake in Gannett when we acquired Eller's Combined Communications. Lindner was CCC's major shareholder, and in our stock exchange he ended up with over 4 percent of Gannett's stock.

His Goal Was Control

The year following the merger, he and his company president and henchman, roly-poly Ron Walker, came to see me and Doug McCorkindale. Lindner said he liked our company very much and would like to "increase my position." It didn't take a genius to figure out he was after control of the company.

His initial target was the Gannett Foundation, the company's biggest shareholder, with about 11 percent. Doug and I were among the fourteen trustees of the Foundation.

"Would the Foundation sell me its block of Gannett stock? I'd pay a premium over the market price. How much of a premium would it take?"

Our answers to all his questions were the same: We couldn't speak for the trustees. We didn't think they were interested in selling. But his route would have to be through then Foundation president John Scott.

We alerted Scott. When Lindner approached him, Scott, an outspoken Hoosier ex-Marine, showed him the door. "The stock's not for sale," Scott said. No further discussion.

That later sent Lindner into the open market and sent us looking for an antitakeover lawyer. We hired one of the best, Marty Lipton, of the New York firm of Wachtell, Lipton, Rosen & Katz.

Lipton proposed two amendments to our bylaws similar to those being adopted by more and more corporations to discourage or fend off fast-buck artists:

▷ A so-called fair-price amendment, to help ensure that all shareholders must be paid substantially the same price as any other shareholder in a tender offer. That makes it potentially costlier for a raider because he cannot squeeze smaller shareholders to sell their stock at a lower price after acquiring control from major shareholders.

▷ A staggered board of directors. Having only one third of the members stand for re-election each year guards against an abrupt change in management and makes it more difficult for a raider to gain board control.

A little more than a month before the May 21, 1985, meeting of shareholders, Lindner filed notice with the Securities and Exchange Commission that he had acquired additional Gannett stock, putting his holdings over 5 percent. That's the level that triggers an SEC filing. Lindner's filing said he might acquire more from time to time.

His intentions were as clear and classic as those of any corporate raider. He intended either:

▷ To acquire enough stock to force his way onto the board and ultimately gain control of management.

▷ Or to become enough of a threat or nuisance to force the company to buy back his stock at a huge profit for him.

When our proxy statement containing the two antitakeover amendments arrived in his mail, Lindner called me from his Cincinnati headquarters. His usual soft, low voice was several octaves higher:

"Al, I'm shocked. I can't believe you're doing this to me. I can't believe you didn't ask me about it first. We've got to sit down and talk. Can you come to Cincinnati?"

He loved doing business on his home grounds. I didn't buy it.

"I'm tied up in meetings all week in Washington. But I'd be glad to see you if you want to drop in here sometime," I said.

That same afternoon he called me from the lobby of our Washington headquarters and said he'd like to come upstairs to visit. All his meetings were called "visits." His style, as we learned over and over the next few weeks, was to dog you at your office, home, or hotel with an unannounced visit. It was a form of intimidation. He tried to wear you down or frustrate or irritate you. But I didn't let his style get to me.

I summoned chief financial officer Doug McCorkindale to my office. I expected Lindner would have Ron Walker by his side. He did.

He was very direct.

"We're here as major shareholders to ask you to withdraw the amendments. You would be disenfranchising us. We can't stand for that," Lindner said.

"Carl, this is a policy move carefully considered and unanimously approved by the board. We think it's fair to all shareholders. I'm sorry you feel so strongly about it. But we're going to try to get it passed," I said, politely but firmly.

He toughened a little.

"I'm requesting you to poll your directors and tell them of my opposition and see if they'll change their minds. Will you do that?"

"Sure," I said. "You know they're scattered all over the country, and it may take a day or two to reach them. But I'll tell them of this meeting and of your request."

"Will you support my position when you talk to them?" Lindner asked sharply.

I smiled. "Of course not, Carl. I recommended the amendments to them and I'll recommend we stay with them."

Lindner shifted to his Plan B. He turned and motioned Ron to do the talking.

Ready with a $228 Million Check

"As we see it, there is no point in holding our Gannett stock with these provisions. You are trying to disenfranchise us," he said. "So we would like for you to buy our stock back."

I was ready. Doug and I had discussed that possible move by them.

"That's certainly worth talking about." I said. "I'm not very good at arithmetic and I don't have a calculator. But you own about 4 million shares. At today's price of $57, that would be about $228 million. We'll be glad to write you a check for that amount this afternoon."

"Well, that's not quite what we had in mind," Walker said sharply.

He proposed that Lindner would sell all his stock back to

Gannett for $70 a share—about $50 million more than market value.

I turned to Lindner, with a smile and then a smirk.

"Carl," I said, "isn't that something I keep reading about that's called 'greenmail'?"

Lindner bristled. "I'm sorry to hear you use that word. We don't do greenmail."

"Whatever you call it, I call it greenmail, and the answer is no," I countered.

"Well then, you leave us no alternative but to fight you," Lindner said as he and his henchman departed.

A proxy fight, the thing that strikes fear into the heart of any corporate CEO, was on.

We expected the fight to be a tough one. A majority of Gannett stock was held by big institutional investors or pension funds of major corporations. More and more managers of portfolios were opposing antitakeover amendments. They like to see takeover attempts so they can reap profits on a price runup.

Doug and I discussed strategy for the fight. It was five weeks until the annual meeting. We figured Lindner would quietly and privately solicit big institutional shareholders to support his position.

We preferred the quiet and private route also. Unless the going got tough. If it looked as though we were losing the proxy solicitation, we might want to go public to try to drum up support. In that case I thought Lindner's greenmail attempt would play into our hands, if we used it right.

Greenmail Made "Official"

But I didn't want it to be just our word against his. So we prepared an affidavit recounting the greenmail conversations. To give it an official stamp in case of future use, I had it notarized and filed under seal with the Securities and Exchange Commission.

We prepared a series of press releases and newspaper ads for possible use in the proxy fight. They were labeled "nice" and "nasty." All were ready to use at a moment's notice.

One labeled "nasty" started out: "An affidavit on file with the Securities and Exchange Commission dated April 18, 1985, outlines a greenmail attempt by Carl Lindner against Gannett in which he demanded $50 million more than market value for his stock holdings in the company."

Because the proxy vote went our way, we never had to use it.

While we were prepared to get nasty, I kept up a friendly stance with Lindner. He stepped up the frequency of his visits. We were both practicing the Sicilian policy of holding our enemies close.

Our meetings had their comic moments. Because Lindner didn't drink, Doug and I would show up ahead of the appointed hour at restaurants for lunch or dinner and order a glass of ice and gin that looked like ice water before he arrived.

On a Sunday night at the Sign of the Dove restaurant in New York, about thirty minutes after Lindner and Walker arrived, the waiter noticed my glass was empty.

"Would you like another martini, Mr. Neuharth?" he asked loudly.

Doug broke up. Lindner pretended not to hear. But he was hearing the vibes from shareholders. His proxy fight was not going well. So that night he tried another tactic.

"Al, you know that Ron and I admire the way you and Doug run the company. We really don't like to be in a fight with you. We'd be willing to drop our proxy fight if you will put the two of us on your board," he proposed.

I told him I'd pass his request along to the board.

"Will you support it?" he asked.

"I'll be glad to put it to a board vote," I hedged. "You don't know all those members well. We're meeting here in New York Tuesday morning. Why don't you and Ron come to the meeting. I'll introduce you to everyone and you can make some remarks. Then they'll know who they're voting on."

The shark went for the bait. I had told the board members earlier that to know Lindner is to dislike him. I knew if he appeared, he'd unsell himself. Lindner's self-serving, greedy motives were obvious to anyone of intelligence. I knew the board members would spot his phoniness as quickly as I had.

I also figured if he saw any hope of the directorship he would be diverted from the proxy fight for a few days.

Lindner didn't disappoint me. He showed up not only with Walker, but with his son Keith, twenty-five. I introduced them all, then invited Lindner to speak. He made a ten-minute pitch for himself and Walker as directors. He invited questions, but didn't get any.

After they left, the first question asked me by a director was: "Why did he bring his son along?"

Perfect question. Perfect answer: "That's so you could see the next person he'll ask you to put on the board if you elect him," I replied. "And probably the next CEO."

A Toy for His Boy

And I added truthfully, "He told me at one of our dinners that he's always thought it would be nice if someday he could give one of his sons a media company to run."

The sentiment against Lindner joining the board was so strong that we didn't even vote on it.

During the three days Lindner had the board seats uppermost in his mind, McCorkindale and his proxy solicitation team stepped up their efforts. They went over the 50 percent mark. The proxy fight was over. And we had kept the bastards off the board.

With the fight won, I decided to go public. We ran a series of full-page ads in *The Wall Street Journal, The New York Times, The Washington Post,* the *Chicago Tribune,* the *Los Angeles Times,* and, of course, *USA TODAY.*

The ads saluted the Gannett shareholders for their support. They attacked "funny money financiers" for fanning "media merger mania." And they hit hard at junk-bond takeover techniques.

No names were mentioned in the ads. But they drew two quick phone calls. One was from Lindner. The other from Fred Joseph, head of Drexel Burnham, the junk-bond kings. Both were upset at the publicity our ads were generating about their types.

Joseph invited McCorkindale and me to lunch with him in his private dining room at Drexel.

"How could you say things like that about our firm?" Joseph wanted to know when we met with him.

"I didn't mention anyone by name," I smiled.

"But everybody knows we're the junk-bond kings. What I

want you to know is that we never have and never will do a junk-bond deal to finance an unfriendly media takeover.

"We've been asked to and said no. Ted Turner wanted us to work with him when he went after CBS, but we turned him down. You guys in the media really have no reason to attack us or to fear us," Joseph said.

"That sounds nice from you, but what about Mike [Milken]. Can you control him?" I asked.

"Of course—I'm the CEO," Joseph responded.

Four years later Joseph agreed to have Drexel pay $650 million in fines and fire that same Mike Milken because he apparently was out of control.

Lindner's call took a similar thin-skinned approach.

"Al, how could you say terrible things like that about me," Lindner asked.

"Why, Carl, I didn't even mention your name," I replied. Then I added, in a not-so-friendly tone, "But if you keep this bullshit up or ever talk about a big buyback bonus again, I may have to." I told him about the greenmail affidavit I had filed with the SEC. He hung up on me without a word.

No more reasons for me to be Mr. Nice Guy. I was trying to rid the company of a greedy S.O.B. The time had come to switch from niceness to nastiness.

And Lindner switched out of Gannett stock. Over the next several weeks, he unloaded all of his Gannett holdings—at the market price.

The shark was eager to swim away from me.

PLAIN TALK:

Beware of sharks in sheep's clothing.

V

**WHEN THEY
TELL YOU IT
CAN'T BE DONE,
CHANCES ARE
YOU'VE GOT
A WINNER**

"When you win, nothing hurts."

JOE NAMATH

Life is a game. It is not an undefeated season. You win some. You lose some. To enjoy life to the utmost, you must play every game to win.

Winning is the most important thing in life. And the most rewarding. Everything else pales in comparison to the feeling of winning. That's true whether you win:

▷ A Girl Scout cookie sale.
▷ A Little League baseball game.
▷ The love of your life.
▷ The office pool.
▷ Bingo at church.
▷ The job of your dreams.
▷ The business deal of your schemes.

The goal should be to win 100 percent of the time. But don't expect to. And be glad that you don't. Winning them all means you haven't taken enough risks. And that takes the fun out of life.

Your won-lost record is the most important thing on the report card for how you have lived your life. One hundred percent is too much. Ninety-nine percent is great but unlikely. Ninety-five percent is good. Anything below 90 percent is unsatisfactory.

While winning is the best feeling in the world, losing need not necessarily hurt either. Losing should be a lesson in how to win more often. I learned a lot from my failures. Losses fed my fervor to win.

The most satisfying victories are those where the odds against your winning are the greatest. But long odds don't necessarily make the job more difficult.

In fact the more that people tell you it can't be done, the more likely that you have a winner. That usually means you know something they don't know. Or that your idea is so different or so daring that they can't comprehend it.

If your sights are clearly set on a goal, the fact that others say it can't be done shouldn't slow you down. It should spur you on.

"There is no substitute for victory."
GENERAL DOUGLAS MACARTHUR

REINVENTING
THE NEWSPAPER:
REENACTING
A DREAM

"Over the years, Neuharth concluded that there were millions of potential readers with neither the time nor the inclination to read the kind of newspapers that already existed."

PEOPLE MAGAZINE
September 28, 1987

Why did we do it?

That question has been asked over and over. Why in the world did Gannett undertake a high-cost, high-risk new venture like *USA TODAY*?

In 1981, when we announced it, most critics said we were crazy. They wrote our obit before we were born.

In 1982, after we published Vol. 1, No. 1 on September 15, many said we had aborted on the launchpad.

The whole idea was simply too big and too bold for the newspaper establishment club and the journalism critics to accept.

They had their own answers for why we did it: Neuharth's huge ego. The company's naïveté. Just plain stupidity.

Not many people realized that *USA TODAY* was a dream being reenacted. A thirty-year dream of mine of starting new newspapers. A dream that had given me both a nightmare and a new vision:

▷ In 1952 that dream became *SoDak Sports*, a loser.
▷ In 1966 *TODAY* in Florida, a winner.

Like most dreams or visions, the notion of a new national newspaper didn't appear full-blown all at once. But once it got inside my head, it wouldn't go away.

For more than ten years, it was coddled inside me. Petted. Pampered. Nourished. Over the next three years I shared it with others. We planned. Plotted.

Five years after the reenactment of an old dream in a big, new way, *USA TODAY* became the most widely read newspaper in the USA.

These are the answers to why and how the nation's newspaper moved from dream to reality.

The "why" falls into two general categories:

▷ Professional
▷ Personal

Personally I had the world by the tail in 1979.

I was fifty-five, CEO of the USA's largest newspaper company, making more than a million dollars a year. Company jets flew me wherever I wanted to go, whenever I wanted. Limousines eliminated the hassle from ground travel.

I had pretty fancy offices and/or homes in New York City; Washington, D.C.; Cocoa Beach, Florida; and Lake Tahoe, Nevada. And staffs to look after my care and feeding in Gannett locations from the Virgin Islands in the Atlantic to Guam in the Pacific, and nearly everywhere in between.

Presidents and prime ministers, sports and entertainment heroes and heroines were among my friends or acquaintances. The best seats were mine at the Super Bowl or the World Series.

Gannett was on automatic, grinding out bigger profits year after year, even quarter after quarter, by then forty-six quarters in a row.

I had a long-term employment contract. If I wanted, I could coast for ten years, then retire in 1989 to collect a pretty pension and other perks for the rest of my life.

Two things kept me from taking the road most might have traveled by:

▷ I wasn't satisfied with the job being done by my profession—journalism and newspapering.
▷ I was getting bored again, on easy street.

A lot of my critics say I have a low boiling point, a temper. Actually my *boring* point is much lower than my boiling point. That may be my strongest characteristic.

Once an objective is achieved—large or small—repetition or routine drives me up the wall. As soon as things are under control, I leave others to watch the store. I go seek new adventures.

A Pipe Dream Updated

By 1979 I commanded the wherewithal to put into play the pipe dream that had become a vision—some said an obsession. I told my early confidants there were two prime goals:

▷ A national newspaper so informative and entertaining and enjoyable that it would grab millions of readers, including many of the television generation who were then nonreaders.

▷ A newspaper so different, so advanced in design and appearance and content that it would pull the rest of the industry into the twenty-first century, albeit kicking and screaming.

"We'll reinvent the newspaper," I said with my usual modesty.

I knew it wouldn't be easy. But I figured we had a reasonable chance. A better chance than anyone else. And I was sure it would be a helluva lot of fun.

The vision I put into play in 1979 bore little resemblance to my pipe dream of 1952.

Back then, during the final days before *SoDak Sports* went belly-up, a sportswriter friend from Mitchell, S.D., Jerry Tippens, stopped by to see me on his return from the Korean War.

He was hoping I might have a job for him. I confided in him that *SoDak Sports* was on its last legs. But, over martinis in the Westward Ho bar in Sioux Falls, we toasted that small dead dream and talked of bigger ones.

"If we could figure out how to finance it and find a delivery system, I think a daily version of the national weekly *Sporting News* might work," I said.

Tippens, also a sports junkie, agreed. But our technical know-how was even weaker than our financing knowledge, so we saw no magic way to deliver anything nationwide on a timely, daily basis.

Just a pipe dream. Two decades later the magic of satellites meant that kind of dream and many others in communications could become reality if the dreamers could be realists, too.

My yearning for a new national publication got stronger as

Gannett broke out of its northeastern nook. The successful launch of *TODAY* in Florida in 1966 was followed by our acquisition of the *San Bernardino* (Calif.) *Sun-Telegram* in 1969. Now we were in New York State, Florida, and California, cornerstones to the rest of the country.

When I became president of Gannett in 1970, chairman Paul Miller and I were off to the races together. We nearly always agreed on targets, even though we differed on long-term goals.

▷ He was a buyer, period.

▷ I enjoyed buying, but I much preferred building.

During the decade of the seventies, we acquired forty-six daily newspapers. Each was bought as a good investment on its own. But from the time I became CEO in 1973, any available newspaper that geographically fit my hope of building a truly nationwide base of printing plants and distribution systems became even more desirable and commanded an even higher offer from us.

That's why by the time we launched *USA TODAY* in 1982, we were positioned with modern, offset printing plants that not only served our community newspapers but gave our new national newspaper easy entrée to most of the metropolitan markets.

We could print *USA TODAY* on our own presses, within an hour or two drive-time of such major markets as New York, Philadelphia, Pittsburgh, Detroit, Minneapolis, Seattle, San Francisco, Los Angeles, Denver, Indianapolis, New Orleans, Atlanta, or Miami.

That network didn't cover all the country, and we had to make contract printing arrangements in other markets. But it was enough of a nucleus to give us a strong advantage over anyone else thinking about a national newspaper.

Common Sense Beats Strategic Planning

Some CEOs call that strategic planning and employ a squadron of MBAs to tell them why—or generally why not—to do it. I never did that.

Instead I relied on common sense. The CEO should have the smarts and instincts to plan ahead, then employ experts to help him figure out "how" to do "what" his vision envisions.

That "what" for Gannett—a new national general-interest daily newspaper—became crystal clear to me in 1978–79.

Before that, I wasn't sure exactly what our developing nationwide base of printing plants and distribution systems would lead to. I saw three possibilities:

▷ A stand-alone national sports daily, à la the weekly *Sporting News, Sports Illustrated*, and my defunct *SoDak Sports*.

▷ A daily and/or Sunday supplement or wraparound section for all our community newspapers, with strictly national news and advertising.

▷ A full-scale, stand-alone national general-interest daily newspaper.

In 1978 I began a one-person nationwide survey to decide which of those options to exercise.

I had just been elected chairman and president of the American Newspaper Publishers Association, the granddaddy of newspaper industry groups.

That role for me was as controversial as most of my associations with establishment clubs have been. I'd been on the ANPA Board for eight years. But most of my time was spent kidding the club members about their silly and staid traditions.

If the democracy I preach had been practiced there, I never would have made it to the top among the majority of blue bloods or bluenoses on the board. But the publisher in Alexandria, La., Joe D. Smith, was ANPA boss in 1976–77. Under the club's traditions he was entitled to pick his successor.

Joe is a regular guy. We both liked Beefeater martinis and solved many of the world's problems over them. He got a kick out of picking a once-poor kid from South Dakota to run the nation's most elite newspaper club.

After the ANPA board routinely, if a bit reluctantly, rubber-stamped Smith's selection of me as chairman and president, I pledged in my acceptance speech:

▷ To travel to all fifty states as chairman.

▷ To speak on First Amendment issues of the day.

Over the next fifteen months, I did that. I spoke to and met with many dozens of local, state, and regional groups—newspaper people, readers, advertisers, college and university students.

My message in my speeches was always a local adaptation of the public's stake in free press and free enterprise. But my mission was mostly self-serving.

Learning from Listening

I carried my vision of a national newspaper everywhere I went. But only inside my head.

I listened more than I talked. The message I was hearing over and over was that newspaper people thought they were putting out better newspapers than newspaper readers thought they were reading. I was reading them, too. By the hundreds. My jet was loaded down with every area paper available everywhere we went.

Some were real rags. Many were pretty good. A few were outstanding. But not one was as good as its editors thought it was. And very few gave readers the total satisfaction they were seeking.

In addition to close reading of all the local papers, I looked for *The Wall Street Journal* and the national edition of *The New York Times* everywhere. I formed these conclusions about those two prestigious publications:

▷ *The Wall Street Journal* had a surprisingly sophisticated distribution system across the USA. It was popular among many moneyed people in medium-size cities as well as in major metropolitan centers. But it didn't reach the multitude of small towns across the USA. And its narrowly specialized content kept it from generating much interest among the general public anywhere.

▷ The national edition of *The New York Times* had surprisingly sparse sales—still only 181,000 at this writing. A limited number of thought leaders, or those who wanted to be, read it in major cities, or pretended they did. But *The Times* was so hidebound in its approach that readers in Battle Creek and Boise and Baton Rouge simply had no interest in fighting their way through this dull, gray old lady.

Besides, *The New York Times* distributed nationally is not a national edition at all. It is a cutdown version of the Big Apple metropolitan edition, dropping some of its most interesting advertising and reassembling a hodgepodge of all the news that fits.

By the summer of 1979, I'd seen, heard, and read enough to convince me that there was indeed a vacuum out there for the right general-interest national daily newspaper.

And it was clear to me that no company or no individual was as well positioned as Gannett or I to undertake the venture.

▷ We had more newspapers with more printing plants in more states than anyone else did.

▷ We had a coast-to-coast network of more than three thousand journalists.

▷ We had deep pockets, with Gannett revenues over $1 billion a year.

▷ We had solid experience in starting newspapers. *TODAY* in Florida from scratch. Other new editions and Sunday editions of our newspapers from New York to California.

▷ We had the benefit of my own failure with *SoDak Sports* to remind us what not to do.

Even so, I knew the idea was so daring it would be a very hard sell, inside and outside the company.

I decided on a simple strategy of spoon-feeding. I hoped to build support steadily, if somewhat slowly. By starting where the sell would be easiest, I hoped to enlist supporters that would help me where and when the sell was harder.

It worked. Two years later, when the Gannett board voted to launch *USA TODAY*, director Julian Goodman, former head of NBC, said, "A vision has a way of becoming infectious, particularly when it is engendered by the chairman."

My family was informed and enlisted first. Then a few close confidants at Gannett. Very gradually, a broader base of working associates. Later, the board of directors. Ultimately, my critics. Finally, the potential consumers.

Getting the Family in Tow

It was important that members of my family know what was up. If we went ahead with *USA TODAY*, it would mean an absolutely total commitment of my time and effort for several years. And I knew I would be subject to public jeering and sneering from critics. The family needed to understand and be able to handle that.

I was fortunate because both my children had been through such situations before. They had learned to stay cool when their father was under fire. They were ready for a new wave of adventure—and abuse.

By then Dan was twenty-six and a journalism educator. After some very rocky relationships while he was in his teens, he and I had become very good friends.

Jan, then twenty-four, was a law student at Vanderbilt University. After majoring in football players and fraternities at the University of Florida, she had become a serious scholar. She shared in and took satisfaction from her dad's adventures.

I was then in the final year of my marriage to Florida Senator Lori Wilson. Even though the romance was gone, we shared in each other's professional projects. She has a keen mind and her perceptions about *USA TODAY* were extremely helpful.

With the family in the know and in tow, I turned next to my closest confidants within Gannett. In this order and in entirely different ways:

▷ John C. Quinn, then fifty-three, chief news executive. Quinn is a kindred soul. He served as my point man to keep the financial types at bay in their constant pressure to put profit before product. And he became the conscience of our company.

▷ John E. (Jack) Heselden, then fifty-nine and president of our newspaper division. He was steady. No show, but substance. A compromiser.

▷ Douglas H. McCorkindale, then forty, chief financial and legal officer. A brilliant strategist in financial and legal matters.

Those three and I were members of the Office of the Chief Executive, which I formed and chaired. For years this trio gave me a balanced supporting cast for my varied acts.

Quinn: farseeing and foresighted, hungry but humane, passionate.

McCorkindale: button-down cautious, conservative, cold, passionless.

Heselden: the ponderous compromiser.

Every major corporation should have some such mix among its top management.

It's important that a CEO of any company not pretend he can run a one-man show successfully. It's equally important that he not surround himself with people who think and act the same way he does.

That's why my troika was so helpful. I could always count on someone wanting to push ahead, someone wanting to pull back, someone steering a middle course.

Later, while *USA TODAY* was in the formative stages, I added a fifth person to that office of the CEO—Madelyn P. Jennings, then forty-six, the human relations director at Standard Brands, to be VP/Personnel and a member of the OCE. She brought a much-needed people and female perspective that went beyond the all-male circle of advisers.

I enjoyed and benefited from playing Quinn and Mc-Corkindale against each other, in private and in public. They enjoyed it too. Their contrariness stimulated thought and thorough examination of issues large and small.

The Benefits of Debate

Even when I was pretty sure which decision I would make, an open debate benefited everyone.

During confrontations between Quinn and McCorkindale, the compromiser, Heselden, was always ready to step in just before polarization peaked. His compromises nearly always coincided with the chairman's wishes, because he read me very well. Or he had been told by me in advance which way I was leaning.

Since I was seeking support for *USA TODAY*, not caution or compromise, I went to Quinn first. I was direct and spelled it all out.

It didn't take him long to jump aboard with both feet: "An opportunity to be taken," he said. Quinn quickly grasped what such a major venture, if successful, would mean to Gannett professionally. Quinn never worried about profit. He left that to McCorkindale. And Doug obliged by never considering anything but profit.

Quinn's professional instincts were churning: It would mean an outlet, or haven, for the dozens of Gannett journalists who then were leaving annually for major metropolitan newspapers, or magazines, or the networks, after having been trained on our farm systems in Chillicothe or Chambersburg, Reno or Rochester.

It would help us attract and hold the best journalistic talent from colleges and universities. It would move Gannett, in one step, from the minor leagues of newspapering to the majors.

Quinn and I began plotting how we would spoon-feed the idea to others. And planning the research-and-development program that would lead to the launch.

Step by careful step, I guided that process for a full two years, before asking the board of directors to make a "go" decision.

November 18, 1979: I called the members of the Office of the Chief Executive together—Heselden, McCorkindale, Quinn, and me—for "some year-end reviewing and planning."

On a cold and dreary Sunday morning in Rochester before a crackling fire in the twenty-fifth-floor boardroom fireplace of our corporate headquarters, the four of us talked about the year that was ending. Another good year, we agreed. Indeed it was.

We had acquired Combined Communications for a $362 million bargain, bringing us seven TV stations, major newspapers in Cincinnati and Oakland, and the largest outdoor advertising company in North America—then 38,000 billboards.

"Business as usual" had brought us over $1.065 billion in revenues—our first billion-dollar year—and $135 million in profits, up more than 19 percent from the year before.

McCorkindale loved dwelling on numbers. I changed the subject.

"Let's talk about next year and the future," I said. I got up from my seat, paced back and forth in front of the fireplace. My walking the meeting rooms as I often did always made McCorkindale—and others—nervous. They knew it was a sign I was either bored, or thinking, or about to spring something on them.

I rarely sit through an entire meeting of any kind. I think better on my feet. Walking. Stretching. Moving my body not only keeps me awake, but helps my perspective on the people or things under discussion.

"Our business is changing," I said. "We can't just keep on buying the same old things. If we want to stay in front, we've got to be building more—either on what we already have or some new ventures from the ground up."

McCorkindale, perceptive as always, asked, "What do you have in mind?"

"I'm not sure," I replied. "But we need to spend some money and time on research. Figure out how to harness the satellite to help us deliver and sell more of what we have or can produce. Maybe Super-TV. Maybe Sunday newspaper supplements. Maybe a national newspaper."

"How much money?" Doug asked pointedly.

"I'm only thinking of a million or so for research next year," I replied, low-key.

Doug didn't bat an eye. He knew a million for research and development for a company our size was peanuts, even though most media companies spent little if any in that area.

But he wanted to know more. "How will the money be spent? Who will you hire? What will you explore?"

"Doug, I'll figure out how to spend it. You figure out how to budget it," I said.

When the meeting adjourned, I figured my three key associates left with these diverse thoughts:

▷ Quinn: Neuharth's national newspaper project just got bankrolled. The train is rolling and it will be hard to stop.

▷ Heselden: It really makes sense to carefully research some possible new opportunities as long as we don't rush into anything.

▷ McCorkindale: I'm not sure what he has in mind, but a million dollars isn't that much, and if he comes up with some crazy idea there's plenty of time to kill it.

December 18, 1979: the year-end meeting of the Gannett Board at the Capital Hilton Hotel in Washington. It had been a good year, a good meeting, and everyone felt good. When board members are feeling good, it's easy for any CEO to inject casually new ideas or projects that may be much bigger than they sound.

Downplaying the Dream

Near the end of the meeting, matter-of-factly under agenda item "Other Business," I reported that the Office of the Chief Executive had decided to get into some research-and-development work next year.

"We're going to establish a task force of a few of our brightest young executives. They'll study what's new in newspapers and television. And especially whether we can harness the satellite to deliver more news to more people in more ways. We've set aside about a million dollars for the R & D work.

Hopefully before the year is out, we'll have some interesting possibilities to kick around with you."

No big deal. No vote necessary. Just a tiny spoonful. It's important not to tell people more than they should know before they're ready to understand it. Especially corporate directors.

March 5, 1980: a Gannett news release gave the press and public its first spoon-feeding. The release read: "Establishment of a research-and-development task force on new ventures for Gannett and appointment of two general executives were announced today."

The two rather routine appointments took the emphasis off the real thing. The release continued: "The task force will explore any and all possibilities for new ventures in the entire communications field which might even better serve readers, advertisers, viewers, and listeners."

No mention of a national newspaper.

That smokescreen was an important part of the spoon-feeding. I didn't want directors or other insiders to ask a lot of questions too soon as that might lead to polarization. And I didn't want competitors to know we were looking seriously at a national newspaper just yet.

At that time, *The New York Times* was gradually but guardedly expanding its national edition. I knew *The Washington Post* was thinking about and talking about a national edition. (It ended up being a weak weekly tabloid.) Rupert Murdoch, with his big-circulation national weekly *Star*, had a huge appetite for nationwide and worldwide ventures.

Because I knew the blue-blood owners of *The New York Times* and *The Washington Post* very well, I really didn't expect "Punch" Sulzberger or Kay Graham to do anything very bold or risky. But Rupert is a character of a different complexion. I didn't want to give him—or anyone else with guts—a reason to hurry up any plans of their own.

The week before the press release, I had assembled the task force for the first time. The group was put together with help from Quinn and Heselden. I didn't consult McCorkindale because I didn't want any financial nay-sayers putting the idea down at that early stage. Later, of course, I'd bring them in to help develop a business plan.

The cast of characters, all with Gannett backgrounds:

▷ Tom Curley, then thirty. A smart and aggressive newsman like his brother, John, who is now Gannett CEO. A proven record in news research.

▷ Paul Kessinger, twenty-nine. A research and marketing whiz from our Reno newspapers.

▷ Larry Sackett, thirty. An expert in technology and satellites, whom I stole back from the *International Herald Tribune.*

▷ Frank Vega, thirty-one. A tough-talking, circulation streetfighter. I liked him especially because he did not hesitate to talk back to me.

Average age of this foursome: thirty. I wanted to make sure these were young visionaries with their eyes on the future.

To baby-sit them and pull them together as the task force coordinator, I named Vince Spezzano, fifty-two, then publisher of *TODAY* in Florida. He is a long-time trusted friend and coworker. If I told him which way I wanted the train to head, he would keep it on track.

I decided to headquarter—and/or hide—the task force in an out-of-the-way cottage in Cocoa Beach, Fla., five blocks up the street from my own Pumpkin Center hideaway.

Since this was in effect a small think tank, I didn't want the members working where there was a lot of diversion. For six months or so, I wanted them thinking nothing but "Project NN."

When I labeled it that, I told the task force and the OCE members, "You and I know 'NN' stands for 'National Newspaper.' Others probably will think it simply means 'New Newspapers,' and we should encourage that thinking."

"Neuharth's Nonsense"

It wasn't long before word got back to me that many wags, especially outside Gannett, had dubbed Project NN "Neuharth's Nonsense."

I laughed. The less seriously our competitors viewed what we were up to, the better.

The five-member Project NN task force met at Pumpkin Center for the first time on February 29, 1980.

I had already briefed them individually that our goal was to figure out how Gannett could successfully launch a new national newspaper.

At the first group meeting, I gave them a pep talk and spelled out the mission:

"We're only a few miles away from where some of us successfully launched *TODAY* fourteen years ago. We're also only a few miles away from the launchpads where the USA has sent people into space, and to the moon and back.

"Now I want to harness our vision to see if we can do something nobody else has ever attempted—launch a truly national general-interest daily newspaper for all the USA.

"If we do it and succeed, we'll make history. If we try and fail, we'll still make history. Even if we decide not to, we'll have a helluva lot of fun exploring it."

I outlined four key questions to be thoroughly explored and answered, one of which fit the area of expertise of each of the four futurists:

▷ Can we design a daily newspaper that will grab readers around the country in sufficient numbers to make it worthwhile? What is that number?

▷ Can we produce and print such a newspaper?

▷ Can we distribute and sell it nationwide?

▷ Can we get the necessary advertiser support?

While I used "if" and "whether" in making my charge to the task force, the emphasis was on "how." They heard that and got it.

Tom Curley later said, "While Al asked us to find out whether or not this could be done, he phrased most questions in such a way that it was clear he expected the answer to be 'yes.' "

Vega later recalled, "It was a really inspirational meeting. Al kept referring to us as 'geniuses' and 'whiz kids.' I had goose bumps during the whole meeting. It was like we were the four chosen apostles for a new era in our business."

Project NN was poised to reinvent the newspaper.

PLAIN TALK:

A dream is the mother of invention.

BRIDLING BEAN COUNTERS

"There is a fear of Al. He strikes you as a person who has the capability and mind-set and sometimes willingness to fire your ass or demote you so low in the company you'll never be seen again."

JIMMY THOMAS
Gannett treasurer

Bean counters. Money crunchers. No matter what you call them, they're all alike. They can work in a shoe factory or a newspaper company. Doesn't matter to them.

They're intelligent. Well educated. Well intentioned. Office walls displaying MBA degrees.

All of them know how to count money. A few of them know how to manage it. Very few know how to earn it. None of them is willing to risk it.

Conservative, up-tight S.O.B.s. Narrow-gauged and no vision beyond the next quarterly earnings report. The creation of *USA TODAY* brought out the worst in Gannett's bean counters, even though they are among the best in their business.

During most of 1980, while the Project NN task force was trying to figure out how to launch a national newspaper, I spent much of my time keeping a tight rein on the bean counters who were trying to bomb it.

On Tap, but Never on Top

Smart financial people are very important to any business operation. But a CEO who permits the bean counters to set company policy or make long-range decisions is condemning that company to the status quo and ultimately to a slow death.

The specialists in finance must be on tap, but they should never be on top.

Most of them think they can save their way to prosperity. Unless the CEO redirects their efforts, they're likely to spend as much time policing pennies and peanuts as they are managing or trying to make millions or billions of dollars.

I've always tried to make it clear to the bean counters that they are a service department, not a police department. But they have trouble getting it.

Gannett's top bean counter, Doug McCorkindale, is the best in the business. He also is one of the smallest thinkers. When the CEO doesn't keep him busy on big deals, Doug busies himself being a pest about peanuts.

Two of many, many examples:

In 1980 I was flying around the country and around the world much of the time. I often had aboard would-be sellers of newspapers, domestic or foreign business executives, or government dignitaries. To make a classier impression, I decided to order uniforms for the members of our flight department.

McCorkindale held up the purchase and sent me this memo:

"Flight department uniforms . . . at $1,450 per set per person . . . are an extraordinary cost. I've tried to think of a better example of corporate waste, but have not been able to come up with one."

At that time our revenues were over $1 billion a year.

I fired back this reply: "I disagree! It's peanuts. It will finally make our flight operation look first class. This is a very good example of how a very minor expense can enhance a company's image. It can't be measured on the bottom line, but it's important and you ought to understand that."

We bought the uniforms.

Once bean counters become prisoners of their penny-pinching tunnel vision, they can't help themselves. It's second nature. They look for smaller and smaller peanuts to police.

It was my custom to order special gifts for all Gannett directors and their spouses for all our meetings. They were relatively inexpensive, but generally fit the motif of the place where we were meeting.

For my final regular board meeting as chairman in February

1989, we met in the Virgin Islands, where Gannett owns the *Daily News*. I ordered twenty-five pairs of $102 Porsche sunglasses for our seventeen directors, spouses, and special guests to enjoy the St. Thomas sunshine.

After the meeting McCorkindale checked to see how many sunglasses were left. He was unable to account for two pairs. He sent the special assistant to the board a memo demanding a list of every recipient.

It turned out the missing sunglasses he was concerned about had been given to our *Virgin Island Daily News* publisher and his wife, who were our hosts.

The CFO of a $3 billion company, wasting his time trying to find two pairs of missing sunglasses!

Keystone Cops See Their Image

I've concluded this is one of the reasons most financial officers play keystone cop: They spend so much of their own time finagling, scheming, sometimes fast-talking others—the government, the banks, the brokers—that they assume others operate the same way. As a result, they spend endless energy looking for evidence that others are as tricky as they are.

Through the years some of my senior associates became so annoyed at the antics of Doug and his financial aides that they urged me to get rid of him. I didn't, for these reasons:

▷ He is a top-notch deal analyzer and financial manager, when properly supervised by the CEO.

▷ I used his penny-pinching approach to point out, not so subtly, to employees that company policy was to be creative and sell our way to prosperity, not to hunker down and try to save our way there.

▷ Dissent in a major company leads to dialogue that leads to good decisions, if the CEO has the smarts and the balls to make the right decisions.

Because Doug was so blatant in displaying his bean-counter mentality toward *USA TODAY* and in urging his associates to do likewise, he and they became the bad guys in the eyes of those in other departments who were working hard to give the idea a fair test.

It was a snap to rally others, especially in the news departments, behind any idea that the bean counters opposed. That became critically important when the going got tough with *USA TODAY.*

A "them" vs. "us" attitude developed. "Us" were employees in news, advertising, circulation, production, promotion, and personnel. "Them" were the small group of financial executives.

There is no doubt many *USA TODAY* employees performed better than they otherwise might have, sometimes better than they knew how, because they were determined to show that the bean counters were wrong.

I kept our financial people out of the initial research about *USA TODAY.* From March until October 1980, none of them was involved. I would bring them in when/if we got around to developing a detailed business plan. When it comes to crunching the numbers, the bean counters are absolutely essential.

But while we were dealing with concepts and measuring prospects about product, production, promotion, and sales, I didn't want penny pinchers around debunking all the ideas and fretting about the price tag before they could possibly know what they were talking about.

A new idea, particularly one that puts money at risk, is the last thing a financial officer wants.

The financial types are orderly analysts. They hate any degree of risk. That makes it impossible for most of them to measure truly any risk-reward ratio. They can only measure numbers, not ideas.

Every company has its problems with bean counters. The degree of the problem depends on the CEO. It's the CEO's job to keep the financial people in their place, to take advantage of their strengths, to ward off their weaknesses.

PLAIN TALK:

Keep bean counters on tap, never on top.

STROKING BOARD MEMBERS

―――――――――――――――――――――――――

"I admired that while Neuharth was driving this enterprise, he was also cautioning the board, 'We don't know if this is going to make it, but if it doesn't we have the outs.' Seldom do you meet a salesman who points out the downside."

THOMAS A. REYNOLDS, JR.
Gannett board member and
Chicago attorney

The key to selling *USA TODAY* to the board of directors was managing their expectations.

I made sure they understood that *USA TODAY* was going to take time and money. Lots of both. And I built in escape hatches so that if *USA TODAY* went belly-up, Gannett would still salvage something from it.

The board was as helpful as the bean counters were hostile. Gannett's board members are a diverse group of men and women, heads or former heads of business or government operations, all with top-level experience and expertise.

The most fascinating thing about dealing with the board and the bean counters in the early eighties was that both had exactly the same information about *USA TODAY* available to them, but they reacted totally differently.

▷ The bean counters wanted to stop me from launching *USA TODAY* but couldn't.

▷ The board members could have stopped me, but didn't want to.

By spoon-feeding the board members for two years until I was ready for them to make the decision on *USA TODAY*, they became my strong allies in this adventure.

Many CEOs fall short of their personal and professional goals because they overlook the importance of their relationship with board members.

From the time I became CEO in 1973, I spent a lot of time developing and promoting my partnership with the board. Each member was handpicked for maximum diversity of philosophy, geography, expertise, experience, race, sex.

▷ I inherited a board of twelve white males, most from the East and most golf-playing buddies of my predecessor, Paul Miller. When I retired as chairman sixteen years later, the board had four women, three minorities, and was representative of the country from New York to Hawaii.

▷ I made sure that board members understood their role: general oversight and policy formation, not management. The only thing outside directors should really be totally involved in is the hiring and/or firing of the CEO and in his/her compensation. They cannot be, and should not pretend to be, as qualified as the CEO to make management or operating decisions.

▷ I courted and charmed board members. Their relationship with Gannett needed to be enjoyable as well as stimulating and rewarding. I planned or checked every detail for board gatherings—lunch and dinner menus; wine selections; limo, hotel, and airplane arrangements; seating arrangements at meetings and at social functions.

▷ I never surprised the board. I may have overinformed them, with comprehensive monthly mailings when they didn't meet, and by covering everything of interest when they did.

But there is a clear line between information and action. Many, many times I brought up subjects and said, "This is informational or advisory only." That way they felt included, but weren't prematurely or unnecessarily asked to take a position.

That overall approach is what made the board members my strong allies on the *USA TODAY* adventure.

There were four important dates for dealing with the board on *USA TODAY*:

▷ December 18, 1979, when I advised the board of the $1 million R & D project. No vote was taken.

▷ October 28, 1980, when the Project NN report was presented and I advised them that an additional $3.5 million was budgeted for planning and prototypes in 1981. No vote was taken.

▷ August 25, 1981, when outside research was presented and prototypes were thoroughly discussed. No vote was taken.

▷ December 15, 1981, when the board was asked to vote whether to launch *USA TODAY* or not.

Knowing When to Count the Votes

If a vote had been taken at any of the first three meetings, the board probably would have approved my recommendation, but without enthusiasm or proper understanding and with premature attention to the details of the project. Then, when the going got tough two or three years later, they probably would have pulled the plug.

If I had not taken a vote in December 1981, nearly a full year before *USA TODAY* was actually launched, they would have felt excluded and resentful. Instead they were all excited and enthusiastic, and felt included and involved.

As a result no matter how cruel the criticism or how red the ink got in those early years, they were determined to stay with "their" project until it succeeded.

The switch from spoon-feeding the board to stroking members with a light but steady diet of information and involvement came at a regular meeting in Reno, October 28, 1980.

The Project NN task force members, after six months of study, were ready to make their preliminary report. I had each director sign a nondisclosure agreement before the meeting began.

But I low-keyed the importance of the meeting by pointing out all findings were very preliminary and in-house, and they would be followed with much more detailed research and planning.

The reports by the four Project NN whiz kids were complete with slides and boards of satellite sketches, demographic data, maps of possible print sites, expenditures of national and multinational advertisers, and readership and viewership figures on national magazines and TV shows.

But I coached the kids not to try to translate those figures into potential *USA TODAY* circulation or advertising or revenues.

I always coached and critiqued the people who were making board presentations. By the time I got through with them, their facing the directors was a piece of cake.

"Stick with the concept. Don't get into a discussion or debate on details," I instructed them before that meeting.

▷ Sackett, the technology whiz, reported that the state of the art with the satellite was indeed such that we could transmit any number of newspaper pages from one location to any number of print sites anywhere simultaneously. And we could do it with quality color, something *The Wall Street Journal* or national edition of *The New York Times* did not offer.

▷ Vega, the circulation street-fighter, displayed maps showing Gannett print sites within a two-hour drive of at least forty very big markets. And some potential contract sites near the others. He pinpointed 105,000 possible sales outlets in fifty states.

▷ Tom Curley, the reader researcher, highlighted results of reader surveys various Gannett newspapers had taken in recent years. Across the country a sampling of about 40,000 readers indicated they were especially hungry for more sports, entertainment, and business news. That was especially true of the 1.75 million people who stayed in hotels or motels every night and the 850,000 who traveled daily on airlines.

▷ Kessinger, the marketer, reported that most major national advertisers or ad agencies were unhappy with the quality of newspaper printing. "Their money goes mainly into TV and magazines because there they get colorful impact. A newspaper that is exciting and colorful, instead of dull and gray, could grab a lot of that money if it reaches the right audience," he concluded.

Head Off Hasty Judgments

Before taking any questions, I emphasized again the very preliminary nature of the reports.

"This is encouraging enough to keep looking. But it will take at least another year of stepped-up research and work to develop prototypes and test them and prepare a business plan. We won't be asking you for any 'go' or 'no-go' decision until all that has been done," I promised.

I said I would recommend we go ahead with *USA TODAY* only if the next year's work convinced me we could develop a five-year plan with the right risk-reward ratio.

The board members listened intently, but not many questions were asked. Most were noncommittal and generally neutral, which was what I hoped for at that point.

But two very diverse reactions demonstrated why I had determined not to take any votes or let polarization set in prematurely.

Director E. J. "Jack" Liechty, a personable ex-president of the thirteen-newspaper Speidel chain, which Gannett acquired in 1977, was enthusiastic. A former circulation executive, he quickly sensed the reader potential.

"Only Gannett could do this," Liechty beamed.

Wes Gallagher, the former president of the Associated Press, was skeptical. Gallagher is gruff and direct. Since retiring from the AP and joining our board, he had moved to Santa Barbara, Calif. He asked:

"Why should I want another paper? What are you going to offer me that the *Los Angeles Times* or *The Wall Street Journal* don't already give me?"

I explained that that's exactly what the upcoming development and testing of prototypes would answer.

"If we can offer people another read that will grab a million or two of them, we'll recommend doing it. If we can't, we won't."

Then, informationally, I told the board we would budget about $3.5 million for 1981 to complete the R & D phase of the project, including development of a business plan.

"We'll move the Project NN team from Florida to Washington, D.C., expand it, and tap some outside expertise," I said.

I pointed out that meant we would also have to go public with what we were studying. We'll announce it at the next board meeting in Washington in mid-December, which coincides with our year-end meeting of several hundred Gannett executives, I advised them.

"Once we make the public announcement, we should all be prepared for a little internal and external skepticism and criticism," I warned.

That may have been the understatement of my career.

PLAIN TALK:

Keep the board informed and in line.

BACKBONE BEATS BACKBITING

"Neuharth never gave a good goddamn about the critics."

CATHIE BLACK
publisher, *USA TODAY*

When I was a poor kid living on the wrong side of the tracks, I acted up a lot at school, at church, and at home. Not dangerously but differently.

I felt it was better to be noticed, even criticized or attacked, than to be unnoticed or unknown.

As an adult, I've often plotted how to get attention and criticism. And especially how to use my adversaries to an advantage.

Because I've worn a bull's-eye on my chest all my life, criticism doesn't bother me the way it does most people.

I'm interested in what people think. But I don't take personal offense at criticism. Consequently I'm able to be more objective about the criticism and the critics.

My style has encouraged some of my critics to climb way out on a limb. When they are wrong, I don't have to saw off the limb. They do it for me.

By the time I tackled *USA TODAY*, I had developed a very thick skin. Criticism amused me. I listened to or read it all. But I was able to separate the wheat from the chaff.

Good thing. Because *USA TODAY* drew more criticism—and more chaff—in volume and intensity than any media venture in the history of the USA.

It started even before we announced we were thinking about launching a national newspaper.

Following the Reno board session, we began planning for

our December meeting and announcement in Washington. Everyone in Gannett had been sworn to secrecy until then.

But ten days ahead of schedule, a weekly newsletter, *Satellite Week,* put out an extra edition that said: "Gannett plans a national daily newspaper. The start-up cost will be mammoth, possibly around $100 million."

The fact that the emphasis was on the cost tipped me off that one of our own financial people had leaked the item. Not surprising. It was their first of many efforts to sabotage the project.

The next day *The Washington Post* quoted Wall Street media analyst John Morton as saying, "A national daily newspaper seems like a way to lose a lot of money in a hurry."

Gannett stock dropped 1.25 points on the New York Stock Exchange. The same day, other media stocks were basically unchanged.

When I made the official announcement the following week, critics really came out of their holes.

My announcement was low-key and left a lot of outs. It read in part:

> Preliminary research indicates favorable response to the concept of a national daily newspaper.
>
> It is envisioned as a "different" newspaper, which would neither compete with existing metropolitan newspapers nor Gannett community or regional newspapers.
>
> The next step will be developing and field-testing prototypes with potential readers and advertisers. If the response to the prototypes tested is favorable, a 1982 launch of the new newspaper is a possibility.
>
> For planning purposes, the projected publication has been given the title *USA TODAY*.

Protecting the Franchise

I wrote the news release myself. I wanted to give the press, the public, and Wall Street just enough to substitute fact for rumor, and especially to establish the franchise and protect it with a trademark register for the *USA TODAY*.

We dropped the Project NN label and called the next phase GANSAT—Gannett Satellite Information Network. That emphasized we might explore other forms of satellite news distribution, in addition to the national newspaper.

I asked members of the OCE—Heselden, Jennings, McCorkindale, and Quinn—to help me put together a GANSAT staff. Quinn became totally involved. He, Heselden, and Jennings helped pick the best and brightest from our Gannett news, circulation, advertising, production, and promotion staffs. McCorkindale adopted a different attitude. His financial candidates for GANSAT were second-level or castoffs. He didn't want his best to get dirtied in what he was sure would be a failure.

GANSAT's key players were:

▷ Moe Hickey, forty-six, president. His job was to supervise all business-side planning for *USA TODAY*. The job was too big for him, and we transferred him before publication began.

▷ Ronald Martin, forty-three, planning editor. His assignment was to develop the prototypes that would be tested on potential readers. He did a superb job, became the first executive editor of *USA TODAY*, and held that position for our first six-and-a-half years.

▷ Chuck Schmitt, thirty-three, finance director. His job was to crunch the numbers to help Hickey develop a business plan. He was caught in the middle in the bean counters' sabotage efforts and was replaced after two years.

▷ Vega, the circulation whiz kid who had been part of Project NN. His street smarts made him the most valuable member of that group.

From the beginning I worked very closely on news product and circulation planning. Quinn devoted nearly full time to prototype plans with Martin. My instructions to them were pretty simple:

USA TODAY had to be different, in appearance and content. Wrapped in color. Four sections. Everything organized and in a fixed place. Short, easy-to-read stories. Lots of them. Heavy use of graphics and charts. Heavy emphasis on sports, TV, weather. News every day from every state.

"Steal and adapt the best of everything that's on TV or in the magazines or in other newspapers," I told Martin and Quinn.

They went one step further and also stole the best news

talent from Gannett newspapers in an ingenious plan that Quinn called the "Loaner Program."

Intrapreneurship Opens Opportunities

I later called the program "intrapreneurship" and expanded it to other *USA TODAY* departments and ultimately throughout Gannett. It's the use of internal talent, internal equipment, and internal money to create a new product.

Most large companies have a huge and generally untapped pool of underutilized talent and equipment that can give them a great financial advantage over others in undertaking major projects or new ventures.

Intrapreneurship helped make *USA TODAY* possible and greatly reduced Gannett's incremental costs for the new venture. "Loaners" to *USA TODAY* generally did not have to be replaced on their hometown paper during the time they were away. As is the case with most successful big businesses, some of our newspaper staffs had become a bit fat.

The use of loaners drove the bean counters crazy. They saw the practice as simply a financial dodge to reduce *USA TODAY*'s cost. They couldn't see the overall advantage to the company because their neat little square money boxes were being disturbed.

We worked out an arrangement with local newspapers whereby they would continue to pay the salaries of their employees who were loaned to *USA TODAY*, usually for three- or four-month periods.

In exchange the local newspapers received the benefit of having their employees participate in the most sophisticated and exciting newspaper training program in the country. And the employees had the assurance of jobs back home if the bean counters were right and we went belly-up.

Dozens of news people who learned from this loaner experience went on to bigger jobs on their own or to other Gannett newspapers. It was the most economical and effective management training program we ever devised.

USA TODAY's loaner program continues today, on a reduced scale. Importantly it has led to a cross-fertilization of talent among Gannett newspapers, broadcast stations, and other operations. The individual employee benefits from these broadening experiences. So does the employer.

By 1981, twenty-two loaners from Gannett newspapers had been called into Washington to help Martin and Quinn tackle the development of prototypes.

First they produced stories and columns in a new *USA TODAY* style. Then cover pages of sections. Finally entire sections. Page after page and section after section underwent change after change. Because there was no daily deadline, pages were displayed on the wall, critiqued, then revamped.

Because this was a brand-new newspaper, there were no sacred cows. Nobody warned that "we've never done it that way before," which so often inhibits change on existing operations.

Our target was to print two different versions of a few thousand prototypes in April and test them on potential readers, advertisers, opinion leaders, and the media.

During the final month of prototype development, I couldn't resist getting totally involved. I wanted to leave nothing important to chance or to the judgment of others. I read most of the stories for the prototypes several times, sending them back for rewrites. Some of the reporters who didn't know me as well as others were surprised that the CEO would get involved in editing stories. Not all of them liked it.

Some stories had to be rewritten ten to twelve times before they satisfied me. This drove some reporters crazy. In some instances I didn't know what I wanted myself. But I recognized it when I saw it.

Making Reporters Out of Essayists

USA TODAY's terse writing style emerged from these exercises. A maximum of facts in a minimum of words. Some reporters couldn't live with that approach. They saw their jobs more as essayists than as reporters. About 15 percent of the original reporting staff at *USA TODAY* left because they couldn't adjust to the writing style.

When the prototypes were ready, we handled their public distribution in a way far different from start-ups in our local communities.

For example, at *TODAY* in Florida in 1966 those prototypes

were produced in strict secrecy. They were done for internal purposes of practicing for the real thing.

USA TODAY prototypes had several different purposes:

▷ To gain media attention for this possible new newspaper.

▷ To get thought leaders in business and government talking about it.

▷ To get advertising decision-makers thinking about it.

▷ Most importantly to measure reaction from potential readers.

To meet the first three objectives, we sent the prototypes to thousands of opinion leaders—publishers, editors, business executives, government leaders.

With each prototype, we included a return postage-paid postcard that gave them two choices to check:

▷ I hope you start publishing *USA TODAY* regularly.

▷ I hope you forget about the idea.

The response from journalists was swift—and predictably negative. They didn't like the way we had redefined the informational mission of a newspaper. Facts rather than endless prose. Graphics as important as words. They were resisting a new generation of readers—the television generation—as much as the new newspaper.

They were afraid we might be right.

The *Los Angeles Times* interviewed people who received the prototypes and concluded, "The vast majority of those polled by the *Times* said they would recommend that Gannett scrub the idea."

Publisher's Auxiliary, a trade publication for weekly newspapers, said the prototypes were too shallow. Its editorial asked, "How stupid do they expect their readers to be?"

Other reactions:

▷ John McMullan, executive editor of the *Miami Herald* and my old city desk associate there: "I don't think it has much chance. I give it two years. Al Neuharth's ego will keep it going that long."

▷ Mike Davies, then editor of the *Kansas City Times and Star:* "I don't see how they can make it. I don't expect it would have more impact in Kansas City than *The New York Times,* which sells about five hundred copies." (*USA TODAY*'s average daily paid circulation in the Kansas City market now is over 50,000.)

▷ Ralph Otwell, then editor of the *Chicago Sun-Times:* "National publications must fill a need. *USA TODAY* redundantly adds a general, all-purpose layer to the newspaper scene. My sad prognosis: Here *TODAY,* gone tomorrow."

With *USA TODAY* prototypes publicly available for inspection, journalists who were not too keen on my brand of newspapering anyway were able to attack the idea and me at the same time. Since I had been a lightning rod for criticism all my life, it didn't bother me.

Media critic David Shaw of the *Los Angeles Times* discussed how my identity with the newspaper was affecting its reception in the industry: "A few editors and publishers have to admit— off the record—that they would like to see *USA TODAY* flop, if only to humble Neuharth. That's an unlikely occurrence, no matter what happens to *USA TODAY.*"

Many in the newspaper establishment had never appreciated my maverick style. Some viewed my efforts to promote and push Gannett—and myself—into the big leagues as unseemly or unbecoming a journalist.

Jerry Friedheim, president of the American Newspaper Publishers Association, said, "Many in the publishing establishment were saying that Al has finally bitten off more than he can chew. They figured the time had come when he had over-reached."

Lou Harris: Another Bull's-Eye

The reaction of journalists was amusing to me, but not really meaningful. Obviously we never designed *USA TODAY* for journalists. We were after readers.

That is why I turned to my old friend Lou Harris, the nationally known pollster who had worked with me in Detroit, Rochester, and Florida.

Harris conducted four thousand reader interviews with the prototypes and reported strongly optimistic results. His interviews found that 21 percent who had read a prototype said they were "certain to buy" *USA TODAY*. He projected *USA TODAY* could achieve a circulation of 2.2 million daily.

"I went into the bull's-eye twice in my life," Harris recalled. "The first time was when I predicted Jack Kennedy would win the West Virginia primary in 1960. The second time was with *USA TODAY*. Both turned out pretty good."

Harris's research group is owned by Gannett, so we had separate surveys done by Simmons, whose research results are the bible of Madison Avenue. Twenty-seven percent of the people surveyed said they "definitely would buy" *USA TODAY*. The Simmons figures were even more optimistic than those by our own Lou Harris.

The results of these two somewhat scientific samplings by two highly regarded research firms were my major weapons for the next updating to the board.

Most of the director discussion concerned the proposed newspaper slogan, "The Nation's Newspaper," and the two versions of the Page One nameplate we had tested.

Young and Rubicam, the nation's biggest ad agency, had been hired by us to work on the prototypes as well as to test advertiser reaction. "The Nation's Newspaper" slogan was Y & R's idea. I bought it immediately. It said it all. I often joked afterward about how our modesty had led us to that line.

The Page One nameplate was a much more difficult decision.

For the prototypes, we tested two versions: one stretched across the entire top of page one in more traditional fashion, although on a blue background. The other was a rectangular block of blue in the top center of page one. No other newspaper had a nameplate that looked anything like it.

I liked it. I thought it would be a grabber for new readers. Designer Matsuo Yasumura of Y and R, Quinn, and I were the only ones strongly in favor of this offbeat design.

There was no vote, of course, but the directors clearly favored the more traditional approach. Even Harris was worried about our being too different. "You go with the block nameplate at your own peril," he told us at the board meeting.

My mind was made up, but there was no need to announce my decision. I just said we'd keep considering the two options.

At the August meeting I clearly sensed a more positive attitude developing on the part of most board members. They had been able to read and feel and share prototypes with family and friends. *USA TODAY* was being talked about. Because of our ongoing discussions they felt they were in on the action.

Of course they still had no financial figures on which to base a decision.

I told the board we would now use the Harris and Simmons circulation projections to develop a business plan. That would be in their hands before the December meeting, when I would make my recommendation whether to proceed with *USA TODAY* or not.

A business plan for any new venture is much more difficult to develop than a budget or profit plan for an ongoing operation.

In an ongoing business, the bean counters can simply apply percentages to last year's costs and revenues, allow for what are usually minor assumptions of changes in volume as projected by the operating executives, and you have a plan.

Through the years at Gannett, our annual overall company profit plans usually came within a percentage point or two of the actual results. I knew that would not be the case with *USA TODAY* and told everyone so. At best the cost and revenue projections were educated guesses.

Those who favored the idea—Curley, Quinn, and company—guessed too optimistically. Their revenue projections were too high and their cost estimates too low. Those who wanted to kill the project—McCorkindale and company—did just the opposite.

Testing the WIMME Factor

I understood the game being played in both camps and was amused by it. The preciseness of projected quarterly or annual losses—or what I called investments—during the start-up years, were not nearly as important to me as something we called "WIMME."

Will It Make Money Ever? was the key question.

No CEO, no CFO, no board can answer that question with certainty or preciseness on any new venture. When you offer a new product or service for sale, the consumer ultimately decides whether you'll succeed with it. It can only be tested in the marketplace.

All of our surveys indicated a national newspaper was an idea whose time had come. My instincts told me *USA TODAY* was that idea, if, as Lou Harris had warned, the editors do not screw up the idea. And if we could produce a product people would want and charge a price they were willing to pay.

We had an advantage over others who were wrestling with this idea because I had founded:

▷ *SoDak Sports,* which failed.

▷ *TODAY* in Florida, which succeeded.

I wasn't about to repeat my mistakes of *SoDak Sports.* And it seemed pretty sure to me that I could multiply my Florida *TODAY* success on the *USA TODAY* scale.

Before making my recommendation to the board, I wanted the members of the OCE on record, for their own peace of mind, if not mine. I sent Heselden, Jennings, McCorkindale, and Quinn a note asking each to give me a private memo on his/her go/no-go vote.

"No ifs, ands, or buts. Just tell me whether, if you were the CEO, you would or would not go ahead with *USA TODAY.*"

Their answers were predictably different.

Heselden, the compromiser, came down near the middle. He voted a reluctant *no.* But he added, "If you decide to do it, I'll support you all the way. I've seen you take a lot of things that looked chancy and make them work."

Jennings, the people person, voted *no.* She said the idea was so big and would be so demanding, she was afraid it "may elicit ennui" among employees. That sent me to the dictionary. Ennui: weariness. I thought to myself: Furchrissake, does she want a guarantee that employees will never get weary?

McCorkindale, the head bean counter, voted *no.* He said launching *USA TODAY* "could mean two down years in a row" in Gannett earnings. Fact is, we never had a down year, or even a down quarter, in spite of *USA TODAY.*

Quinn, the visionary, voted *yes.* "Go like hell; it's a matter of pride, passion, and honor for Gannett."

Both Quinn's and McCorkindale's reactions were glandular. John was for it, no matter what. Doug was against it, the facts be damned.

Heselden and Jennings, despite their intelligence and competence, followed the safe status quo route that most executives take.

Even though my four OCE associates voted 3–1 against the idea, I knew I had the votes on the board to go ahead. Private discussions with each of them in the summer of 1981 told me that most, maybe all, of the outside directors were ready to support a "go" vote.

Before I took that step, I wanted to make sure the personal side of the decision was in hand.

By then I had been separated from Senator Lori. But daughter Jan and son Dan and I had become closer than ever. I invited them to join me for a World Series weekend in Los Angeles, October 23–25, 1981. Jan came from Nashville, where she was in law school at Vanderbilt; Dan from Honolulu, where he was a journalism professor at the University of Hawaii.

Thumbs Up from the Kids

The morning before we went to the game, we talked over brunch in my usual suite at L'Ermitage in Beverly Hills. I told them of the negative 3–1 OCE vote. I also told them I could get the board to approve *USA TODAY*.

"But if I go ahead, the backbiting will really start, inside and outside Gannett. A lot of people will be after my blood. Do you and I have a backbone to put up with that backbiting?"

They didn't hesitate. Both gave me the thumbs up. We laughed about how we would laugh at the critics—and we figured we'd get the last laugh.

We spent the afternoon at Dodger Stadium watching the Yankees lose to the Dodgers (5–4) in World Series Game 3. Even though we were all Yankee fans, we were on a high over our *USA TODAY* decision and had an afternoon of great fun.

In preparing for the December 13 board meeting, I left nothing to chance and took nothing for granted. Even though I knew I had the votes, I prepared and distributed to the directors two press releases.

One was based on a "go" decision. The other said the board had abandoned the idea. I figured it would not hurt psychologically at that point if they read a release that would make them appear lacking in backbone.

When Hickey presented the preliminary business plan to the board, I said it was "by guess and by golly." But I added that was all you could expect when venturing into the unknown.

Hickey's plan called for losses totaling about $100 million in 1982, '83, and '84, with the red ink ending in 1985.

When he left the room, I told the board, "If we do this and stay with it, the losses will be much bigger than that, and it will take longer to turn the corner."

But I emphasized that a "go" decision simply meant we would launch in the fall of '82. It did not commit us to any specific period of publication.

"If *USA TODAY* doesn't catch on, we can pull the plug at any time, while the losses are modest, and salvage some parts of the venture. We simply cannot make precise predictions unless we try it in the marketplace. If we choose not to try it, I think we'll miss the opportunity forever, because someone else will certainly pick up on the concept."

After two years of talk, it was now time to count votes for the first time.

I decided against just a voice vote or a show of hands. Instead, I would go around the table, having each person vote *yes* or *no*, and make any comments he or she wished.

There were twelve directors. I knew from my private discussions the vote at worst would be 10–2, maybe 11–1. But I preferred 12–0.

Leave Nothing to Chance

So I arranged the seating with four sure *yes* votes coming first. The question marks were in seats number five and eleven.

McCorkindale was a possible *no*. I seated him as number eleven, at my left. He told me in advance, "If you want me to vote for it, I will. If you want me not to speak at all, I won't."

I told him to do whatever he thought was right.

All along I had encouraged him to speak out about the downside risks of this new venture. His dissenting voice showed directors that dialogue and difference were encouraged by me. CEOs who welcome that are much better off than those who try to squelch the opposition.

A second *no* vote might come from J. Warren McClure. He joined our board after Gannett acquired the Burlington, Vt., and Chambersburg, Pa., newspapers, which he had acquired by marrying the daughter of the owner.

McClure is not my kind of guy. We are opposites on everything, personally and professionally. He brags that "money isn't everything; health is 2 percent," and nothing else matters.

My predecessor, Paul Miller, had named McClure vice president of Gannett and put him on the board. Mac spent full time trying to become president. At a showdown luncheon he requested in 1975, I told him there was no way he would ever be promoted by me. He retired as veep soon thereafter.

Continuing as a board member, he often expressed concern about why we kept putting expensive fruit like fresh strawberries on the Gannett airplanes. He basically opposed anything with my stamp on it. I knew he wanted to vote against *USA TODAY*, but I also doubted he would have the balls to do so, if I handled the meeting right.

I put Mac in seat number five, so that his voice and vote would be heard only after four prestigious members had already voted *yes*.

The first was Andy Brimmer, former member of the Federal Reserve Board. *Yes*. "The company has used a classic Harvard Business School approach to introducing a new product," he said. I thanked him and squelched my laughter, for I hadn't used a single Harvard Business School idea or any of their MBAs in arriving at my decision.

Next banker Bill Craig, the most conservative member of the board. *Yes*. "The project has been thoroughly researched," he said.

Julian Goodman, former head of NBC, could not attend because he was at a meeting involving merger discussions of Gulf Oil, on whose board he served.

But Goodman left me his proxy and a letter for me to read. I put that in the number three spot. *Yes*. "It would be wrong for a growing company like Gannett to shrink from an opportunity it is so uniquely qualified to undertake," I read from Goodman's letter.

Next Wes Gallagher, the curmudgeon who had been most skeptical a year earlier. He had become a strong convert. *Yes*. "I hope you go first class and do whatever it takes to do it right," he said.

Now it was McClure's turn. I smiled at him. He grimaced. "I could vote against this, and if it fails I could say 'I told you so.' I know you've got the votes. So I vote *yes*. But remember, it's pretty damn risky and I've got a lot of money at stake in this company."

I continued around the table, but it was over. The only other question mark, McCorkindale, voted *yes*.

He later said, "Al permitted me, even encouraged me, to speak out against this. I still don't think it's a good investment. But I'll do what I can to make it work."

Final vote: 12–0.

Arranging a Spontaneous Reaction

We adjourned and went down to the ballroom of the Capital Hilton Hotel, to join four hundred Gannett executives in town for year-end meetings.

The scene: a huge chandeliered hall that had hosted presidents and domestic and foreign kingpins for a half century.

Traditionally at this Tuesday luncheon of the year-end meetings, I had delivered the state-of-the-company address.

This time the only thing the audience was really interested in was whether *USA TODAY* was a "go" or not.

But I kept them waiting.

"It's been another very good year for Gannett: $1,367,171,000 in revenues, $171,506,000 in net profit. The number of newspapers has increased to eighty-five. TV and radio stations now number twenty.

"In people, product, and profits, you have again delivered."

Then I turned to the future.

"As you know, we've spent nearly two years looking at the possibility of Gannett starting a new national daily newspaper.

"This morning your board of directors voted unanimously to go ahead with the *USA TODAY* launch."

They were on their feet. I had told Moe Hickey before that a "spontaneous standing ovation" seemed appropriate when I made the announcement. He arranged it by putting a few coworkers in the crowd at strategic locations in the ballroom. When they stood, so did everybody else—a typical crowd reaction.

After the prolonged applause, I said, "Many of you have helped us arrive at this decision. The work of you and your associates gave us the courage to tackle what is clearly a risky venture.

"Over the next year, until we're ready to launch in the fall of 1982, we can expect our critics and competitors to try to make things tough for us. But I know your backbone will be stronger than their backbiting.

"If this little experiment works, we'll all benefit from it, personally and professionally. If it doesn't, I hope we'll all have a helluva lot of fun trying it."

Our adventure in journalism was officially under way.

PLAIN TALK:

Illegitimi non carborundum.
Don't let the bastards get you down.

SHOWMANSHIP AND SALESMANSHIP

"Even Neuharth's critics acknowledge his marketing genius."

NEWSWEEK
September 20, 1982

We stood on a platform under a tent with the U.S. Capitol behind us and the Washington Monument in front. We were:

▷ The President of the United States, Ronald Reagan, and First Lady Nancy.

▷ The Speaker of the House of Representatives, Tip O'Neill of Massachusetts.

▷ The Majority Leader of the U.S. Senate, Howard Baker of Tennessee.

▷ The founder of *USA TODAY*, Al Neuharth, country boy from South Dakota.

The three most powerful men in the USA and our First Lady had joined me at the microphone to celebrate the launch of *USA TODAY*, September 15, 1982.

Under the huge tent around us were hundreds of members of the House and Senate, Cabinet members, ambassadors, media executives from across the country, and working journalists.

The President had come to salute the launch of the nation's first general-interest national daily newspaper.

USA TODAY "is a testimony to the kind of dream free men and women can dream and turn into reality here in America," Reagan said.

The President of the United States, huckstering for my new newspaper for free!

Tip O'Neill's House of Representatives was in session late

that day. But he recessed it for an hour so he and others could join the tent party at 6:30 P.M. O'Neill, a Democrat, noted that he and the President and Senate Majority Leader Baker, both Republicans, didn't often appear on the same platform together.

Indeed, they didn't. And especially not to plug a commercial product.

"How did you get the President and the others to do that?" I was asked over and over that night and in the weeks that followed.

"I invited them," I quipped.

Actually there was a message in that. It's like "Ask and ye shall receive" from John 16:24 in the Bible.

Far too often we fail to get what we want, especially in dealing with VIPs, simply because we are afraid to ask or don't ask the right people.

Of course, in the case of the President, it took more than just an invitation. For months I had used contacts and charm to get the President's people to put the *USA TODAY* launch party on his schedule.

It was a classy party. Red, white, and blue banners and balloons greeted the guests. Like our newspaper, the food and drink had an "across the USA" theme.

King crab from Alaska and crab cakes from Maryland, clams and oysters from New York, walleyed pike from Minnesota, pheasant from my home state of South Dakota, barbecued beef from Texas, poi from Hawaii.

All washed down with wines from California.

Getting Ten Times Your Money's Worth

The price tag: less than $100,000.

Not even our bean counters objected to that. They knew, as we all did, that we got more than a million dollars worth of free publicity.

Pictures of the President, the Speaker, the Majority Leader, and me, displaying the first issue of *USA TODAY*, were on the tube and in print across the country. The party got as much attention from the columnists and commentators as did the newspaper itself.

And it set the pattern for similar launch affairs as we rolled out the newspaper market by market across the USA over the next eight months.

The huckstering and hype that went into *USA TODAY* was an important part of its success. But the most important aspect of it was that the promotion reflected the product.

USA TODAY was designed to be different. Breezy. Bright. Colorful. Attention-getting. Sometimes irreverent. Always up-beat. Most of all, fun. All of our promotions combined some or all of those features.

A lot of promotions miss because they don't reflect the product. That can easily happen when outsiders—even at the best of creative ad agencies—call the shots on a company or a product they don't fully understand.

That's why the CEO must be involved. No one has as good a feel for a product as its creator or founder or boss.

A CEO must make sure that the hype isn't overdone. Too much promotion is as bad as too little. Some hucksters think there's no such thing as too much hype. A CEO must watch them as closely as he does the bean counters.

The entry of *USA TODAY* into local markets wasn't always a welcomed event—certainly not by some local newspapers.

The local launch parties were important to show the community that other parts of the establishment were glad to welcome *USA TODAY*. It became the in thing for political leaders or sports and entertainment celebrities to join us and plug the paper.

Governors and mayors actually made their appearances at some peril, because local newspapers sometimes boycotted the events.

Sometimes we were criticized by the local press for the way we moved our blue-and-white vending machines onto their street corners. New York was an example.

The weekend before our launch in the Big Apple, circulation chief Frank Vega's troops stormed the city and bolted three thousand vending machines to the sidewalks of New York.

At a press conference that Monday morning, reporters from *The New York Times,* the *Daily News,* and the *Post* goaded Mayor Koch into criticizing the *USA TODAY* machines as "unsightly." He said he would have his legal department look into whether he could force us to remove them.

But that night Koch showed up as scheduled at our big bash

at Radio City Music Hall. He followed a spectacular All-American performance we had arranged by the Rockettes.

Chutzpah à la Ed Koch

With his usual chutzpah, Koch welcomed us to New York and wished us well. "I don't know too much about Gannett. But any outfit that can bolt down three thousand vending machines on the sidewalks of New York overnight can't be all bad," he wisecracked before the audience of several hundred of the Big Apple's big names.

The vending machines became a huge part of our nation-wide hype. Ultimately we put over 135,000 of them in place. Not only do they serve as sales outlets, but they are minibillboards that millions of people see daily.

We had carefully researched and been convinced that local politicians or competing media could not prevent their installa-tion or force us to remove the boxes. They are a vehicle for distributing news and the First Amendment protects them. That argument prevailed at several locations where a legal challenge against them was launched.

Even the controversy over the vending machines generated a lot of free publicity. "I'm giving you a hundred thousand dollars of P.R.," Mayor Koch joked.

Some local newspapers were so bitter they carefully cut out or brushed out our newsboxes in pictures of street accidents or other such scenes. Or published them only in scenes depicting slums.

But television stations loved showing the boxes on their TV news bites. Movie producers soon panned street corners across the USA showing this new blue-and-white landmark.

CBS's Charles Kuralt said, "Meandering across the land seeking out 'On the Road' stories, I have plunked quarters into *USA TODAY* vending machines outside the Holiday Inn in Klam-ath Falls, Oregon; the 7-Eleven stores in Great Bridge, Virginia; at the last bus stop as the road runs out at Homestead Valley, California; chained to the light pole at Eighth Avenue and Fourteenth Street in New York City; in Lincoln, Missouri, right under the only stoplight in town.

"I have reason to think Al Neuharth has made a bright and inventive addition to the newsstands and light poles of America."

The vending machines probably were and are the biggest single ongoing free promotion any company ever was able to design for a new commercial product. But they didn't just happen.

From the beginning I knew we had to design a *USA TODAY* newsrack that would be different, one that would really catch the eyes of passersby, as well as dispense newspapers.

Newspaper vending machines had looked the same for decades. Studying how to modernize them was Frank Vega's job. I wanted something that looked like a TV set on street corners, with newspapers displayed so that people would stop and look at them the way they do at TV screens.

Vega traveled across the USA looking at different newsracks and brought dozens back to Washington.

Defying the Laws of Gravity

The traditional, most commonly used racks all had a coin box at the very top. The front page of the newspapers was displayed well below the coin box so that people couldn't read it without bending down at the knees.

When I told Vega I wanted to promote the paper, not the coin box, he didn't get it right away. He said if we were going to display the front page the way I wanted it displayed, we would have to build racks with electric motors in them.

"And Al," Vega said, in his usual smartass way, "there aren't electrical outlets on every street corner of the country."

Because of the laws of gravity, Vega explained, we would have to keep the coin mechanism on top.

"Mr. Vega," I said, with an edge in my voice, drumming my fingers on top of a rack as he and a half dozen associates listened, "I understand the fucking laws of gravity. But I want that coin mechanism out of the way of the newspaper display!"

Besides rattling a few coins, I had rattled Vega's composure. He returned to the drawing board with a renewed sense of imagination and determination.

Again I had had to resort to a little drama to make a point.

Vega took my concept to Fred Gore, a Texas product designer. Vega told Gore that we wanted a rack with a Space Age look, one that would appeal to a television generation.

Gore came up with a winner: Our new rack was on a

pedestal, and the display window was tilted back at a slight angle. The front page was presented to the reader in an inviting way—it said, "Read me, buy me."

And Gore found a way to move the coin mechanism.

We had our unique vending machines, and Gore gave Kaspar Wire Works and the city of Shiner, Texas, a new industry employing 450 to manufacture them exclusively for us.

Our main strategy during the early years of *USA TODAY* was to get as much free publicity as possible. Dozens of launch parties, hundreds of TV, radio, newspaper, and magazine mentions, thousands of vending machines, all free or low-cost ways to attract readers. And they worked.

But to attract advertisers in our developing years I knew we would need a carefully planned, high-cost promotion campaign.

In our prepublication planning, I set this general timetable:

▷ 1982–83: the years of the readers.

▷ 1984–85: the years of the advertisers.

▷ 1985–86: the years of cost control and effective management.

▷ 1987 and beyond: the years of the shareholders.

We knew we would not to able to attract many paid advertisers until we got high-profile readers in big numbers. But making believers out of advertisers took longer and was much tougher than we thought it would be.

After we passed the 1 million mark in paid circulation in 1983, we had hooked readers on Elm Street, leaders on Main Street across the USA, and we were even beginning to win over some analysts on Wall Street. But advertising decision-makers on Madison Avenue were sitting on their hands.

The Cowards of Madison Avenue

The truth is they were afraid of *USA TODAY*. Advertising agency executives are comfortable with the status quo. Despite their reputation for imagination and creativity, they are not quick to go for any new advertising medium. In many ways they resented *USA TODAY* as an intrusion into their comfortable and traditional view of media buys.

Columnist Nicholas Von Hoffman commented on the reluctance of advertisers, "All kinds of reasons are given, but what it boils down to is innate timidity: 'This is a new thing. Dear, oh dear, if we advertise in it, we might be criticized for taking a risk.' "

Most agency executives thought there were enough newspapers already. And besides, they weren't sure *USA TODAY* was really a newspaper.

Advertising agencies generally allocate dollars by category: television, magazines, billboards, radio, newspapers. The agencies saw *USA TODAY* as a mix of newspaper and news magazine and didn't know how to react.

Through the years at Gannett, I had been involved closely with our advertising agency, Young and Rubicam. Y & R had done good work for us, largely because of the effective leadership of then chairman Ed Ney.

In the beginning days of *USA TODAY*, when Ney was directly involved, Y & R very effectively captured the essence of *USA TODAY*. Their slogan and nameplate were winners. Their early reader promotion was satisfactory, if not outstanding.

But when it came time to pitch the advertisers to use *USA TODAY*, Y & R bombed.

Ney himself was no longer directly involved. The key Y & R people on the *USA TODAY* account were Ivy League yuppies. *The New York Times* was their bible. They had trouble relating to *USA TODAY*. Therefore they couldn't figure out how to sell it to media space buyers.

The tip-off was when they presented an expensive ad campaign proposal that was to feature me on TV and in newspaper and magazine ads. When an agency can't figure out how to sell a product, it tries to appeal to the CEO's ego by featuring or selling him.

Such promotion seldom works. It did with Lee Iacocca at Chrysler. But it failed with Frank Borman at Eastern and with dozens of other companies.

I refused to accept the bait. Despite my close identity and association with the newspaper and despite my critics who enjoyed claiming I was on an ego trip, I knew it would be a mistake to sell Neuharth rather than *USA TODAY* in our ads.

That proposal from Y & R convinced me we needed to look elsewhere for an agency. I knew it would be a risky decision, because Y & R had a lot of clout. The agency represented many clients who could have and should have been advertising in *USA TODAY*.

But I had more confidence in dealing with Madison Avenue after I recruited Cathie Black to become president of *USA TODAY* to run our advertising sales effort. Black had been one of Madison Avenue's rising stars. Now she was pumping new life into *USA TODAY*'s sales efforts.

"Your Advertising Sucks!"

I told Black of our problem with Y & R. She recommended that we consider a small agency headed by an iconoclastic genius, George Lois. Black wasn't sure how Lois would play with me and my colleagues. A profane and prolific ad writer, he represented the opposite of the button-down Y & R crowd.

One of Lois's claims to fame was a TV spot for Xerox that showed its copier was so simple to operate a chimpanzee could do it. When Cathie Black met with Lois, he had a simple message for her. "Your product is better than the competition's," he said, "but you're not communicating that to the advertiser. The truth is your advertising sucks."

To see if Lois could improve things, we arranged a competition for the *USA TODAY* account. First Y & R made its presentation. Then George Lois came into a room of poker-faced Gannett executives—many of them skeptical journalists—to hype his ideas.

One proposed print ad Lois prepared tackled the question of *USA TODAY*'s identity head-on. Was it a newspaper or a news magazine? The ad showed a drawing of a creature that had a body of a rooster but the tail of a fish.

"A lot of media people are saying *USA TODAY* is neither fish nor fowl," his copy said. "They're right."

"The truth is," the message ended, "we don't much care what you call us. Just as long as you call us."

I liked Lois's bright new approach. But it left us with a dilemma—it wasn't easy for a new product to ditch the country's largest ad agency. And we would be switching from the largest to one of the smallest—Lois Pitts Gershon.

I asked Lois what people would say if we did that. "They'd probably say you're finally getting your heads screwed on straight," Lois replied. "You're doing pussy advertising now. You ought to be doing triumphant fucking advertising." The man spoke my language.

I decided to give Lois part of the advertising—the part aimed at the trade press. It worked. Combined with continuing circulation gains, *USA TODAY*'s advertising linage began to pick up. Within a short time, Lois had won the entire *USA TODAY* and Gannett account.

Lois's most creative and effective work came in television commercials aimed at both readers and advertisers. He created a series of TV spots which used such celebrities as: Joan Collins, Joe Namath, Diahann Carroll, Willie Mays, Mickey Mantle, Willard Scott.

He put the celebrities on screen, displaying a section of *USA TODAY* and singing a new jingle.

Most of them couldn't sing, but the sight of Willard Scott ogling the camera, waving our weather map, and crooning, "I read it every day," got a lot of attention.

The celebrity ads were so successful that we still use them from time to time, updated with new stars in sports, politics, business, and entertainment.

Dealing at the Top

We also found out that when *USA TODAY* sales executives could pitch the newspaper directly to top executives of companies, their success rate for selling ads was much higher than when they went through agency decision-makers. Many of the CEOs themselves read the newspaper everyday. Often they talked about how their spouses and children liked it. Our product was our best promotional vehicle.

Black felt we were missing a bet by not having me engage in CEO-to-CEO talk about *USA TODAY* advertising. From the beginning I had resisted pleas of ad sales executives to sell ads. I said that was their job, not mine.

I also felt they were better at it than I was. I was perfectly comfortable in the newsroom rewriting stories or headlines. That was my bag, and I usually improved what I played with there.

And I loved the P. T. Barnum promotional part of the job.

But I am not an ad salesman. I was uncomfortable at the thought of trying to become one. I am a better showman than salesman.

After a lot of urging from Cathie Black, I agreed to meet with high-ranking company executives and advertising agency bosses at dinners around the country to discuss the philosophy of *USA TODAY* and to answer questions. But I told her I wasn't going to ask for the order.

That was fine with Black. She could handle that expertly. So we devised a routine where I represented the soft sell and she handled the hard sell.

"One of our secret weapons in attracting advertising was using Al at dinners," Black said. "His presence would guarantee the attendance of top-level decision-makers. And he could deliver the message about *USA TODAY* so that advertisers really paid attention."

My standard pitch included:

"*USA TODAY*'s news columns practice a journalism of hope, not just despair. People say it is an 'enjoyable experience' to read *USA TODAY*. Our readers are upbeat, outgoing. *USA TODAY* makes them want to do more, go more, be more . . . *buy* more."

Because most of the key executives of our advertising clients were our readers too, they got it. They believed it and gradually bought it.

Because *USA TODAY* is fun to read, I wanted our promotions to reflect that zest.

Vince Spezzano, in my book the best newspaper promotion executive in the country, had worked with me for more than twenty years in developing promotional campaigns and gimmicks.

Spezzano loved gadgets. He put the distinctive *USA TODAY* logo on mugs, glasses, pens, paperweights, caps, jackets, gym bags, matches, lighters, golf balls, sweatbands, T-shirts, even aprons and book bags.

A Robot as a Spokesman

But two of Spezzano's best ideas involved machines: a robot and a badge machine.

The robot resembled a *USA TODAY* vending machine on wheels. The robot with the operator and his microphone out of sight attended launch parties, major sporting events, political conventions. It attracted lots of attention as the hidden operator engaged guests in conversation with the robot.

Frequently local television news reporters looking for a good visual and a different angle would interview the robot. The operator, fully prepared to answer questions about *USA TODAY*'s outlook and mission, generated lots of favorable, and free, publicity.

Sometimes the robot appearance for *USA TODAY* got better press than I did.

I thought from the first that the robot would be fun, but I wasn't so sure about Spezzano's desire to buy a badge machine. Since Spezzano has been right more than he has been wrong on promotion, I told him to go ahead.

The badge machine, designed for use at our parties, converted photos of our guests into metal buttons, like campaign buttons. We took pictures of people in front of a large *USA TODAY* Page One with a headline to suit the occasion. The machine produced buttons with the pictures, delivered to guests within minutes.

Dignitaries at our social functions often stood in line to have a personalized button made.

We introduced the button machine at the Democratic National Convention in 1984. When former President Jimmy Carter, *Washington Post* chairman Kay Graham, and *New York Times* publisher Punch Sulzburger waited to have their pictures made, I knew we had a winner.

PLAIN TALK:

A little bit of P. T. Barnum will carry you
a long way.

MOTIVATE AND MANIPULATE

"Neuharth has an ability for histrionics, like in the old movies. But he also has the ability to massage people, to handle them in a way to get the best out of them."

JOHN C. QUINN
former editor, *USA TODAY*

It takes different strokes for different folks.

Some people are motivated or moved to action by a pat on the back.

Others respond better to a kick in the ass.

Just being tough is never enough. Neither is just being a nice guy.

Many bosses make the mistake of trying to be just one or the other. What they don't realize is that most people are best manipulated to produce results by a combination of soft soaping and tough talk.

The job of the boss is to figure out which approach to use, when, and in what doses. The goal, of course, is to get people to do as well as they are able—hopefully even better than they know how.

From the newsroom to the pressroom at *USA TODAY*, our adventure demanded that people stretch themselves to their professional and personal limits, and beyond.

Some could be led to do that. Others had to be driven. I was both the leader and the driver.

The strong and the steadfast—the vast majority—stayed with me, step by step and threat by threat. A few of the weak or the wimps fell by the wayside.

I admit I was always demanding, unrelenting, maybe a bit obsessive. With the lazy I was sometimes insulting or abusive. But I also praised good performers and often promoted or rewarded them beyond their highest hopes.

Hiring and Inspiring

My style might not work at every company. But it worked well at *USA TODAY* and Gannett.

An important ingredient is hiring people that fit the product. In background, outlook, and objectives. Then inspiring them.

USA TODAY had something to prove to the world: that it could beat the odds and succeed. So did many of the members of the staff.

Most had not yet established or peaked with their professional reputations. Many were women and minorities who had run into the glass ceiling elsewhere. They saw *USA TODAY* as their ticket to the top. Others had left jobs they weren't enjoying very much to seek a new adventure. They were there for the fun of it.

Their adventuresome spirit created a counter establishment to the media establishment.

Whether they had left dull or dead-end jobs, they brought with them a highly motivated work ethic. That became an essential part of the *USA TODAY* cult or culture. And a key to its success.

Another key was learning to laugh. While I was deadly serious about the success of *USA TODAY*, I cajoled and joked a lot. I never permitted us to take ourselves too seriously.

I was having a helluva lot of fun, and it showed. All my life I had used self-deprecating humor to make my points or win over audiences. Now, with *USA TODAY*, our critics made it easy for me. They played right into my hands. They gave me lots of self-deprecating material to use.

During the early days of *USA TODAY*, I would speak before various outside audiences and read the most caustic criticism—exact quotes—and smile. Invariably the audience would laugh. Instinctively people pull for the underdog. The critics helped make us a celebrated underdog.

Most of the early criticism was directed at our news and editorial product. Our bright and breezy new brand of journalism brought nothing but sneers and jeers from traditionalist journalists.

At first our editors and reporters were bitterly resentful. I told them to relax and enjoy it.

When *Washington Post* executive editor Ben Bradlee snipped: If *USA TODAY* is a good newspaper, "then I'm in the wrong business," I told our editors at the next news conference, "Bradlee and I finally agree on something. He *is* in the wrong business."

My associates laughed and loosened up. From that point on, our critics became as much a motivator for our news people as I was.

Nancy Woodhull, then managing editor/news and now president of Gannett News Service, said, "Neuharth was so confident and cocky when he was around us. He knew we were changing the world of journalism and laughed at the critics. That made me confident too. It was a classic example of the effect a leader has on people in uncertain times."

Critics of *USA TODAY* tried all kinds of demeaning labels for our brand of journalism. But the one that caught on best—and helped us most—was inspired by this column by Jonathan Yardley in *The Washington Post* when we first began publication:

> This is the real revolution of *USA TODAY* . . . Every day, newspapers give their readers a large serving of cod liver oil; it may taste awful, but it is good for them. *USA TODAY* . . . like parents who take their children to a different fast-food joint every night and keep the refrigerator stocked with ice cream, gives its readers only what they want.

Again some of our editors were miffed. I loved it. I told them we should relish a reputation for giving readers what they want. And I said the "fast-food" comparison would help us much more than it could hurt us.

The Making of McPaper

Yardley's column inspired the label or nickname that did more to motivate our news people than anything I could have done and became the identifier we used to good advantage: *McPaper*.

A hint at it first showed up in *Newsweek* with this headline: "The Big Mac of Newspapers."

Other journalistic critics latched on to the McPaper label quickly. They used the term to show their contempt for our brand of journalism. I saw it as a shorthand way to communicate to the public what we were trying to do:

Lots of news, in interesting bits and pieces. Tastes good and makes you feel good. In a colorful, smooth, slick package with ink that doesn't dirty your hands the way many gray newspapers do.

Linda Ellerbee, TV gadabout and media commentator, said of *USA TODAY*, "It doesn't rub off on your hands, or on your mind."

I quoted her over and over, in a semi–self-deprecating way. But I always used the opportunity to point out that *USA TODAY* "informs, entertains, and debates. But it doesn't dictate. We don't force unwanted objects down unwilling throats."

The staff began turning the other cheek after one editor noted, "They call us McPaper, but they are stealing our Mc-Nuggets."

Turning the snide comments of our adversaries to advantage not only helped morale internally, it amused the general public. Most admired that we were able to laugh at ourselves.

Said editor John Quinn, "Neuharth developed a practice and style of putting himself and *USA TODAY* down in a very effective way. He could stand up in front of a group of advertising executives or truck drivers and say things about himself that would make any group respond favorably to him."

One of our many opportunities to cash in on laughter came when the editors of the *Harvard Lampoon* decided they wanted to do their annual parody for 1986 on *USA TODAY*.

Previous *Lampoon* "victims" included *Time, Cosmopolitan,* and *People* magazines. Most publications parodied by the *Lampoon* considered it a putdown. Many executives of the target publications nervously resented or resisted the idea.

I thought it was another great opportunity to direct attention at *USA TODAY*, especially with a young, bright audience. And most importantly, I thought it would be fun.

So I invited the young Harvard editors to Washington for lunch. I was impressed with their imagination and irreverence. They seemed to understand *USA TODAY* better than their older counterpart editors in the establishment press.

After the meeting I asked all our staff to cooperate with the *Lampoon* editors. We opened many of our files to them. Let them borrow typefaces and graphic devices.

Their spoof featured headlines like:
▷ "Four Out of Three College Jocks Can't Count"
▷ "Judge Wapner Elevated to Supreme Court"
▷ "Kissing Ass: The Key to Corporate Success"

We even bought a full-page color ad in the edition to congratulate the *Lampoon* editors on their cleverness.

Learn to Laugh at Yourself

When the *Lampoon* edition was ready for distribution, key *USA TODAY* editors and I joined the *Lampoon* staff in laughing at us at a black tie bash at Harvard's Lampoon Castle in Cambridge, donated by William Randolph Hearst. We reciprocated by hosting the Harvardites at dinner in Washington, which several hundred government and media biggies attended. Our media critics had another opportunity to laugh at us. But we were laughing with them.

"Al's attitude toward our parody showed self-confidence and a sense of humor," said *Harvard Lampoon* editor Dan Greaney. "I couldn't help but admire a company that is both gung ho and irreverent."

They printed 750,000 copies of this witty parody that sold mostly on college campuses. It was a reflection of the success *USA TODAY* itself enjoyed as a hot publication on most college and university campuses. One indicator: 30 percent of *USA TODAY* circulation is now in the 18–38 age group, an encouraging forecast for future readership.

While critics helped boost morale and motivate our newsroom people, we didn't get many such opportunities in circulation, advertising, and other departments.

With people in those departments, the key to motivation was in clearly setting very high goals from the beginning, spelling them out publicly, and then working like hell to meet or beat them.

Before *USA TODAY* began publication, I publicly announced the five-year targets I had shared with the directors:
▷ Average daily paid circulation of 1 million to 2 million.
▷ A price of 50 cents per copy.
▷ Twelve to fifteen paid pages of advertising daily.
▷ At least $200 million in annual revenues.
▷ Turning a profit.

I could have kept those goals a secret. It would have taken a lot of pressure off me and my colleagues. But announcing them publicly was as important as establishing them. Telling the world about these expectations forced everyone—including myself—to buy into them.

Private objectives don't really mean much to anybody. They are for wimps. They're easy to forget, or to change when the going gets tough.

USA TODAY's goals were aggressive, clear-cut, and communicated broadly to everyone. That gave us, our board, our public, and our critics clear bench marks against which to measure our performance.

The major challenges to *USA TODAY*'s long-term success were circulation and profitability. It was important for everyone in all departments—from the pressroom to the newsroom—to understand that.

The most important circulation number for *USA TODAY* was 1 million. That was the magic number our advertising sales staff said was needed to really interest national advertisers. And it was important for the 1 million to come as quickly as possible. National advertisers were sitting on the sidelines waiting.

Once we started publication and realized the importance of breaking into the million-circulation club, I moved up our target. I didn't change our five-year goals, but I told our key people we had to hit 1 million before the end of the first year.

No small task. At that time there were only three daily newspapers in the country with over 1 million circulation:

▷ *The Wall Street Journal,* 1,925,722. It was founded in 1889.

▷ New York *Daily News,* 1,544,108. Founded in 1919.

▷ *Los Angeles Times,* 1,052,637. Founded in 1881.

Most people assumed the venerable *New York Times* had a daily circulation of over a million. But even with its national edition, it fell short. Other fairly well-known names like the *Chicago Tribune* and *The Washington Post* aren't even close.

I knew if we were going to have a shot at reaching a million in a year, we'd have to perfect every little thing we were doing in circulation. I appointed myself a one-person circulation checker in every market we entered.

During my early morning jogs, I would carry quarters and paper and pencil. I checked vending machines to make sure that day's newspaper was on display by 6 A.M. and that the machine was operating properly. If anything was wrong, I made notes.

Nothing turns off potential purchasers of a newspaper on a street corner more than to have the machine gobble up coins without returning that day's paper.

The Lazy Won't Last

A month after *USA TODAY* was launched, I found a machine with day-old papers in it in downtown Washington near the White House. After dressing down circulation boss Frank Vega personally, I used the opportunity to prod others as well with this memo to department heads:

> This is only one example of a lackadaisical attitude and performance which is slowly creeping in around here. Some people think they and we already have it made.
>
> Please let this be a reminder to all of you to remind all of those who work for you that the lazy, the sloppy, the unenthusiastic, the uninspired will not be working for *USA TODAY* very long.
>
> If the above is not clear or if you have any questions about your individual responsibilities to see that the proper attitude and performance is maintained here, please ask me.

The first launches in 1982 went well. We exceeded circulation expectations in Washington-Baltimore, Minneapolis, and Pittsburgh. We did okay in Atlanta and Seattle. But the San Francisco numbers were our first disappointment.

The San Francisco operation was important because it was the first market that had two existing newspapers serving it. My observations were that local planning and implementation of the launch were ineffective. I also thought our top executives were beginning to think circulation was on automatic and were giving it routine attention.

After the San Francisco launch I summoned Vega and publisher Phil Gialanella and president Vince Spezzano to my Florida home/office for a Sunday morning meeting.

All I asked them was "Who screwed up in San Francisco and how are you going to fix it?"

"When we sat down in Al's office at Pumpkin Center, it was like a scene out of *Doctor No* and James Bond," Vega said. "He had his two white Maltese puppies in his lap, stroking them gently but piercing us with cold stares.

"I'm looking at Phil and Vince to see which one of us is going to take the fall for San Francisco. You can just sense one of us is sitting over a trapdoor that will be opened at any minute to send us below to our fate in a pool of alligators."

Vega, Gialanella, and Spezzano dreaded being in my disfavor. I had learned that kicking them in the ass is what motivated them. Others could be moved by milder admonishments, but it took tough stances to get these tough guys' attention.

Before the meeting broke up, I told them their explanations sounded like excuses, not reasons. "If you guys expect to stick around, I expect no repeat of such screwups."

The next launches in Houston, Denver, and Los Angeles were very successful. By the end of January 1983, our circulation topped 530,000. After only four and a half months of operations, we were halfway to our million goal.

I sent Vega one of my peach-colored notes after Los Angeles: "You done good, kid. Another half million and you'll come of age."

Motivation by Deprivation

I made it a point to praise good work, but usually by citing the next challenge.

"Al doesn't give many compliments, so they mean more when you get them," said Vega. "He's the greatest motivator I've ever known. He has the ability to make you want his approval. You have to work for it every day because he parcels it out bit by bit, like one commandment at a time. At least God gave Moses all ten commandments at once."

When praise is specific and not overdone, employees value it more. I call that motivation by deprivation.

Now that we seemed on a good roll in circulation launches, I decided to press for the million mark even sooner. The big annual meeting of newspaper publishers—ANPA—was coming up in April in New York City.

I told our executives I wanted to be able to announce that we had hit the million mark at that time, even though we would be only seven months old. That added new excitement and recharged some batteries that were beginning to run down.

We moved up launch dates in Miami, Detroit, Chicago, Philadelphia, and New York. The stepped-up schedule was back-breaking for everyone. But it worked.

On April 24, 1983, in the ballroom of the Waldorf-Astoria, before hundreds of newspaper executives, I unveiled a huge *USA TODAY* banner with this number: 1,109,587.

Gannett publishers stood and cheered. Others in the industry were more reserved. And many didn't believe us.

USA TODAY's seven-month circulation story was the topic of the week among the nation's newspaper publishers. Many of them concluded we were "cooking the books." They said, not so politely, that I was a liar and that we had inflated our circulation by claiming phony sales.

The newspaper industry has a way of verifying circulation claims. The Audit Bureau of Circulations (ABC) audits the books, makes field inspections for each member newspaper, and then issues a number that is considered gospel by the industry and by advertisers.

That should have been an easy way to certify our claim. Trouble was the ABC has an archaic rule that says no newspaper is eligible for an audit until it has been publishing for a year. Another way for the Old Boys' Club to protect itself.

I figured a way around it. I hired the nationally known auditing firm of Price Waterhouse to do an independent audit of our circulation books. No newspaper had ever done that.

The result: Price Waterhouse said our million-plus number was correct.

That should have ended the sniping, but it didn't. Competing publishers kept saying the only circulation audit that counts is one by ABC. Many advertising decision-makers agreed. But the smart ones figured we would not be stupid enough to lie publicly about a number as important as this one.

Going public with the million-plus number was a great morale booster, internally. And it motivated circulators to keep the numbers up. The million-plus figure was becoming fixed in advertisers' minds.

When the long-delayed first ABC audit finally was announced, it made believers out of everyone. The official number: 1,179,834. That was about 70,000 more than any unofficial number we had announced.

Report Cards for Grown-Ups

With the numbers guessing game finally over, I turned my attention to other departments as well as circulation. I snooped into everything everywhere.

Then I began a series of management meetings with key executives of each department and issued their first year's report card.

I issued lots of report cards over the years. Grown-ups aren't used to getting report cards. If grades work to measure school performance, they mean even more in the workplace.

Life is a test. Every job is a test. With me every day is a test. So grades and report cards are important.

Highlights from those first-year report cards:

▷ ADVERTISING: "The *USA TODAY* advertising performance gets an A or A-plus for promotional activity. It would be lucky to get a C-minus for actual sales effort and results. We need new approaches and new thinking. Unless people at the top level do effective selling, the target accounts won't be cracked. If you can't do that, you don't belong in this million-circulation league."

▷ CIRCULATION: "You deserve an A or an A-plus in sales. Keep in mind I don't give many A's and damned few A-pluses. But you also get a C or C-minus in marketing strategy and pricing. More and more, you're trying to figure out deals to literally give the paper away. That won't work. From now on, the strategy is on selling more newspapers at higher prices. We're going to 35 cents next year and 50 cents the following. So get ready!"

▷ NEWS: "You're doing the best job of any department at *USA TODAY*. Day in and day out your overall product is on target. It's a strong B-plus from front to back. But you keep screwing up the top half of page one. That's the most important part of the paper. It's the only thing the potential buyer sees. And it's the poorest-edited part of the paper. That gets a C-plus."

I walked from my seat and paced the conference room. I knew where I was heading and what I had in mind, but no one else did. My target: the vending machine in the corner. We had them in the newsroom and meeting rooms, so that day's newspaper was always on display for our staffers to see exactly what our potential readers saw on the street corner.

I staged another of my planned dramas, controlled temper rising.

Stopping at the vending machine, I rattled the door, jabbed at the top half of the newspaper on display. Then I reached in my pocket, pulled out a quarter, and bought a paper.

I unfolded it so the entire page was showing. That day's cover story was about basketball tournament fever, with a color picture of a beautiful, blonde, tight-sweatered high school cheerleader leaping in the air. But only her head and shoulders showed in the top half of the page, which was on display in the machine window.

Tits Above the Fold

I jabbed my finger at the page for emphasis and growled, "The next time you run a picture of a nice, clean-cut All-American girl in a tight sweater, get her tits above the fold!"

The men and women news editors in the room roared. They got it. The message didn't have anything to do with tits. It was designed to leave a lasting impression—all the best of Page One had to show in the vending machine.

Our treatment of the top half of page one improved after that.

Gradually operations improved in all departments. And inevitably the emphasis had to shift to cost control. In the beginning we threw money at most problems. Ultimately I knew we'd have to substitute smart management for money. I also realized it would be tough to get everyone to shift gears.

The time came at the end of our second year of publication.

I was at my Pumpkin Center hideaway for the weekend when the October 1984 financial statement arrived. That was the first month of our third year of operation.

USA TODAY had lost another $10 million that month. Losses had been at that level during most of 1984. I had promised the board they would see improvement by year end. I had talked again and again with our key management people about it. But they weren't listening.

I had to get their attention—one way or another.

I called President John Curley in Washington midday Saturday and told him to bring the eight-member *USA TODAY* management committee to Pumpkin Center for a meeting at noon on Sunday. It was his problem to round up the executives and have them on a Gannett jet Sunday morning. I said 100 percent attendance was mandatory.

He found them scattered near and far. Cathie Black was the last one to be found, late Saturday night. She and her husband were enjoying a weekend in the Blue Ridge Mountains. Curley brought them down from the mountaintop.

That Saturday evening I had dinner in Cocoa Beach at my favorite seafood restaurant, the Surf, with a frequent companion, Barbara Whitney.

Whitney, a New York designer and building contractor, had moved to Cocoa Beach a few years earlier. Her construction company built homes and offices, and she also owned the Whitney Art Gallery. I hired her to design and supervise a new building for *FLORIDA TODAY.*

I liked her style and her results. We became very close friends. We were both twice divorced, but our relationship was not a romance. As close friends we had a lot of fun together, personally and professionally. She has rich tastes and is given to going first class. But she can upscale or downscale as circumstances warrant.

She has designed projects for me ranging from the multimillion dollar *USA TODAY* and Gannett office towers in Washington to the $30,000 overgrown tree house at Pumpkin Center in which I'm writing this.

At dinner I told her of the meeting I had arranged for the next day with the *USA TODAY* executives and the reason for it. "I've got to jar them into realizing that the days of an open cash register are over," I said.

She thought awhile, then suggested, "If you really want to get their attention, why don't we stage something like a 'Last Supper' for them?"

I laughed and said, "Sounds great. But I don't know enough about the biblical details to do it. If you arrange it, I'll stage it."

She said, "You're on. I'll get the wine, the unleavened bread, a cross, a crown of thorns, the works."

Whitney is English-Polish-American. I often called her the

Polish Princess. She teamed up with Rusty Fischer, the owner of the Surf restaurant, who provided the Jewish text for the ritual.

The next day, while I was delivering my own Sunday sermon to the *USA TODAY* executives at Pumpkin Center, Whitney and Fischer were busy preparing for the Last Supper.

When the *USA TODAY* executives arrived at Pumpkin Center, they sensed right away that things were different. It was noon. But no sign of lunch. I had even removed the usual candy dishes from the long conference table. No drinks or amenities were offered.

Quit or Start Over

We got right down to business. I said, "We can no longer afford to run *USA TODAY* the way we've been running it. We can't afford it financially. We can't afford it in terms of our credibility. We can't afford it emotionally.

"I promised you and myself this adventure would be fun. Losing money at the rate we are is no longer fun. We have two alternatives. We can quit. Or we can start over. Here's what that means:

"▷ If we quit, we declare defeat for *USA TODAY* and spend the rest of our careers doing dull things.

"▷ If we start over, it means drastic policy changes. The days of wine and roses are over.

"Since I don't know how to quit, I'm starting over. I'll be making the policy changes. Those of you who stay will implement them. It won't be easy. It may not even be pleasant. Some of you may not want to play under those new rules. If so, I understand."

I got up and walked the room. I looked at each person. I gave them plenty of opportunity to leave. They were all where I wanted them: transfixed.

I returned to my seat, with these few brief, simple statements:

"The ruthless realities are that overall, we must now substitute management for money.

"We must produce and present even more news, with fewer people, in less space, at lower cost.

"We must sell and publish even more advertising, at higher rates, with fewer people, at lower costs.

"We must produce and print more newspapers, with even better quality, with fewer people, at lower cost.

"We must circulate and sell even more newspapers, at higher prices, with fewer people, at lower cost.

"You must figure out how to do all that. I'll help you by declaring a 5 percent reduction in each of your payrolls for next year. Effective today there will be no new hires without approval in writing by Curley or me. We won't approve any.

"So all you have to do is figure out how to do more with less. I'm going to give you the afternoon off to think about it. We'll reconvene tonight at the Surf at seven."

That was our usual way to end the day when we had Pumpkin Center meetings. They were all expecting the same thing. A fancy dinner of stone crabs or oysters; Florida red snapper or pompano; French wine. A little pleasant business and social talk. But they were in for a surprise.

When they arrived at the Surf, they were directed to a private dining room. The door was closed. Some waited outside for twenty or thirty minutes. No drink orders were taken. When all were assembled, Barbara opened the door to the private room.

Sunday Night Theater

As they filed in, I was seated at a long, barren table. I was wearing a flowing robe and a crown of thorns. A large wooden cross rested on the wall behind me.

The guests were silent. They didn't know whether to cry, laugh, or leave.

At each setting there was a glass of Manischewitz wine and a piece of unleavened bread. Also, a brief script from which I later read and they were to respond. Barbara and Rusty had arranged a loose adaptation of the Jewish Passover and the Christian Last Supper, with emphasis on theatrics.

I began reading from a script headed "The Service for the Passed-Over."

It was a mix of religious metaphors. The setting was that of Jesus at the Last Supper. The script was from the Jewish feast of Seder, a Passover ritual.

I read this ritual question from the Seder service: "Why, on this night, do we eat especially bitter herbs?"

Then I asked them to join me in the answer: "This bitter herb is eaten because we are threatening to embitter our lives and the lives of our children."

As the service went on, some laughed. Others were silent and stony-faced. But they all got the message. Unless things changed, this might indeed be the last supper. And all of them would be passed over.

To make sure none of them forgot the message, I had a photographer on hand to record for posterity this somber setting. I later gave them autographed copies.

A picture of their boss wearing a crown of thorns with a cross in the background and them seated at the Last Supper was an effective reminder of the ruthless realities—even years later.

I was told later that on the two-hour jet ride back to Washington, some were pissed, some were praying.

But the cost-cutting started in earnest the next morning.

After they left, I went home to Pumpkin Center and stopped at my little oceanfront chapel. "Thanks," I said, looking up to Him or Her, smiling.

I went to bed thinking about these words which Whitney had given me along with the script for the service:

▷ From the Greek fabler, Aesop, who wrote in 550 B.C. "The gods help them that help themselves."

▷ And, from Ben Franklin, the S.O.B. who stole from Aesop, paraphrased it slightly, and wrote in *Poor Richard's Almanac* in 1736, "God helps them that help themselves."

Either way I figured I had called on the right helper(s) to motivate and manipulate the people on whom I was counting to make *USA TODAY* a winner.

PLAIN TALK:

Praise the Lord and pass the inspiration.

MEA CULPA AND
BON APPÉTIT

"Like most people, I doubted USA TODAY
*would succeed. But I hedged it by saying,
'Never, never bet against Al Neuharth.' "*

KAY GRAHAM
chairman of The
Washington Post Company

The King Midas of the USA is Warren Buffet. Everything he touches on Wall Street turns to gold.

When I invited this witty and lovable S.O.B. billionaire boss of Berkshire Hathaway to *USA TODAY*'s fifth-anniversary celebration, he accepted but said he wanted to be served crow.

"You should have two menus," Buffet wrote. "One should feature truly elegant fare and be served to those who were believers right along. The other should be crow for the skeptics. If you follow this suggestion, you probably should reserve the largest, toughest, and ugliest crow for me.

"I thought *USA TODAY* would fall on its face—editorially and financially. It now appears that you have created a product at a cost of about $300 million . . . that has a potential to gross over $300 million a year in the near future. As we both know, this is incredibly better than can be done by waiting for the next auction from Morgan Stanley . . .

"I hope you will be charitable and supply a lot of A-1 or Worcestershire sauce on my crow."

Crowing is not my style. Neither is gloating. Laughing is what makes my world work.

So when *USA TODAY* celebrated its success on its fifth anniversary—September 15, 1987—we served up fun and fine food for friend and foe alike.

Five years earlier on this same evening, we had celebrated the launch of *USA TODAY* under a tent on the grounds of the nation's Capitol. On this night we celebrated in the glitzy Gannett and *USA TODAY* headquarters, thirty-one stories above the west bank of the Potomac, overlooking Washington and the White House.

What a difference five years had made:

▷ Then, polite offers of good luck. But whispered wisdom by nearly all who knew that what we were trying to do couldn't be done.

▷ Now, messages of *mea culpa*. Those who were early skeptics or critics offered hearty congratulations for our success.

President Ronald Reagan, who also had been on hand for the launch party, led the salutes of anniversary celebrants:

"Your success is truly a turning point in the news business. You're leading a whole industry into the twenty-first century," said the fortieth President of the USA.

Other guests included two hundred leaders of government and industry, sports and entertainment: media biggies Walter Cronkite, Malcolm Forbes, and Helen Thomas; Supreme Court Chief Justice Warren Burger and House Republican Whip Dick Cheney (now Secretary of Defense); race car driver Mario Andretti; author Kitty Kelly; and businessman Bill Marriott.

Forbes, one of the most colorful and lovable multimillionaire S.O.B.s I know, had expressed the mood this way:

"When Gannett and Neuharth first got started on this project, I was among the multitudes who thought there was no way it could succeed. How wrong can one be?

"Can you think of any newspaper anywhere, anytime that has enjoyed such phenomenal success?"

Champagne and Laughter

The tributes were nice to hear. But I didn't want the celebration to get maudlin or mushy. So we cut out the speeches, laughed, and lifted our champagne glasses.

No crow and no crowing. Never take yourself too seriously.

But turnabouts and mea culpas continued, with the most surprising reversal coming on the eve of my retirement.

The prestigious and independent *Washington Journalism*

Review reported in its March 1989 issue on a poll of its 30,000 readers—mostly journalists from across the USA and many of them early and ardent critics of *USA TODAY*.

WJR's survey question: Who has had the greatest impact on print journalism in the last decade? The results:

▷ Al Neuharth . . . . 44.6 percent
▷ Ronald Reagan . . . . 13.4 percent
▷ Abe Rosenthal (former *New York Times* executive editor) . . . . 8.4 percent

Commented *WJR*:

"The man most readers think has had the biggest influence on print news in the past decade is also one of the most controversial: *USA TODAY* founder Allen Neuharth . . . Perhaps more than anyone in journalism, Neuharth has made the newspaper industry take a long, hard look at the nature of its product. That may stand as Neuharth's lasting legacy, more significant even than *USA TODAY* itself."

At the *WJR* awards presentation in a room full of former doubters or critics, I accepted with this brief tongue-in-cheek thank-you: "Without the constant encouragement of everyone in this room from the beginning, *USA TODAY* never could have made it."

Everyone laughed and applauded. The jeers had turned to cheers.

PLAIN TALK:

The last laugh really *is* the best laugh.

VI

MIXING MONEY,
MUSCLE,
AND CHARM

"I'm against any deal that I'm not in on."

THOMAS P. "TIP" O'NEILL
former speaker of the
U.S. House of Representatives

I've always liked bigness. Big opportunities. Big jobs. Big deals. Big companies. Big league.

When I was working for Knight newspapers in Miami and Detroit, I was proud of their big newspapers in big cities.

When I joined Gannett in Rochester, New York, things were different. Mostly small newspapers in mostly small towns.

We were treated like country bumpkins: What is Gannett? What does it do? Why should we care?

I could predict the question I would get first from most strangers: "How do you pronounce Gannett?"

The accent is on the *net*.

The *net* is what first got Gannett its attention. Net earnings made Gannett a darling of Wall Street. With the resources from going public, we began buying and building our way to bigness.

Long before the creation of *USA TODAY*, I knew what I wanted: the biggest newspaper company in the country.

A lot of people can claim they're the best. That's an opinion. Only one can claim the title of biggest in any ratings category. No argument. Bigness is easy to measure objectively. Most other ratings are subjective.

In a single decade—1970 to 1980—Gannett went from number seven to number one, the nation's biggest newspaper company.

In the early days, charm and friendship weighed heavily. Newspapers were a very personal thing, and most sellers put them in the hands of only those buyers they liked and trusted.

Later, as the competition caught on to what we were doing and sellers became less sentimental, we had to substitute more money for charm. And sometimes add a little muscle.

The mix worked. Country bumpkins no more.

"Fortune favors the bold."

VIRGIL
Roman poet and author

THE WOOING OF
WALL STREET

*"Wall Street seems to approve of
Neuharth's aggressive stewardship."*

BUSINESS WEEK
June 2, 1986

When Gannett decided to become a public company in 1967, I didn't know much about Wall Street. I knew where it was. Narrow street. Tall buildings.

I knew what it did. Let people gamble on companies and stock prices. I preferred the casinos and poker.

In the next twenty years, I learned a lot about Wall Street. It changed Gannett's fortunes, and mine. It made Gannett successful. It made me—and a lot of others—rich.

The biggest thing I learned: the mystique surrounding Wall Street is unnecessary.

Many CEOs are afraid of Wall Street. They forget an important element—the human touch. Stock market analysts are people, too.

Wall Street is home for a marvelous mix of people—some very talented, many hard workers, some greedy, some sloppy, most honest, a few bad apples. And many are a lot of fun to work and play with.

Figuring out how to deal with those people helped me enjoy my Wall Street experiences. But more important, it helped make Gannett one of the darlings of the investment world.

None of that happened by accident.

The wooing of Wall Street was one of my most important jobs as CEO. I didn't need an MBA or an accountant's understanding of finance. Something far more important was required: an understanding of people.

That is true for CEOs of any public company. That's why a generalist is better at it than is a specialist.

As a generalist, I wooed Wall Street by:

▷ Meeting the analysts face to face. Anywhere. Anytime.

▷ Bringing them in to check out our operations.

▷ Giving them straight answers to straight questions.

▷ Sticking to a no-surprise policy on company results.

▷ Trading wisecrack for wisecrack when appropriate. An irreverent style and spirit that showed I didn't take them—or myself—too seriously, while being very serious about company successes.

In 1967 when Gannett went public, Wall Street knew very little about newspaper companies. We launched a major propaganda campaign—based on hard facts—that changed Wall Street's perception of the newspaper industry.

Only two newspaper companies preceded Gannett in the public arena: Dow Jones, which owned *The Wall Street Journal*; and Times-Mirror, owner of the *Los Angeles Times.*

Life Beyond the Hudson

Those two companies were doing okay. But most analysts who followed the newspaper business at all viewed it through the tunnel vision of New York City, where most of them lived and worked. Some seemed to think life ended at the Hudson River.

Newspapers were in trouble in New York City. Four Manhattan dailies had died during the decade. Those remaining were plagued by the combination of labor problems and readers fleeing to the suburbs. The same problems haunted metropolitan papers elsewhere.

I set out to convince Wall Street that small- and medium-size newspapers across the country were alive and well. By praising the newspaper industry generally, it was easier and more credible to talk about Gannett. "If you like the newspaper industry, you'll love Gannett," was the message.

We invited analysts to our headquarters in Rochester. We conducted tours of our highly profitable suburban dailies in Westchester County, just north of Manhattan. We showed off our new Space Coast success in Florida. We highlighted our entry into California, with our acquisition at San Bernardino.

We accepted every invitation to meet and speak with financial analysts in New York, Boston, Philadelphia, Chicago, Los Angeles, San Francisco.

In the beginning, we traveled as a trio of pitchmen: Paul Miller, our then chief financial officer Jack Purcell, and I.

We soon learned the Wall Street types were not interested in how many Pulitzer Prizes Gannett had won (a lot), or how good our reporters and editors were (very), or about our personal lifestyles.

They wanted to know:

▷ What made Gannett different from the troubled *New York Times* and newspapers in other metropolitan areas?

▷ How much would our earnings improve this quarter, this year, next year?

▷ How aggressive and effective would we be in acquisitions and growth?

▷ How much pricing flexibility was there in our products?

▷ Could we weather recessions or economic downturns?

Miller had trouble focusing on such business specifics. At an early meeting of analysts in Boston, he talked on and on about what a great week he personally had had:

"I played golf for three days in California. Then I flew in the Gannett plane to Columbus, Ohio, picked up my mother-in-law and flew to Oklahoma. We visited my sister and family and I played golf with my old Okie buddies. Then we flew back home to Rochester for the weekend."

That travelogue didn't impress the Wall Street types. Purcell and I caught the disapproving glances. From that point on, we reduced Miller's role to handshaking and then soon reduced our team of touts to just two.

Miller was great at charming publishing pals. He worked the cocktail crowd as well as anyone I've known. But talking specifics of the business with analysts was not his bag.

Later, when Purcell left us to seek fame and fortune at CBS, I replaced him with Doug McCorkindale, who had been our chief legal officer. Doug, a slick Scotsman, fit the team even better.

Jack, then Doug, and I developed a simple standard speech for the Wall Streeters. The heart of my persuasion:

"Newspapers are an indispensable part of the lifestyle of most Americans, especially in small- and medium-size communities.

"Because they are a small ticket item, there is very little consumer or reader resistance to newspaper price increases.

"In most markets, the single daily is the primary advertising vehicle for the Main Street merchants. That permits pricing flexibility in advertising."

After selling the newspaper industry in general, I would pitch Gannett's special strengths:

"Importantly, and by design, Gannett newspapers are in medium-size communities. Many of them are near, but not in, major metropolitan areas.

"Our emphasis is on local news and advertising. No nearby larger daily newspaper or TV station can compete with that."

A Nonstop Money Machine

Gannett could manage its profits better than most companies, I explained.

During good times, revenues from advertising and circulation increase steadily. During economic hard times, we can easily reduce expenses, especially through use of less newsprint. And revenues can still be increased by modest price adjustments without consumer resistance.

Gannett was a dependable profit machine in good times or bad.

I was able to quote competitors to back up our claims.

Example: "Norman Chandler, patriarch of the *Los Angeles Times* and Times-Mirror family, understands Gannett strength. He has said: 'Metropolitan dailies can't compete with local newspapers. We tried it and it didn't work.' "

Soon Wall Street media analysts and publications began hyping our Gannett stock. Examples:

▷ John Kornreich, Neuberger & Berman: "Gannett's basic media business is awesome. It is virtually an unregulated monopoly."

▷ *The Wall Street Transcript:* "Gannett's management lives, breathes, and sleeps profits and would trade profits over Pulitzer Prizes any day."

Gannett began hosting dinners in connection with analysts' meetings. We even invited our competition, and many of the CEOs of major media companies began attending on a regular basis.

It was all part of my strategy to establish Gannett as the leader of the industry.

The dinners and the give-and-take exchanges afterward gave Gannett a more human identity. That human element is much more important than most CEOs realize.

When I made my first appearance before a Wall Street group, PaineWebber analyst Ken Noble told me a story that I never forgot:

He said that when the CEO of a certain manufacturing company made a presentation at a luncheon for analysts, "He was so bad that people began slipping out before it was over to phone in their sell orders."

Analysts pay attention to the style and personality as well as the substance of CEOs. If you're good, it helps. If you're not, it hurts.

I realized that my personal contacts with the analysts also helped give them credibility. Analysts like to be able to say, "Al Neuharth (or any CEO) told me . . ." It doesn't matter that you tell them that in a room with a hundred other analysts.

The personal touch in a business that is largely viewed as impersonal can be a big plus.

Most company presentations to analysts—particularly the CEO comments—are duller than the college classroom lectures that I remember. Some CEOs refuse even to go. They don't belong at the head of a public company. As Harry Truman said: "If you can't stand the heat, get out of the kitchen."

I found most analysts to be a lot like newspaper reporters. They really want the facts. At first, they're skeptical, sometimes cynical. But if they become convinced a company and its CEO are okay, it takes a disaster to dissuade them.

Once we had the analysts listening to us, they believed us in good times and bad times.

I never shaded the truth. I figured the facts would help us in the long run. And I made sure I had the appropriate facts on hand. The chief financial officer briefed me before analyst meetings the way the President of the United States is briefed before a press conference.

Bad News Can Be Fun

I didn't try to hide the bad news. In fact, I made fun of it.

In February 1983, I warned at an analyst meeting that we could be facing our first down quarter. The start-up costs of *USA TODAY*, plus the usual first-quarter doldrums, cast a shadow.

"After our long, boring, repetitive string of up quarters," I told them, "Gannett may have its first down quarter. If we do, we'll invite you all to a party to celebrate the end of one string and the start of another string of up quarters."

Silence. Then laughter. And at the next analysts' meeting in April, I apologized for a modest gain in the first quarter that cheated them out of a down-quarter party.

Because the analysts knew I was open and honest with them, they were in a better position to make forceful recommendations.

The analysts liked Gannett for its consistency of earnings. This track record from 1967 to 1987 helped:

▷ Annual revenues increased from $186 million to $3.1 billion.

▷ Annual earnings jumped from $14 million to $319 million.

▷ Shareholder dividends increased twenty times in twenty years, from 4.8 cents to $1.00 a share.

We not only had twenty consecutive years of earning gains, but also eighty uninterrupted quarters. By the time I retired as chairman, that streak had hit eighty-five consecutive quarters.

Someone who bought 100 shares of Gannett the day it went public in 1967 saw the value jump in twenty years, with stock splits, from $2,900 to $74,588.

The analysts looked good in recommending Gannett stock. And so did we.

For Gannett, the wooing of Wall Street worked wonders.

By 1972, just five years after going public, Gannett stock was selling at a price-earnings ratio of 36—twice the then average of other companies measured by Standard and Poor.

The goals we had in mind in taking Gannett public were realized even more quickly than we had hoped.

Of course, there are pros and cons of being a public company. Advocates of private companies see these advantages:

▷ Business can be run in a highly personalized way, almost

as a private fiefdom if the boss chooses to operate that way.

▷ The company is not accountable to Wall Street and is under less pressure to produce consistent increases in profits.

▷ Financial information about the company and its top executives is not a matter of public discussion.

None of those so-called advantages mattered to me. I believe accountability is a good thing, so I welcomed the broader scrutiny that Gannett got.

Most private companies go public for two reasons:

▷ To provide family members or other insiders a ready market for their stock, so that those who wish can cash in.

▷ To give the company much greater resources with which to grow, through acquisitions or new ventures.

In the case of Gannett, both those objectives were present. For the first time since I had joined the company, money-men Bitner and Williams and newsmen Miller and Neuharth were in complete agreement. But for different reasons:

▷ Bitner and Williams wanted to make themselves, their families, co-workers, and friends very rich.

▷ Miller and I wanted to gain for Gannett and for ourselves greater financial resources and professional power and prestige, although we didn't mind the prospect of making some money personally.

Those in Gannett who wanted to go into the public arena to sell out and get rich quick made out very well. But I had a helluva lot more fun and ultimately cashed in even bigger.

Frank Gannett owned all of the common voting stock in his private company while he was alive. He willed it to the Gannett Foundation when he died.

But he had created a class of nonvoting preferred stock for members of his family and for sale to some executives and employees. The preferred stock had very little market action, except in sales from and back to the company, at carefully controlled prices. But it paid a pretty high dividend.

A Big Political Payoff

Most of the preferred stock sold was to help Frank Gannett's ill-fated campaign for the Republican presidential nomination in 1940. That was the year such heavyweights as Dewey, Taft, Vandenberg, and Willkie were in the race.

Gannett made his bid as a prohibitionist and free enterprise candidate. He crisscrossed the country for over a year in his company plane seeking support. He entered the Philadelphia convention as the low man on the list and dropped out after getting just 33 delegate votes on the first ballot. Wendell Willkie ultimately won the nomination on the sixth ballot.

To finance that campaign, Gannett sold preferred stock in blocks of 5, 10, and 100 shares. Under present-day election laws, his financing would have been in trouble.

Printers, pressmen, reporters, editors, salesmen, friends, and relatives bought stock, generally considering it a campaign contribution. If they could have looked twenty-seven years into the future, they would have mortgaged their homes and bought all the stock they could as an investment.

As printer Frank Fantanza told me at a shareholder meeting years later, "Thanks for making me rich. Now don't change a thing you're doing."

Here's how a holder of the Gannett preferred stock made out at the time of the public offering:

Each share of preferred stock was converted into forty shares of common stock. That meant each preferred share originally bought at $110 became worth $1,160 overnight—40 shares at the opening market price of $29 a share.

Those who cashed in reaped an instant bonanza. Those who held their new common stock became much richer.

Twenty years later, by 1987, each share of converted preferred stock had grown in value from $110 to $29,835.

The wonders of Wall Street not only made individuals rich, but made it possible for the Gannett company to spend billions on acquisitions and new ventures. And to become the industry leader we set out to be.

PLAIN TALK:

Wall Street is a little dicey, but better than a crapshoot.

THE JOYS OF
DEAL MAKING

*"Neuharth glows like an ember when he
describes the deals he has brought off."*

NEW YORK TIMES MAGAZINE
April 8, 1979

I've never made a deal I didn't enjoy doing. For me, every business deal combined the art of games I had played at home—checkers, chess, poker, Monopoly.

During my years as chairman or president—1970 to 1989—Gannett made deals to acquire:

▷ 69 daily newspapers.

▷ 16 TV stations, trading up to meet FCC ownership limits.

▷ 29 radio stations, selling some as the FCC required.

▷ North America's biggest outdoor business, now with 45,000 billboards in the USA and Canada.

Every deal was different.

Price is always important, but not always overriding. Some sellers want an ongoing association with the successor owner. For them, friendship and trust count. Others seek community approval or a prestigious new owner. Some sellers, of course, just want the top dollar.

For the buyer, the trick is to figure out what mix of ingredients will open the door and close it.

At Gannett, we approached most deals with these key players:

▷ A deal door opener.

▷ The deal analyzers.

▷ A deal maker, or closer.

Each role is important. The art of good deal making depends on teamwork, blending the knowledge and skills and instincts of a variety of people to come up with the right approach and the right results.

The door opener can be anyone—from the boss to a bosom buddy to a banker. In our case, when Gannett really began its buying binge in 1971, the door opener usually was Paul Miller, then the CEO.

Miller had spent a lifetime befriending publishers and owners of newspapers. His dual role as president of Gannett and president/chairman of the Associated Press, which he was for fourteen years, put him on a first-name basis with most newspaper owners in the country.

He had a delightfully disarming Oklahoma country boy personality, polished a bit by his stints in New York and Washington. He played smart games of politics and golf. Most owners in our business liked and trusted him.

Miller wanted to buy everything available. While Gannett was a private company, limited resources and the nervous nellies in the financial department kept a rein on him. After we went public, the resource restraint was gone. But we had to make sure our acquisitions made sense to Wall Street.

That's where the deal analyzers came in.

That team was headed by our chief financial officer, backed up with experts in accounting, production, sales, and research.

Miller never saw a newspaper he didn't like. He really didn't know or care about price. He just wanted to buy. CFOs Purcell and McCorkindale, on the other hand, felt most available newspapers or stations were overpriced. So they often waffled on deals.

What Makes a Good Deal

That's when the deal maker had to take over.

During the thirteen years I was CEO of Gannett, deal maker was one of my key roles. Every decision to buy or not to buy was made by me, then presented and recommended to the board of directors.

By the time it got to the board, it had been so thoroughly thought out that in all those years our directors approved every buy or sell recommendation I made.

My favorite deals were one-on-one: the seller and me. The

more people you have around a negotiating table, the more chances the deal will be screwed up.

Of course, after the buyer and seller agree, lawyers are a necessary nuisance. In our push to grow bigger, these considerations were important:

▷ Does it fit our plan to develop a geographically diversified nationwide media company?

▷ Is it the dominant newspaper or station in its market, or could we make it that?

▷ Is it in a good growth market?

▷ How good is the present management? Would key players stay? Sometimes you want them to. Sometimes you hope they'll leave.

▷ Can we make the investment pay off in a reasonable time?

▷ Will it be fun to run?

The last two weigh heavily with me.

If it isn't going to be both fun and profitable, why do it? It makes no sense to buy incurable headaches. That's why we turned down repeated chances to acquire such longtime losers as the *New York Post,* the *Washington Star,* and others.

While the financial aspects of a deal are very important, they were not the most interesting or most intriguing for me.

Deals allowed me to play fun-and-games with some of the bigshots of the media business.

Kay Graham stormed out of a meeting of twenty media moguls and mcmoguls on a brilliantly beautiful Monday morning at the Mauna Kea Beach Hotel in Hawaii.

I had just slipped her a note that prompted two hurried and harried phone calls—one to her office at *The Washington Post.* The other to the headquarters of the DuPont Company in Wilmington, Delaware.

After hanging up the pay phone on the flagstone terrace next to the men's room, she reentered the meeting, sallied to where I was sitting, leaned over my chair and hissed:

"You son of a bitch. You knew all about it Saturday night. You led us on."

The grande dame's unladylike comments were on target. I had acted my playful S.O.B. part.

The "it" she bashed me about was the acquisition by Gannett of the Wilmington newspapers. They had been a prime target for months by many in our business, including Kay Graham.

When DuPont Chairman Irving Shapiro decided that the company would sell the newspapers, which dominated Delaware, he invited inspections and sealed bids. The deadline was Friday, January 27. Late that afternoon, DuPont informed us privately that Gannett was the winner.

Our lawyers and theirs were to put the commas in the contract over the weekend. The public announcement would be Monday, when the stock market closed—4 P.M. in the East, 10 A.M. in Hawaii. In the meantime, we agreed, mum's the word.

That same weekend, the elite directors of the American Newspaper Publishers Association gathered for what was a traditional annual midwinter meeting—this year in Hawaii—as always, somewhere in the sun. Expense-paid. IRS-approved.

At the opening dinner on the terrace under a full moon with the balmy breezes of the Pacific paradise providing natural air-conditioning, topic number one was the Wilmington deal.

Who would win?

How much money would it take?

Because I knew our winning bid was $60 million, I speculated that the price couldn't possibly top $50 million. That encouraged Kay and others who had bid more than that to think they might win. Or at least that Gannett had lost.

I fanned the fever of speculation. Playfully. It didn't concern me that thirty-six hours later some would call me an S.O.B.

You Lost—Love and Kisses

I had been hanging around this ANPA establishment for eight years, but the elite never really considered me an insider. I liked it that way. If you're not really in the club, you're not bound by its laws or its lores.

In short, you can play the game your way. And have more fun.

Deals like the Wilmington newspaper acquisition are fun. Especially when you win. And if you know you've won before anyone else knows.

The fun of that deal reached its peak when I left the Hawaii meeting at 10 A.M. to call my Rochester office. I was assured everything was on schedule. The press release would be out momentarily—4 P.M. in New York as the market closed.

I returned to the meeting, sent Kay this love letter on one of my familiar peach-colored memo pads:

"Kay: Irv Shapiro just announced that Gannett wins the Wilmington newspapers. $60 million. Hearst was 2nd. You were 3rd. Love & Kisses, Al."

That's what sent her scurrying to the phone. She was hoping to find out I was teasing her, as I often did. But her office and DuPont confirmed that the deal was done.

She was still livid when our group broke for coffee thirty minutes later.

"What really pisses me is that my board authorized me to bid $60 million," she told me.

"Why didn't you?" I asked.

"Because I thought I could get it for less."

Lowballing it. And thinking her insider club membership would protect her interests. She undoubtedly expected her longtime friend Irv Shapiro to let her know if the bid fell short, so she could increase it. She didn't want to risk leaving a million or two on the table.

But Shapiro played by the rules. Sealed bids were sealed bids.

As the full impact of how many newspapers Gannett was buying, and how well they were paying off, hit home with other media company managements, more scrambled to get into the act.

With more available buyers, more sellers put their property in the hands of investment bankers. That led to more and more sealed bids—either from anybody who had the wherewithal, or from a list of acceptable buyers.

"Acceptable" meant a seller was willing to put his or her media company into your hands as the successor-owner. Gannett was on nearly every seller's acceptable list, but so were eight, or ten, or sometimes a dozen other reputable media companies with deep pockets.

That meant that sizing up our competition on a deal became as important as sizing up the seller.

We compiled voluminous books on other companies that would be competing with us. The books provided important statistical data. Most of that was public information but the psychological "poker playing" analysis was included, too. The books revealed:

▷ Relative interest in the size and geographic location of properties for sale.

▷ The style and reputation of their investment bankers.

▷ The company's financial track record, cash flow, and availability of resources for acquisitions.

▷ Whether their plate of late was full or empty of other deals that needed digesting.

▷ Most important—the background, personality and style of the CEO.

Making Book on Other Bosses

The CEO decides how far to go on a deal. Insight about him or her, more often than not, helped us best other bidders.

I viewed the other media CEOs like players in a poker game.

To win in poker, you have to understand and anticipate the other players' actions. Who will bluff? Who will hold? Who will fold?

A few highlights from my book on the bosses of the competition:

▷ *Warren Phillips,* boss of Dow-Jones, publishers of *The Wall Street Journal, Barron's,* and other newspapers:

Tout le monde as an editor. But no stomach for brawling with the bursars who are the real S.O.B.s in our business. Missed most of the big deals because he is too genteel.

▷ *Alvah H. Chapman, Jr.,* boss of Knight-Ridder, publishers of newspapers in Miami, Detroit, Philadelphia, St. Paul, San Jose, and elsewhere:

Canny and cagey. But a careful, cautious member of the church consistory. Delay and pray is his style. If in doubt, he won't reach for a deal.

▷ *Stanton Cook,* boss of the Tribune Company, publishers of the *Chicago Tribune,* New York *Daily News,* and others:

Organized, orderly engineer. Loves to kick the tires, shift the gears, check the foundations. Unfamiliar and uncomfortable with the heart and soul of newspapers—the newsroom. So he won't be aggressive.

▷ *Kay Graham,* boss of the Washington Post Company, which publishes that newspaper and *Newsweek* magazine:

Often called the most powerful woman in the USA. She publicly pooh-poohs the label but privately it pleases her. Outwardly gutsy and glamorous. Loves to talk like a truck driver around the guys. But inwardly very shy. She relies on her financial people, who study the past, not the future. They lowball nearly all deals.

▷ *Arthur Ochs "Punch" Sulzberger,* boss of *The New York Times:*

His prestige opens doors. But his president, Walter Mattson, is an engineer who overexamines everything, finds a lot that's broke and figures it's too expensive to fix. Watch out if Jack Harrison, head of the Times's community newspapers, is involved. He's shrewd, gutsy, willing to pay top dollar.

Such personal profiles helped us zero in on the prices to offer when the sealed bidding got really competitive. The idea, of course, was to win without leaving a lot of money on the table.

Some examples of the fine-tuning:

▷ In Shreveport, Louisiana, we won with $61 million. Harte-Hanks was second with $60 million.

▷ In Louisville, our winning bid was $305 million. The runner-up bid about $300 million.

▷ In Detroit, we won with $717 million, just $17 million ahead of the next offer.

Of course, we didn't win them all. *The New York Times* outbid us in Santa Barbara, California, a market we very much wanted. Billy Morris's Morris Communications Corporation of Augusta, Georgia, topped us in Jacksonville, Florida, a deal we would have liked to add to our other Florida operations.

The Bigger They Are, the Easier They Fall

Looking back over the dozens of deals we made, one thing stands out:

The smaller deals took much more time and effort, proportionately, than the bigger ones. The bigger they were, the easier they fell into place, during negotiations and in running them afterwards.

On the smaller deals, every dollar becomes very important to the seller. And so do company cars and company-paid hide-aways, also wives, and especially girlfriends, on the payroll.

On the big deals, the seller or sellers know they'll end up with enough scratch so that they can afford to take care of those fringe goodies themselves.

Deals bring sellers and buyers together for some of the damnedest reasons:

In Nashville, we bought both papers within a seven-year period. The sellers sold because:

▷ One was told by a seer he had only two years to live.

▷ The other needed big bucks to pay off wife number five and marry number six.

As a result we bought our way into the highly desirable Nashville market by acquiring the afternoon *Nashville Banner* for a mere $14.1 million.

Seven years later, we sold the *Banner*—the number two paper—for a $10 million profit and bought the dominant morning and Sunday paper, *The Tennessean,* for $50 million, a steal.

The ultraconservative, prejudiced publisher of the *Nashville Banner,* Jimmy Stahlman, decided to sell his newspaper after seer Jeane Dixon told him he was going to die within two years. He wanted time to write his book, with the highly irreverent title of *Sons of Bitches I Have Known.*

He was the biggest S.O.B. most of us had known, but he bristled when I asked if he would include himself in the book. "I'm the author," he snapped. He lived more than five years longer, died at the age of eighty-three, and never did the book.

The publisher of *The Tennessean,* Amon Carter Evans, was the second S.O.B. in the Nashville story.

He and his liberal news team had no use for Stahlman. Evans was furious that Stahlman did not discuss sales plans with him in advance. It did not take him long to decide he didn't like me as the successor owner, either. But he liked money and needed a lot to marry for the sixth time and pay off wife number five.

Enter Karl Eller, another S.O.B. who had just joined our management after we acquired his company, Combined Communications.

Eller presented what seemed to me either a very clever or

a very crazy idea: Gannett should sell the *Banner* and buy the *Tennessean,* which clearly was the newspaper to own in that market. The two were part of a Joint Operating Agency agreement.

A joint operating agency is a waiver of antitrust statutes to allow a failing newspaper to merge its business operations with a competitor in order to survive. News and editorial operations must remain independent and competitive.

We took the Nashville proposal to the Justice Department, which must approve joint operating matters. Justice found nothing illegal about it, so we made a dream deal.

We got the big paper in town and Evans got wife number six.

We also acquired *Tennessean* editor John Seigenthaler, one of the USA's best. A former critic of newspaper groups, he became a convert. Later he helped us gain entree to other Southern markets and he also became editorial director of *USA TODAY.*

The Spotlight on "Sin"

Our deal in Jackson, Mississippi, showed how important community approval—or perhaps preacher approval—can be to a deal.

The newspapers in Jackson and nearby Hattiesburg, Mississippi, were owned by the Hederman family, devout Southern Baptists.

The door opener to deal with them was a phone call to me from another devout Southern Baptist, Charles Overby. He had worked for us on *TODAY* in Florida, at Gannett News Service in Washington, and as our city editor on the *Nashville Banner.* Then he went astray for awhile and became chairman of the Republican Party in Tennessee. He later repented and rejoined Gannett.

Overby called to say he knew the Hederman family was torn by internal bickering and that the family patriarch, Robert Hederman, Jr., was ready to sell. Overby offered advice on how to approach the deal. And, knowing me, he also offered a warning: "Remember, these are nice Southern Baptists. No drinking or carousing around them."

After some preliminary discussions, we arrived for a marathon negotiating session. Each member of the Hederman family was present with his own lawyer, his own banker. These Baptists trusted God, but they didn't trust their brothers.

We met from early afternoon until late that night. The only refreshments were soft drinks, coffee, and cookies. But we agreed on all the terms, including $110 million in cash. Their lawyers and ours were to work as long as necessary through the night putting an agreement in principle together for the parties to sign the next morning so we could make a public announcement.

McCorkindale and I escaped shortly before midnight. That was the drinking curfew in Jackson. We dashed to the nearest bar down the street from the newspaper for a couple quick martinis before moving on for a greasy, fast-food, post-midnight snack.

The next morning at 7:30, all appeared for the signing.

Hederman opened by saying sternly: "Mr. Neuharth, before we go any further, I have a very serious matter that I want to discuss with you privately in my office." I followed him.

I thought to myself: "He found out about our drinking last night. I hope this is just a lecture and not a deal killer."

Hederman closed the door, sat very stately at his desk and said in slow, but stern, Southern tones: "Mr. Neuharth, we are religious folks. We don't believe in drinking."

I winced.

Hederman continued: "As part of our deal, I must request of you that you sign a letter of agreement that under your ownership these newspapers will continue for at least ten years our policy of no liquor advertising."

I was uncertain whether the liquor issue could kill our deal. I reached way back for support.

"Mr. Hederman, I understand your feelings fully and sympathize with them. As you probably know, Frank Gannett was a prohibitionist. He would applaud your position. But, when we became a public company, our Gannett board decided we would not refuse advertising for any products that can be legally sold where we do business. Therefore I must reluctantly refuse your request."

He nodded, smiled and said softly, "I understand your

position. And I accept it. Now when I go to church on Sunday I'll be able to tell my preacher that I made this request of you and you refused."

We shook hands, went in and signed the deal.

His conscience was clear. Now if sin came to Jackson, Mississippi, it would be my fault, not his.

I figured both Frank Gannett and God would forgive me, because it was a helluva good deal for the shareholders.

PLAIN TALK:

A good deal-maker is a good poker player.

MONEY IS THICKER THAN BLOOD

"Al Neuharth came to Louisville . . . He strolled through the lobby as if he were a conquistador."

MARIE BRENNER
House of Dreams:
The Bingham Family of Louisville

Most third- and fourth-generation rich kids want it all—and then some.

Good schools in the USA or abroad, cushy jobs, designer clothes, fast and fancy cars, skiing in Switzerland, sunning in Hawaii, pricey playmates. But sooner or later all of that is not enough.

That's when they want to cash in the family jewels.

Grandfathers be damned. Unless the grandchildren are personally involved in the family business—and most are not—there is very little sentimental attachment to the hereditary house.

Descendants of newspaper pathfinders used to be different. But that, too, has changed.

Hundreds of newspapers have been pushed out of the family fold in the past quarter-century. Money was the motivator in nearly every case.

In a one-year period—July 1985 to July 1986—three family feuds put three rich and revered newspaper dynasties up for grabs. The race for these newspapers set off the most intense struggle among major media companies in decades:

▷ The *Des Moines Register and Tribune,* flagship of the publishing empire built by Gardner (Mike) Cowles, Jr., who also founded *Look* magazine.

▷ The *Detroit News,* cornerstone of a company founded by James E. Scripps, which also included five TV stations and four other newspapers in growth areas of the USA.

▷ The *Louisville Courier-Journal and Times,* owned by the most aristocratic family in newspaperdom, referred to nation-wide and worldwide simply, but regally, as "the Binghams of Louisville."

Dozens of newspaper owners were panting for these three proud, prestigious, and generally profitable operations.

Dow-Jones, The New York Times Company, the Washington Post, Chicago Tribune, Hearst, and other giants set their sights on one or more of the targets.

Gannett went after all three. And we won them all. The total price tag: $1.2 billion.

The rewards:

▷ The prestige of winning the equivalent of the newspaper industry's single-year Triple Crown against the best and biggest on our turf.

▷ Purses that paid off handsomely and quickly in Louisville and Des Moines. And a future very big stakes winner in Detroit.

▷ More fun in maneuvering and manipulating to win these three jewels than all the other newspapers we had acquired.

Romancing the Reluctant

The trick to all three deals was courting someone who didn't want a romance. None of the family patriarchs wanted to sell their newspapers. But other paramours were making advances anyway. Children and grandchildren succumbed.

In each case, my strategy was to try to hold the hand of the elder as a friend until he saw the advantage of having me as one of the suitors.

To map a strategy to buy the Louisville newspapers, it was important to understand the Bingham family.

Barry Bingham, Sr., patriarch of the family, came as close to royalty as you can get in the USA. And his father before him.

Barry, Sr., and his family owned both Louisville newspapers, the leading television station, a radio station, plus a commercial printing plant. The family lived on a magnificent estate overlooking the Ohio River.

Bingham was a dignified, patrician man. Tall, with white hair, he carried himself like a Kentucky king.

He and wife Mary had three surviving children:

▷ Barry, Jr., fifty-five, the editor and publisher of the newspapers.

▷ Sallie, fifty-one, who returned to Louisville in 1977 after her second marriage ended in divorce in New York City.

▷ Eleanor, forty-three, who returned home in 1978 after living in California, to marry a Louisville architect, Rowland Miller.

The sibling rivalries got worse with age. The deaths of two brothers had made Barry, Jr., determined to become the head of the family. The two sisters eagerly wanted to fill the void left by those deaths, although in strikingly different ways.

Barry, Sr., put daughters Sallie and Eleanor on the boards of the three family companies. He also added his wife, Mary, and Barry, Jr.'s wife, Edith.

Barry, Jr., didn't like having the Bingham women on the board. He said he didn't think they contributed anything. He wanted them replaced with "respected business professionals."

Finally, Barry, Jr., delivered an ultimatum to his father: Either the women go or I go.

Barry, Sr., was reluctant to choose sides. But he accepted his son's demands. Mary, Eleanor, and Edith resigned from the boards as requested. Sallie refused and had to be removed by board votes. The day she was removed, Sallie quit speaking to her father. She moved back to New York.

Within months, Sallie informed her family that she wanted to sell her 15 percent stake in the Bingham empire. The family hired the New York investment banking firm, Shearson Lehman, to establish a value for her stock. Its estimate: between $22 million and $26 million.

Sallie thought that was too low. So she hired her own investment banker, Henry Ansbacher. He placed the value at $45 million to $50 million.

When her family rejected the higher valuation, Sallie did what other family members thought had been unthinkable: She began to solicit offers from outside the family.

That's when I got into the act.

Cracks in the Palace Wall

The bankers called to see if we would make an offer for Sallie's stock. I had absolutely no interest in her 15 percent ownership. Pursuing Sallie's stock would alienate the rest of the family and a minority ownership never appealed to me. But I also recognized the signs: the palace wall had cracked. It was inevitable it would crumble. When it did, I wanted to able to pick up *all* the pieces.

We didn't turn the bankers away. They not only had solid information about the company but offered an insight into how Sallie was going about selling her shares.

That was information Barry, Sr., would want. I called him. He knew Sallie was in the marketplace but didn't know her strategy. He was deeply grateful for my information. I told him I'd keep feeding him what we learned if he wished. He said he wished. And I assured him we would not buy one share of stock in his empire unless he himself offered to sell it to us.

I was courting Barry, Sr., without pressing him. In any romance, anything worthwhile is worth waiting for.

Barry, Sr., applied pressure by telling the three children privately that if they could not agree, he would put the entire Bingham empire up for sale.

The sibling rivalry became a public spectacle.

At 5 P.M., January 9, 1986, I got a call from Barry, Sr.

"Al, I hoped this moment would never come. But, I have just announced that we're going to sell the family properties. I have told our bankers that I want them to make all of the financial numbers available to you. I hope you will be interested."

I sympathized with him over his painful decision. "But, under the circumstances, and at your invitation, we certainly are interested," I assured him.

Barry, Sr., called several other people that afternoon. But getting the call was important. If you weren't on his approved short list of buyers, you wouldn't even get a chance to bid.

I huddled immediately with John Curley and Doug McCorkindale. "Get all the information available and analyze it. And be sure we schedule our Louisville visit after all the other potential bidders have been there."

We always tried to be the last visitor when a newspaper was up for bids. That gave us a chance of picking up intelligence or nuances about the other bidders.

A parade of media executives began to march through Louisville.

The New York Times sent two of its top executives: President Walter Mattson and vice chairman Sydney Gruson. The Binghams wanted to be impressed with the New York Times executives, but they weren't.

Barry, Jr., said later: "Gruson seemed bored" and "Mattson asked uninformed questions."

A "Pluperfect Jackass"

The Washington Post dispatched publisher Don Graham and executive editor Ben Bradlee. Bradlee met privately with a small group of reporters and editors, leaving mixed reactions. Some in the meetings thought his arrogance showed disrespect for the senior Bingham. He pressed his irreverent style on the staff by referring to Barry, Sr., as "gramps."

Barry, Jr., said later: Bradlee was a "pluperfect jackass."

Representatives from the Chicago Tribune Company and Hearst Company also paid visits. So did Jack Kent Cooke, owner of the Washington Redskins, the *Los Angeles Daily News,* and other conglomerate properties.

When Curley, McCorkindale, our top news executive John Quinn, and I visited Louisville, we asked only for a meeting with all key department heads.

No plant tours. No checking of brick and mortar and hardware. I learned that earlier visitors had gone over all the equipment with a microscope and the Louisville folks resented that.

We made it clear we were interested in the people and the product.

"I know you have mixed emotions about the family's sale. But we are here by invitation only. We're not here to inspect 'a property.' We're here to see whether together we might make these great newspapers even greater," I told the department heads.

When we prepared our bid, I expected the Washington Post

and the New York Times to be our main competition. And I figured it would take an offer of over $300 million to win.

I was right and I was wrong. Our winning bid was $305 million, about $5 million over the next highest offer. But what about our competition?

The New York Times failed to make a bid. Punch Sulzberger knew we would be aggressive, and didn't want to offend his friends, the Binghams, with a lower offer. Elitist to the end.

There were three other formal bids: the Chicago Tribune, Jack Kent Cooke, and the Washington Post. The losing bids were not publicly announced, but here's how they stacked up.

The Post bid of about $255 million was a distant third, ahead of only the Tribune Company. Barry, Sr., was deeply disappointed, and called to offer Kay Graham an opportunity to raise her bid. She declined.

Barry, Jr., later called the Post offer an insult.

The surprise was Jack Kent Cooke's bid of about $300 million.

We bid high to beat the Washington Post and the New York Times. If we hadn't, we would have lost to Jack Kent Cooke.

Buddy, Can You Spare a Quarter?

The morning we came to Louisville to make our announcement, I went for my daily jog. I had decided that afterward I would drop in on the newsroom to surprise the early staff, as I often did when visiting a Gannett city.

It was 6:15 A.M. when I walked in in my jogging outfit. I had purposely not carried any money, not even the "mugger money" I always carry in a wrist band when jogging in New York.

I walked up to the city desk and said, "Hi, I'm Al Neuharth. Can I borrow a quarter for your coffee machine?"

A startled assistant city editor, Pat Howington, reached in his pocket for the quarter. I got my coffee, chatted a bit, looked at the early news reports, and told Pat and others I'd see them in a few hours.

A few hours later Barry Bingham, Jr., introduced me as the new owner. A platform had been erected in the newsroom and a P.A. system installed.

Most of the hundreds assembled had heard of my early

morning newsroom visit. Their faces were tense. The moment they had feared had arrived. Their newspaper had been sold. A new owner was here. A dramatic first experience for them. I had been through dozens such, but nearly always on the buy side.

I thanked Barry, Jr., for his comments. I reported that the deal was for $305 million—a specific the news types wanted to hear. I assured them the check wouldn't bounce. Light laughter.

Then I said:

"The next thing I want to do is pay back Pat Howington for the quarter he loaned me this morning for a cup of coffee." I flipped a quarter at him at the city desk.

Loud laughter. Applause. The tension was broken.

Afterward, the discussions centered on whether I was a good guy or a publicity-seeking eccentric. Many on the Louisville newspaper staff still aren't sure.

A Dunce Cap for Dow Jones

Our opportunity to acquire Louisville was triggered by family members. In Des Moines and Detroit, external factors started the scenario, then family members moved it along.

Des Moines was put into play by Dow Jones, venerable owner of *The Wall Street Journal, Barron's,* and other business publications.

Dow Jones, which analyzes and criticizes everyone else's business moves, made one of the dumbest ploys in acquisition history: putting a target into play and then failing to follow up.

Their move was instigated by Michael Gartner, former *Wall Street Journal* Page One editor who was then editor of the Des Moines newspaper. He convinced Warren Phillips, Dow Jones CEO, to make an unsolicited, unwanted and unfriendly offer for the Des Moines company.

The offer: $112 million—ridiculously low, but enough to attract other unsolicited offers. The predators began moving in.

The move shocked David Kruidenier, Des Moines Register and Tribune Company chairman and CEO. He is a member of the Cowles family, which had owned the properties since 1903.

Kruidenier placed Gartner (now president of NBC News) on "paid leave." He announced publicly and emphatically that the company was not for sale.

But other unsolicited offers kept coming. They quickly escalated.

As I expected, as other family members saw the dollar signs get bigger, the palace wall cracked. The only question was when it would collapse and how much money it would take to pick up the pieces.

I did not have a special relationship with Kruidenier. He is a standoffish loner in the newspaper fraternity—uncomfortable in social and professional settings, not good at small talk. I started looking around for an intermediary.

In my zeal to gain an advantage, I made a costly mistake.

We recruited Otto Silha, retired president of Cowles Media in Minneapolis. Silha assured me he had a close relationship with Kruidenier and the family. We negotiated a deal with Silha so that if we successfully purchased the Des Moines Register Company with his help, he would receive a percentage of the sales price as a consultant's fee. That fee ultimately turned out to be $1,080,000.

The first thing I asked Silha to do was personally deliver a carefully worded letter to Kruidenier so it would carry a special, personal touch from me.

With my midwestern roots, I wanted to try to separate myself from the rest of the pack. I thought the Silha delivery could be important in gaining access to the Cowles family at a critical time.

A Million-Dollar Dunce Cap for Me

As it turned out, Silha didn't have a close relationship at all with Kruidenier. In fact, Kruidenier wouldn't even see him when he flew to Des Moines with the letter. So Silha left the letter on the secretary's desk.

We never used Silha on the deal after that. The result was we paid him more than $1 million to deliver a single letter to a secretary. A 25-cent stamp could have done the job equally well. Better, actually, because I doubt Kruidenier hated the mailman as he did Silha.

I deserve a dunce cap for that one!

When the Register and Tribune Company board voted to seek bids for the company, the usual parade began, with nearly all the biggies looking. But unbelievably, Dow Jones, which had started it all, withdrew without raising its initial bid.

Again, we arranged to be the last ones to visit. We learned what the others had done and focused on people, not the building and presses.

We liked the people we met. So we decided to make an aggressive bid: $165 million. Hearst was second at $130 million. The Washington Post third at $115 million.

We left a lot of money on the table there because I didn't realize how guarded the eastern establishment was about the Farm Belt.

The Washington Post kept sending Ivy League reporters to Iowa to report on the farm economy. Because the easterners didn't understand the Midwest, they criticized it. Kay believed what she read in her own newspaper—always a risk at the *Post*—and lowballed her offer for the Des Moines papers.

Our investment paid off quickly. Earnings quadrupled in our first four years of ownership.

Says Charles Edwards, a member of the Cowles family who remained and is now our publisher:

"If my grandfather had known these newspapers could make this much money, he never would have died."

All in the Family No More

The media takeover world was getting crazy when television producers Norman Lear—famous for the TV series "All in the Family"—and A. Jerrold Perenchio launched an unfriendly takeover effort against the family-dominated Evening News Association of Detroit.

ENA owned the *Detroit News,* four other daily newspapers, five television stations, and two radio stations. I had known Peter Clark, chairman of ENA, since my early days at the *Detroit Free Press.* He is the great-grandson of James E. Scripps, founder of the *Evening News.*

Clark, intellectual and polite, cherished the family tradition of ENA, a closely held company with about 350 shareholders.

The California television producers offered $1,000 a share for a majority of ENA stock. Those same shares had sold less than a year earlier for $250.

It was time for me to swing into my "white knight" strategy again.

I called Clark and asked if there was any way we could help. I assured him that we would not make a move without his permission.

Peter said he hoped to be able to hold things together, but he wasn't sure for how long. Some family members, seeing the price of their stock skyrocket, were reassessing their commitment to keeping ENA within the family.

My customary follow-up letter was similar to my Des Moines message. But this time I mailed it with a 25-cent stamp—no more million dollar messengers.

After a couple of weeks, Lear and Perenchio were offering $1,350 a share, and Clark realized the handwriting was on the wall.

He called me. I assured him we would move quickly and aggressively.

Within ten days he called a special meeting of his board to consider all offers. Again, I arranged for our appearance to be the last one on the list.

We figured it would probably take a little over $700 million to make the deal. Our board authorized up to $750 million.

When we met with the ENA Board, we offered $1,583 a share, or $717 million. Lear-Perenchio, who started it all, finished third. Once again, Jack Kent Cooke was the sleeper, with about $700 million.

Why were there fewer bidders for the Detroit company?

Most of the big players stayed away because they thought the *Detroit News* was a sure loser.

They totally underestimated the other ENA properties, especially WDVM-TV, the number one station in Washington, D.C., which we renamed WUSA. That station alone is worth over $400 million.

Family Jewel Still Sparkles

In putting our price on ENA, we allocated only about $75 million to the *Detroit News*. Some Wall Street analysts thought the value of all the other properties was high enough so that the *Detroit News* was a "freebie."

While only marginally profitable, the *News* had held its number one position against Knight-Ridder's *Free Press.* And I knew Knight-Ridder was ready to throw in the towel, hoping at best for a joint operating agreement that would reverse its losses.

Within three months after we closed the ENA deal, we announced a hundred-year-long joint operating agreement with Knight-Ridder that would guarantee two very profitable newspapers if approved by the Justice Department.

When a hearing judge recommended against approving the agreement, Knight-Ridder announced it would close the *Free Press* if the JOA is not approved.

At this writing, the JOA is still unresolved in the courts. If approved, we have a 100-year guarantee of a highly profitable newspaper partnership. If denied, we'll have the only game in town in the USA's sixth-biggest market. The *Detroit News,* under-valued and underappreciated, is on the verge of generating mega-million earnings for Gannett for years to come.

The family members whose greed forced the Detroit ENA sale will probably buy Gannett stock in the hope of cashing in on the family jewels a second time. Those who haven't already blown their bundle, that is.

PLAIN TALK:

Soft sell and hard cash finesse family feuds.

VII

BIG EGOS MAKE OR BREAK BIG DEALS

"Egomania: an exaggerated appreciation of one's accomplishments and potentialities."

—RICHARD A. SPEARS
Slang and Euphemism

On reflection, I probably should admit to a slight case of egomania by the mid-1980s.

Not as bad as some of my critics laid on me. Probably worse than I realized at the time.

I was feeling my oats and, I thought, with good reason.

▷ Gannett had become the biggest newspaper company in the USA.

▷ *USA TODAY* had become the nation's most widely read newspaper.

▷ My commitment to retirement as chairman at age sixty-five was on track. The next generation of leadership was in place.

I lusted to add a few more jewels to my crown before hanging it on the fireplace mantle. That's when my ego went into overtime.

Ego is important to big deals. It frequently brings people together. Or drives them apart.

On business deals, a lot of egos come into play. The owners. Managers. Bean counters. Bankers. Lawyers.

Controlled egos make deals. Out of control egos break deals.

In the twilight of my career, my ego did both.

"Every man's got to figure to get beat sometime."

HEAVYWEIGHT CHAMP JOE LOUIS

GOODBYE, CBS

"Neuharth's ego makes the average British press baron look like a retiring lily."

THE TIMES OF LONDON
October 7, 1987

CBS was a company under enemy siege in early 1985. And the boss, Tom Wyman, was obviously overwhelmed. I thought I could capture it as a friendly suitor.

Barely five years after taking over the glamorous but arduous job, Wyman was in trouble on two fronts:

▷ Externally: Ted Turner, the Atlanta media maverick who is underrated by everybody but himself, had put CBS in play with a takeover attempt. And North Carolina Senator Jesse Helms was trying to rally conservatives to buy huge blocks of CBS stock so they could "become Dan Rather's boss."

▷ Internally: Operating income was down dramatically. And the premier CBS news division was in near revolt over staff and budget cutbacks.

Something, or someone, had to give. A tempting target for anyone with a major media base and a big till to tap.

The time was right for us to make our move on CBS.

We'd been thinking about it for several years. Unlike Turner, we would not make hostile moves. We only do friendly deals.

In any merger of media companies, it's preferable that the marriage be mutually desirable. A hostile takeover might drive away some of the main assets—creative people.

My "white knight" move on Wyman advanced so fast that it surprised even me. Within eight weeks, we appeared to be within hours of announcing a $9 billion merger that would have been the world's biggest media marriage. Much more quickly, the deal fell apart.

I blew the big one. My ego made me err enormously. Wyman's weaknesses again overwhelmed him.

Paley's Passion for New Presidents

Tom Wyman is tall and handsome. In New York society, on the golf course and the dance floor, he presents a perfect image. Inside Black Rock, as the CBS corporate tower is known, he was a flustered misfit.

How Wyman came to be CEO of CBS tells you a lot about both him and William Paley, the legendary founder.

Wyman caught Paley's eye at a social gathering early in 1980. A few weeks later, Paley called Wyman at his Pillsbury headquarters in Minneapolis and invited him to spend the weekend at Paley's hideaway in the Hamptons on Long Island.

"I thought I was just being invited for a weekend of golf when Paley called me," Wyman told me later. "When we were sitting in his library and he started talking serious business about CBS, I thought he was going to ask me to go on his board of directors. Before I knew it, he had offered me the job of CEO."

Paley was no novice at this. After his long-time associate Dr. Frank Stanton's retirement at CBS as president in 1971, Paley marched three new presidents through CBS in nine years.

Despite Paley's track record in hiring and firing presidents and Wyman's total lack of knowledge about the media, he jumped at Paley's offer.

"I didn't even ask him for a contract," Wyman told me. "I figured he was offering me an escape from Minneapolis and a great job in New York. Why wouldn't I go for it?"

I met Wyman five months after he took over at CBS. He and I were among a dozen guests of Ed Ney, chairman of Young & Rubicam, for dinner at the "21" Club on November 25—the night of the second Sugar Ray Leonard–Roberto Duran welterweight title fight.

After dinner we walked over to Radio City Music Hall to watch the fight on closed-circuit TV. When Duran refused to get up off his stool at the end of the eighth round, we all went back to "21" to celebrate Sugar Ray's comeback.

Over nightcaps, Kay Graham and I sat with Wyman. I tried talking about the media business. He was pleasant and personable. And totally lacking in knowledge or understanding of the company he was running and the business we were in.

Wyman had taken an apartment temporarily in the United Nations Plaza, where Kay also stayed when in New York. Both needed a ride home, having dismissed their drivers hours earlier. That's one of those silly things some CEOs do so they can brag about how they're saving their company money.

I was never guilty of penny-pinching on limousines or anything else that helped make my job easier and/or more effective. That policy paid off again on this night. I offered Tom and Kay a ride home. We had a chance to chat a little longer more privately. It also helped Wyman remember me.

The next day when I saw Kay at a newspaper function, she gushed about how charming and fascinating Wyman was. No hint that she noticed that his fascination was with socializing, not with CBS or the media.

I dropped Wyman my normal note the next day and suggested we stay in touch.

Wyman responded with a polite courtesy note. For the next four and a half years we saw each other infrequently, at social or media events.

I was busy getting *USA TODAY* off the ground. He was busy fighting off foes inside and outside CBS. But I watched his activities a lot more closely than he watched mine.

Ted Turner: "A Pain in the Ass"

The opening came when Turner laid his offer on CBS in April 1985. That coincided with our Gannett annual shareholders meeting, at which we approved bylaw changes as a takeover defense.

Because we were able to do that despite the strong opposition of our second biggest shareholder, we ran full-page newspaper ads patting ourselves on the back and taking swipes at takeover artists and junk bond junkies.

I sent Wyman a letter, enclosing all the ad copy. "Some of

this might help you in fighting off Turner," I wrote. "And, if we can be helpful in any other way, drop me a note or give me a call."

A letter in reply came three days later. Wyman thanked me warmly and added, "Next time you're in New York let me know and drop by. I'd love to talk to you about things."

The door was open and I wasted no time. I called him and said I would be in New York the following Monday and Tuesday. We made a date for midmorning coffee on Monday.

The meeting in his thirty-fifth-floor office at Black Rock lasted an hour and a half. Wyman's frustrations were very apparent. He talked freely and candidly.

"Turner is really a pain in the ass. This damned thing is taking up nearly all my time. You can't run a company when you have to cover your backside against these sharks every day," Wyman lamented.

While he was preoccupied with fighting off Turner, I wanted to make sure the conversation covered a broad range of subjects, so I could ultimately bring it around to Gannett and CBS.

"What else are you up to? Are you buying or selling anything?" I asked.

"Nothing right now. But there are a lot of ways to deal with these takeover attempts," Wyman responded. "One way is recap-italization and borrowing heavily to buy back a lot of our stock. Another thing I considered was trying to do a merger with another big company. Dick Munro (CEO) at Time and I are very good friends. We've talked about whether we could put our two companies together. But Time's cable operations pose an FCC conflict, so our talks never really went anywhere."

"What if Time got out of cable? Wouldn't that make a good fit for the two of you?" I asked, helpfully.

Wyman broke into a broad grin. "I suggested that. I like that idea. That would have made them a smaller company than CBS and then we would obviously run the merged company. But Dick and his people won't have any of that," he said.

Wyman had sent me two signals:

▷ A merger with another big media company appealed to him as a way out of the Turner takeover threat.

▷ In any such merger, he and CBS hoped to be the dominant company.

I felt excited and exalted about the former and figured I could overcome the latter if we got serious with each other.

I didn't want to appear pushy at this first meeting. But his candor about the Time talks gave me a chance to go further than I had planned.

"You know, Tom, your concept of two big media companies getting married has a helluva lot of merit. I realize this is not the time to talk seriously about any CBS-Gannett deal, but the concept is pretty much the same. And I don't think we'd have conflicts or overlap problems as big as those you had with Time."

"Yeah, I know," said Wyman. "I've thought about it."

Again, gently, I said:

"Why don't I have my office take a close look in the next week or two at all your operations and ours to see what FCC or Justice Department problems we might face? We can put an overlay on the map and get the full picture. Then I'll put together a little outline of what you'd have to do and we'd have to do. That will help us decide whether it's worth any serious discussion."

"Let's see," said Wyman. "I'm not ruling anything out."

It was a warm and friendly parting. I told him I'd call in a week or so.

Back in Washington, I called John Curley, then Gannett president and chief operating officer, and chief financial officer Doug McCorkindale together:

"CBS is ready to be had. If we're smart enough, we can pull this one off."

We went to work. McCorkindale's offices put together the nationwide picture of which Gannett newspapers or which CBS television or radio stations would have to be spun off to meet government regulations. Curley and I concentrated on the psychology and operational aspects of a possible deal.

A Public Pissing Match

We were spurred on by the fact that the CBS–Turner fight was heating up.

Turner's now-public offer was announced as about $150 a share. But only $40 was in cash and $110 in junk bonds. CBS at the time was selling at around $115 on the New York Stock Exchange.

Wall Street was beginning to take the Turner bid seriously. While CBS was worried internally, it tried to ignore Turner publicly.

But Turner went on the attack. "There is no corporation in America that is as arrogant as CBS," he said.

I thought that was the pot calling the kettle black.

Wyman lashed back. He charged Turner lacked the "conscience" to run a major TV network.

The public exchanges gave me good reason to call Wyman ten days after our first visit. I sympathized with him about Turner's nastiness, then told him our study was ready.

"Let me drop by and show you what it looks like. Neither of us has anything to lose," I said.

"I'm not sure what we should do or where this will lead us. But it's worth having another talk," he said.

We agreed I'd be there the next morning. He asked me if I could stay through lunch. A good sign.

When we settled into his office, he came right to the point:

"We've got to do something. I don't think Turner can whip us, but I don't want to take it to the shareholders, because then you never know what might happen."

He expressed his feelings of frustration. "I'm spending full time trying to fight this bastard off. Sometimes I wonder if I wouldn't be better off still selling green peas." He wasn't smiling when he said it.

Clearly, Wyman was no longer enjoying his job. He had no roots at CBS. His memories of Green Giant and Pillsbury meant more to him than did those of Edward R. Murrow and CBS.

To him, running a revered network was just another corporate CEO's job. He resented the pressures, albeit he enjoyed the pleasures.

"Tom, you ought to be able to end up in a situation that's a helluva lot better than what you're going through now," I said. "Why don't we look seriously at putting a big umbrella over both our companies? I think both of us and both our companies could benefit."

He responded more quickly and more favorably than I thought he would. The turmoil at CBS was really tearing at him.

I suggested that first we should get a small group of our

key people together to see how the chemistry worked. Then, if the vibes were okay, we could move toward trying to negotiate a deal.

We agreed we'd have a social hour the next night at the Gannett Suite, 38-H at the Waldorf Towers, a big, plush penthouse-like layout at a prestigious address. We used it regularly to entertain—and impress—business associates.

Joining Tom and me from CBS were:

▷ Gene F. Jankowski, president of the broadcast group.

▷ Fred J. Meyer, senior vice president, finance.

From Gannett:

▷ President Curley.

▷ Senior vice president finance, McCorkindale.

A room service waiter served the first drinks on the enclosed balcony. Then I excused him. I did refills to ensure privacy. A lot of business deals are leaked by eavesdropping waiters or maids.

The six of us wandered about the suite and looked out over the lights of lower Manhattan. We walked around the glittery, gold-plated pool table which had replaced the one where Barron Hilton and Frank Sinatra used to play eight-ball before Gannett took over this suite. That impressed Wyman and his associates.

We visited for about an hour, mostly small talk. When the meeting ended, Wyman and I agreed we would have lunch the next day at his office. We told the others that if we were on track after that, the financial, legal, and operating people would get in on the act.

Mergers 101

I began to feel more confident that this deal could work. But I kept my emotions in check. I didn't want to appear overanxious. My poker-playing days were paying off.

Wyman had more reason to be anxious than I did. He and CBS still were being pelted daily in the public arena by Turner and Senator Helms.

When I showed up at Wyman's office the next day, I suggested we concentrate on the three basic questions of any merger:

▷ Who runs it?

▷ What do you call it?

▷ Who pays what to whom for it?

"Tom, as we both know, a lot of deals like this get hung up over who runs it. As far as I'm concerned, no matter what the titles, you and I would have to run this company as partners. Unless we both had a strong voice, it wouldn't work for your company or mine.

"Of course, somebody has to be CEO. I hope we can structure it so there would be a CEO/chairman and a president/ chief operating officer, working in tandem." I paused.

He picked it up.

"I've been thinking about that. Sure, I would like to be CEO. I assume you'd want to be CEO?"

I smiled. "I like being CEO. But more importantly, Gannett has been doing pretty well. I doubt that my board of directors would agree to any deal where I was not CEO."

Then Wyman surprised me.

"Well, the fact is that by experience and age, you deserve to be CEO. I would hope that I could prove that I ought to be your successor when you retire." I was 61. He was 55.

"Tom, I'd be disappointed if you didn't succeed me as CEO," I said. To myself I thought: It is disappointing that he is not qualified for the job. And, I'd make damned sure he didn't get it.

Then, I added: "That was easier than I thought it would be." We both laughed.

Actually, Wyman had been through this before. At Green Giant, he was CEO, but became vice chairman of Pillsbury after the merger.

With agreement on the two top jobs, we turned to the rest of the key players:

"Frankly, I'm not impressed with your financial guy [Meyer] as much as I am with mine [McCorkindale]." I said.

"Oh, shit, that's no question. Your guy's got it all over mine," Wyman replied.

We agreed:

▷ McCorkindale would be chief financial officer of the merged company.

▷ Curley would head the combined publishing division, including all newspapers and magazines.

▷ Jankowski would direct the joint broadcast division with all the television and radio stations.

Wyman hesitated a bit about Jankowski. "Of course, I actually would run the broadcast division," he said. It was clear that Wyman lacked confidence in Jankowski.

We agreed this group would comprise a five-person office of the chief executive. Gannett representatives would control the office, 3–2.

Cronkite Wouldn't Make Wyman's Cut

Then we talked about our boards of directors.

Wyman had told his key directors of our talks. He said he indicated to them that we were in discussions and he might be calling a special board meeting to consider a deal.

I had advised our entire board of the discussions at a regular board meeting. All strongly favored trying to make a deal, but with the caveat that Gannett management emerge in control.

Both the CBS and Gannett boards showed their trustworthiness during the secret negotiations. There were no leaks.

Now Wyman and I began to focus on the makeup of the joint board. We both had a prestigious lineup of directors, but clearly some would not make the cut for the bigger company.

We agreed on a fifteen-member board. Gannett would name seven, CBS seven. We'd jointly select an impartial fifteenth director as a tie breaker. Each CEO would decide which of the present directors to retain.

"Just don't expect me to keep that fucking Cronkite on the big board," Wyman said. "Putting him on the CBS board when he retired as anchorman was the dumbest thing I ever did."

It was clear Wyman blamed Cronkite for many of his problems within CBS, especially in the news division. Again, he showed his lack of sensitivity. Wyman had no understanding of Cronkite's value as "the most trusted man in America."

I smiled but didn't comment. When Cronkite retired as CBS anchor, I had asked him to join Gannett's board because I considered him one of the USA's most outstanding broadcast and print journalists. That invitation, and others, probably helped Cronkite get the CBS directorship, plus a plush post-employment contract. But Wyman resented him deeply.

I moved on.

"We've talked about who will run it. Let's talk about what to call it," I said.

Wyman asserted himself. "There's a lot of CBS pride around here. I think CBS is a better name than Gannett."

I countered: "CBS has been a better-known name than Gannett for a long time. On the other hand, Gannett's a helluva name now on Wall Street. Maybe there should be a new name."

Wyman said he hadn't thought of that. I reassured him: "Whatever we call it, the CBS network is going to continue to be called CBS, and the Gannett newspapers will continue to be known as Gannett. But maybe there's a bigger, more global title we could consider."

Since this subject was sensitive, I dropped it. We agreed we'd both think more about that and come back to it later.

The question of who pays what to whom was easier.

CBS and Gannett could each lay claim to being bigger. But the marketplace had really set the parameters.

In 1984, CBS had revenues of $4.9 billion, compared to Gannett's $2 billion. But Gannett had bigger profits: $223.9 million to CBS's $212.4 million.

Wall Street put a higher market value on our total outstanding stock. Gannett was trading at 61⅝, for a market value of $4.94 billion. CBS had far fewer outstanding shares, trading at 119¾, for a market value of $3.55 billion.

So Gannett had a clear edge, even though the public perception beyond Wall Street probably was that CBS was the bigger company.

Wyman said he thought CBS should get a 10 percent premium over its present market value. I told him I thought it should be at least 15 percent. I put a higher value on his company than he did! But, I was hoping to lock up a deal. Lowballing an offer might encourage other suitors.

We agreed we were on the same wavelength on price and our financial people would work out details.

Wyman said he thought the time had come for me to meet with Bill Paley. I knew the importance of this. Paley is the founder and retired chairman of CBS and still the company's largest stockholder.

"Tell me about Paley."

"Well, he's really having a tough time over this Turner deal. He can't imagine CBS being taken over by someone like Ted Turner."

"How would he feel about a merger with us?"

"I can tell you that when we talked about a merger with Time, he thought that would be a good fit between two good companies."

"What would he want out of this?" I asked.

"He's chairman of the executive committee here and he's still on the board. Does that give you a problem?" Wyman asked.

"Of course not."

Even though Paley was eighty-three, he continued to come into the office every day. He arrived at midmorning, then usually left at or after lunch. Wyman checked with Paley's secretary about a meeting.

"Is Mr. Paley free tomorrow morning? I would like for him to see Mr. Neuharth. He'll know the name."

They obviously had discussed the Gannett deal.

"Paley Never Tied His Own Tie."

William S. Paley was and is Mr. CBS. But, incredibly, Paley didn't get the respect he deserved from Wyman.

In briefing me about Paley, Wyman said irreverently and laughingly: "One of the things Paley has bragged to me about is that he has never had to tie his own necktie since he was eleven."

At Wyman's urging, the CBS board forced Paley to retire as chairman in 1983. Paley was fickle, to be sure. As chairman, he had named four different presidents. He had a hard time letting go. But Wyman forgot Paley was the founder. Chairman and presidents come and go in any company, but there is only one founder.

At our morning meeting, Paley showed me the many mementos of his broadcasting career that were on display in the office. Then he turned the conversation to newspapers.

Paley was proud of his one-third ownership of the *International Herald Tribune*. "But your *USA TODAY* is starting to make our *IHT* people nervous," he said, smiling.

I couldn't resist the opening:

"There's room for both those newspapers worldwide, especially if we had some ownership relationship. What do you think of our two companies getting together?" I asked.

"We'd have some company, some company," Paley replied.

"Would you help us run it?" I asked. "Would you be willing to keep on working? How do you like what you're doing?"

"They're very good to me here," he said softly, glancing at Wyman. "They let me keep this office and they let me use the airplane once in a while."

Imagine that. Wyman and the rest of CBS's executives should thank Paley every day for building them their company. Instead, here's Paley thanking them. A retired chairman and founder with his record deserved better treatment, I thought.

I moved on:

"If we are able to put these two companies together, I certainly hope you would be willing to serve as chairman of the executive committee of the bigger company."

"I'd be honored," he said.

After a little small talk about the media, Wyman and I rose to leave. We knew Paley had a luncheon date. "I hope I'll see you again soon," he said.

Paley had blessed the merger. Wyman agreed afterwards: "That couldn't have gone any better. I know the guy and he liked what he heard."

It looked to me like we had a deal. Wyman was ready. Paley was happy. I was ready to push on. Maybe too ready.

Bankers, Lawyers Farting Around

Wyman and I returned to our offices and waited to hear from the lawyers and financial people who had started their meetings the afternoon before in the offices of Morgan Stanley, CBS's investment banker.

As far as I was concerned, Wyman and I had handled the substance. The lawyers were just filling in the forms.

They made little progress the day before, but that was not unexpected. Lawyers and bankers spend as much time as possible just farting around on deals like this, building up or trying to justify their fees. But I wanted to wrap this deal up while we had the momentum going in our direction.

So I sent word to McCorkindale that I wanted to meet with him and Curley during the lunch break. Their report was less encouraging than mine.

"We've made some progress on the financial side, but we've gone nowhere on how the company will be structured. Their lawyers don't have the message you gave us on who's going to run the company and how it's going to be structured. They don't have a clue about who's going to be the CEO," McCorkindale reported.

I was astonished.

"Tom and I didn't even bother to discuss that this morning, but it was clear yesterday that I was going to tell you and he was going to tell them."

I called Wyman immediately. His secretary put me through to his private dining room.

"Tom, I'm getting a report on things this morning from Doug, and he tells me they haven't gotten into the structure of the company and the officers and so forth. I told my guys last night what you and I decided."

"I'm just going to get into that with them now," Wyman said.

"Okay. Fine."

I turned to McCorkindale and Curley and smiled. "That should all be resolved by this afternoon."

By late afternoon, McCorkindale returned to the Gannett offices dismayed.

"They still haven't got the message. Apparently, Wyman didn't spell it out. He's hedging or they're hedging," McCorkindale said.

"Well, we can resolve that," I replied. "I'll talk to Tom again and he'll take care of it."

McCorkindale wasn't so sure.

"I think you and Tom should come to the meeting either tonight or tomorrow morning and help us get the management and board questions straightened out. That's clearly the hang-up."

By contrast, the financial part of the deal was coming together pretty easily. My suggested premium of about 15 percent over market value looked like it would fly.

I called Wyman again.

"I understand the guys are making progress in some areas but are slow in others. Why don't we meet with them tomorrow morning to kick asses and get them moving toward a wrap-up?"

He agreed that we would meet at 10 A.M. in the Morgan Stanley offices.

Just before the meeting was to start, I pulled Wyman aside and said, "Tom, we need to nail down for the lawyers a clear understanding of how we're structuring the management of the company. I assume that's all right with you."

"Oh, sure," he said.

Time to Seal the Deal

A dozen bankers, lawyers and executives were assembled around the long rectangular table.

Morgan Stanley was their banker. Shearson Lehman was ours. Their law firm was Skadden, Arps. Ours was Nixon, Hargrave.

Tom and I sat side by side at one end of the table.

I was really pissed that the people in this room for nearly three days had been unable or unwilling to do what Wyman and I had agreed upon.

My Gannett colleagues recognized my mood—they had seen it often enough in the past—and anticipated my approach.

When things weren't happening at Gannett, I didn't waste a lot of time with social niceties.

"Tom and I thought it might help if the two CEOs got in on the act and explained to all of you how to get this deal done. It's pretty damn simple."

There was an edge to my voice, but it was well below my often higher, but controlled, irritation level. I moved right to the central issue.

"Tom and I have agreed on the management structure of the company. The directors will be seven, seven, and one. I will be chairman and CEO. Tom will be president and chief operating officer. We'll have a five-member executive committee: two additional members from Gannett and one more besides Tom from CBS."

The CBS guys looked surprised and puzzled. Our people nodded and smiled.

There was no sense in dancing around this issue, so I underscored what I had just said even more firmly: "You don't have to argue about this or even talk about it or think about it. It's all settled. You just work that into the legal structure, along with the financial details, and we can all quit, celebrate, and go home."

I wanted to tie things down once and for all.

Turning to Wyman, I said, "Is there anything you would like to add, Tom?"

Wyman looked uncomfortable. He sat up straight in his chair. "Yes, we've agreed on that," he said a bit hesitantly. "The five-member committee might be subject to change and we're not sure who our people would be or who your people would be on the committee or the board. But basically, it's all right for you guys to work with."

I sensed immediately that I had screwed up. I had come on too directly and forcefully. Wyman's people were hearing this news for the first time from me, not from him.

The message wasn't the mistake. It was the messenger.

When Wyman heard somebody else tell his people that he was going to be number two, it made him feel very different than when we discussed it in the privacy of his dining room.

I should have let Wyman explain the terms. He could have put a more gentle face on it. I had satisfied my ego at the expense of crushing his.

But even though the mood of the meeting wasn't quite as I had hoped, I felt putting the central issue on the table would break the logjam. Wyman had backed me up, even if he did so reluctantly. There may be a few more bumps in the road, but at least now we could move this deal off dead center.

The negotiators worked the rest of the day. They reached general agreement on the financial details. Wyman's representatives still kept legal language on the management matters on the back burner.

But we had come a long way and I thought we could wrap it up in twenty-four to forty-eight hours.

By then, I was ready to write the press release. So I did.

Plain Talk on Paper

I always wrote or rewrote the press releases about major events in Gannett. It helped put things in perspective—my perspective. And it allowed everyone to understand in English— not lawyer's language—what was happening. Once you put plain talk on paper, nearly everyone understands it.

The next morning I called Wyman and told him I wanted to bring over a draft press release to see how it sounded to him. "We've been talking about the name of the company," I said. "I want to see how something wears on you."

Wyman welcomed me as warmly as before. I sensed he had come to peace with himself overnight. I handed him this draft of a release, with blanks for the key numbers to be filled in when they were worked out:

> NEW YORK—CBS and Gannett Co., Inc., today announced that their boards of directors have unanimously agreed to merge the two companies in a tax-free stock exchange.
>
> The current market value of the two media companies combined is about $8.5 billion. Their combined annual revenues are about $7 billion; their combined after-tax earnings last year were $469 million.
>
> The agreement calls for merging of both CBS and Gannett into a new company, with the planning title of Universal Media, Inc. Each share of _____ would be exchanged for _____shares of _____; all _____ shares would then be exchanged for shares of Universal.
>
> CBS closed Wednesday on the New York Stock Exchange at $117; Gannett at $61¾. At those market prices, the after-tax value of each share of CBS stock in Universal Media would be about $ _____.
>
> After the exchange, present CBS shareholders would own approximately 45 percent of the stock of Universal; Gannett shareholders would own about 55 percent.

I noticed that Wyman scanned down the press release to the section that talked about him and me: "Neuharth, 61, will be chairman and chief executive officer of the merged companies. Wyman, 55, will be president and chief operating officer."

Wyman's mood changed only slightly. He didn't seem over-joyed with the press release. But he didn't suggest any changes. I left him a copy.

I explained that I thought Universal Media was a good name, but it wasn't necessarily written in stone. I put it in the proposed press release because I wanted him to be thinking about it or some other new name.

The negotiators worked fewer hours on that third day, but I figured it was because they were tired from the previous two days and nights of negotiations. My goal was to tie up all loose ends the next day.

Wyman and I had discussed calling a special meeting of both our boards of directors in New York during the upcoming Fourth of July weekend. We thought that would make for a nice holiday celebration. Everything still seemed on track for that.

But on the fourth day of the negotiations, McCorkindale and Curley reported at lunch that the mood was entirely differ-ent.

"It's not moving at all," McCorkindale said. "Meyer is being a sonofabitch."

"Do you think Tom and I need to get back in the room?" I asked.

"I don't know," McCorkindale said. "But Tom and you need to be talking or something, because it's not moving."

Blow-Up at Black Rock

As the three of us chatted, the phone rang.

Wyman was calling me.

"Hi, Tom."

"Al, I just want to tell you the deal is off."

I was stunned.

"What are you talking about?"

"The deal's off," he repeated. "So there's no point in going on any further."

"Well, I thought we agreed if we developed any hitches along the way, you and I would sit down and talk about them. We've come a long way in a short time. What's wrong?"

"The deal's off. I just can't deal with you, and I can't deal with this thing anymore."

"Do you mind telling me a little more?"

"Oh, there are several things," he said. "First of all, this crazy idea of changing the name. How could we possibly not call it CBS? We have a long tradition of excellence, and we have one of the best names in the country."

It was clear to me he was talking for the benefit of others sitting in the room with him at Black Rock. On reflection, he obviously used the company title change as a way to turn Mr. CBS, Bill Paley, against the deal.

Wyman's tone turned nasty.

"Also, you know you lied to me."

I checked my temper. I wanted this deal to work. No matter how stupid Wyman was, I was going to try to avoid derailing it by blowing my stack.

In a deliberately even, calm voice, I replied: "I haven't lied, Tom. What are you talking about?"

"You said you weren't talking with anybody else about a deal."

"I told you we weren't negotiating with anybody else. I know that you know that I've been talking to your friend Dick Munro at Time. But those have been discussions, not negotiations."

In fact, I had been having discussions with Munro, because it was clear to me that Time could not stand alone forever. But the talks never were serious in my mind because Munro insisted on co-CEOs. He and I agreed on the merits of a merger. But Munro didn't understand that one person has to be in charge. He was still hung up on co-CEOs during the Time-Warner-Paramount fight in 1989.

When two co-bosses disagree, there is no referee. The buck has to stop with the boss. When there's no clear boss, the buck doesn't stop—usually, it doesn't even get started.

At any rate, Wyman didn't understand the difference between discussions and serious negotiations. Unlike Wyman, I talked to everyone and was always on the prowl for new deals and opportunities.

Wyman was so inexperienced at this that he viewed every conversation as a negotiation.

Wyman was reaching for excuses. It was apparent to me that he was looking for a way—any way—out of the deal.

"You lied to me," he insisted. "I just can't handle that."

"Well, you're wrong. But I've been called worse things than a liar, so . . . no hard feelings. You haven't told me anything big enough to kill the deal. We surely hadn't decided on the name. I just floated a new name with you in the press release to see what your reaction would be."

"Well, the deal's off," he said again. "I don't want to talk about it anymore."

An edge began to develop in my voice.

"It seems strange to me that someone of your stature, running a company the size of CBS, who was as serious as you have been for the last four days, would just pick up the phone and call everything off. I think you've gotten some bum advice from your bankers or lawyers. Why don't just you and I sit down this afternoon and see if we can't work out whatever's really bothering you?"

Wyman shouted into the phone: "There's nothing to talk about. The deal's off."

I believed him, so I calmed down. "Okay, Tom, that sounds pretty final. I assume you'll go ahead with the recapitalization. I hope it works for you. If it doesn't, call me. I'll still be around. I hope you will. Good luck."

Then he cooled off. He got my message. "Yeah, that's what we're going to do. It will either be self-help or self-destruct."

I turned to Curley and McCorkindale sitting across the desk from me: "The game's over. We lose. And he'll lose."

Mom Said: If in Doubt . . .

Wyman's "self-destruct" comment was prophetic.

Within a week, CBS announced it would borrow nearly $1 billion to buy back 21 percent of its stock. That huge debt took CBS out of Ted Turner's reach.

But it opened the door for Laurence Tisch and his Loew's Corporation to take over the company a year later, even though they owned only 24.9 percent of the stock.

Tisch took a full year to outmaneuver Wyman. But when he was ready, the destruction was devastating.

We got the signal two weeks before it happened. Tisch invited Curley, McCorkindale, and me to lunch at his "power" Regency Hotel in New York on August 27, 1986. His son, Tom, was with him.

Father and son talked about their fascination with the entertainment, travel, hotel, restaurant, newspaper, and broadcast businesses. Then, Larry got around to what I felt was the real purpose of the meeting:

"What happened when you guys were talking about putting CBS and Gannett together?" he asked.

I generalized. "We seemed pretty close to a deal. But Tom had other options and took the recapitalization route."

"What did you think of Tom, during your discussions," Tisch asked pointedly.

My mother taught me: If in doubt, tell the truth. So I did. "I thought he was a troubled guy trying to run a troubled company and he wasn't up to it."

Tisch nodded and smiled. Two weeks later, on September 10, 1986, Wyman got the ax. Paley returned as chairman, Tisch became president/CEO. Wyman's self-destruction was complete.

Why weren't we able to put the Gannett-CBS deal together?

Too many egos got in the way. Bankers'. Lawyers'. Wyman's. Mine. Mostly mine. I made two serious mistakes:

▷ Announcing to Wyman's team that I would be running the show bruised his ego badly and unnecessarily.

▷ Putting the plan on paper prematurely in a press release was rubbing salt in his wounds.

If I had taken a lower profile and gentler approach it might have worked. Making a show of too much muscle too soon was self-destructive for me.

PLAIN TALK:

Keep your ego from outrunning your brain.

HELLO, HOLLYWOOD

"Neuharth is my kind of people. He runs his own store and there are no layers of management to go through."

—GRANT TINKER

Grant Tinker walked out of Rockefeller Center at 5 P.M. on September 12, 1986, his last day as chairman of NBC.

Fifteen minutes later, five blocks away in the Gannett suite at the Waldorf-Astoria Towers, I offered him a drink. And a partnership.

Tinker was available because he decided to quit when General Electric acquired RCA, which was NBC's parent company.

Tinker was hot. He had done it all:

▷ The CEO who in five years had lifted NBC out of its last-place doldrums to network leadership.

▷ The Hollywood legend who cofounded the mega-moneymaker MTM with his then-wife, Mary Tyler Moore.

▷ The creative genius who produced a long string of TV hits, from "Hill Street Blues" to "The Bob Newhart Show."

We wanted him as our entré into television program production and/or the movie world.

A lot of others courted him, too, including: MCA, Westinghouse, Disney, the Tribune Company of Chicago. But we were the first he talked with—and the last.

Bagging Tinker would be a coup for Gannett. His stature would bring us into the big leagues of television programming overnight.

My ego heightened my interest in Tinker. I liked being associated with winners. Tinker was a big-time winner.

I had long wanted to get Gannett into the television program production and/or movie business. The synergies between that and our conventional newspaper and broadcast operations were obvious.

But I knew next to nothing about show biz.

My early movie experience was limited to dating the usherette at the Rex Theatre in Woonsocket, South Dakota, in 1941—the pretty, blonde high school junior named Loretta Helgeland, who later became my wife. I saw more movies that year than at any time since.

My first brush with television came when the new station KELO-TV opened in Sioux Falls, South Dakota. In 1953–54 it took away most of what little advertising we had in my first newspaper, *SoDak Sports,* and hastened its demise.

By 1986, Gannett owned eight TV stations. We were in good major markets, including Washington, D.C., Boston, Atlanta, Denver, Minneapolis, Phoenix.

But the FCC limit for ownership of TV stations by any individual or company was twelve. There was no limit on how many TV or cable programs you could produce or how many movies you could make. I've always thought getting bigger is better, if you do it right.

In earlier 1986, I had made two stabs at getting into show biz, one external, one internal:

▷ A flirtation with MCA, long-time Hollywood biggie.
▷ An exploration at developing our own "superstation."
Both failed.

In the MCA deal, price was the problem. MCA boss Lew Wasserman wanted much more money for the company than it was worth.

My Super Station idea was to use WUSA-TV, our Washington, D.C., TV station as the vehicle to imitate and then outperform such national superstations as WTBS in Atlanta, WGN in Chicago, WOR in New York.

The WUSA call letters would be appealing all across the USA, I thought. But there was a flaw in my fantasy.

In 1984, USA network, a growing cable system, had filed suit against KUSA, after we introduced those new call letters for the Gannett TV station in Denver. The suit charged that the use of KUSA created confusion among viewers and infringed on the USA cable network rights.

Super Blunder Kills Super Station

Unknown to me, in settling that lawsuit, Gannett's lawyers agreed not to use KUSA or WUSA in any future regional or national cable operation.

When I learned that, I hit the ceiling.

"The stupid bastards! The dumb-ass lawyers!" I ranted at McCorkindale because he was our chief lawyer. This was further proof that lawyers have no foresight, they wear blinders. No vision and not a hell of a lot of common sense, I told him.

Again I had learned what happens if the CEO doesn't keep lawyers on a short leash.

After the superstation idea was dead, I was even more convinced that we needed some new associate to take us into show biz.

Our first contact with Tinker came through Julian Goodman, a senior member of the Gannett Board and himself a former chairman of NBC.

Goodman is a street-smart Kentuckian who is our inhouse antenna to television. He knows everybody in the business. I sought his counsel on things I didn't understand about television. That gave us a lot to talk about.

Present at the Waldorf social session were Goodman, Curley, McCorkindale, Tinker, and I.

My first impressions of Tinker:

▷ A real gentleman.

▷ Still very energetic at age sixty.

▷ As self-confident as his reputation said he should be.

▷ Cool, cagey, laid-back.

Tinker was cordial, but noncommittal. He knew he would be courted by many and he had been around long enough not to fall quickly.

"I'm sixty and figure I have another good, productive ten years or so. I want to see if I can do it one more time," he said, reminiscing about his MTM days. "I'm not sure just how I want to structure my next venture, but I'm pretty sure I'll need a well-heeled partner."

"How big are you thinking?" I asked.

"Don't know. I sense it will take much more than it did when we started MTM. It will require more than spit," he joked. "Probably many millions."

"No problem," I said. "You come up with the right ideas. We'll come up with the money."

After our meeting, Tinker took a holiday in Paris with his young live-in companion, Melanie Burke, a bright and attractive former secretary.

Three weeks later, he called me.

"I've narrowed my list down. If you still want to talk, come on out."

We met in his hillside home on Lausanne Road, millionaires' row in Bel Air, a stone's throw from what became Ronald and Nancy Reagan's retirement home.

Tinker clearly was more comfortable here than he had been in New York. He hated the Manhattan suit-and-tie environment. He greeted us in an open-collared shirt and sweater. Melanie strolled out in her tennis togs as he showed us around the court area. We moved into the huge, beamed living room to talk.

"I'd like to tell you what I'm thinking. I believe there's an opportunity in developing programs for television networks and/or independents. My specialty is sitcoms. I think I know the weaknesses of the networks. I think I can put together a team that can develop some things that might work. But to do it, I want to have a partner," he said.

"A financial and kind of silent partner that will put up the money and let me run it. I think I will have the opportunity to do that with a number of organizations."

Tinker was a hot property and he was playing it to the hilt.

I told him the concept fit fine for us. We began asking about details. How much money would he need up front? Would he develop a one-year plan? Three-year plan? Five-year plan?

Money Without Meddling

Grant didn't want to get that specific just yet. It was obvious to me he was sizing us up to see how the chemistry would work. He was confident he could get money from several sources. What he clearly wanted was money without meddling.

That was an entirely new concept for Gannett. To us, money had always meant control. But in the world of Hollywood and Broadway, the banker often has little or nothing to say about how the money is spent.

The negotiations with Tinker tested my glandular instincts against my business judgment. Glands won. For the first time since I had been running Gannett, we put up the money without gaining control.

The financial arrangements on the new venture were fairly well established by Hollywood precedents. All of Tinker's suitors were talking pretty much the same deal.

One big difference: His other two finalists, Disney and MCA, had a ready-made home for him to use in his production staging. Gannett didn't. We offered to build or buy him one.

Tinker had a place in mind. Laird International Studios in Culver City was in the hands of a judge on a receivership. It was going to be up for auction. Cecil B. DeMille directed there. Some scenes from *Gone With the Wind* and *Citizen Kane* had been filmed there.

"It's old. It's historic. A good studio. It needs some work, but it would be a home. It would take quite an investment."

"How much?" I asked.

"We think it's probably in the $25 to $35 million range, plus several million in improvements."

"Well, that doesn't scare us," I said. "It's real estate. The right home at the right price is no problem."

Tinker expressed one other reservation:

"These other people are out here. They and I have a lot in common," Tinker said. "You're a great newspaper company and I respect you. But you're not in television programming. And you're in Washington, D.C. They're here."

That was a weakness easily turned into a strength:

"Let me tell you something about our headquarters being in Washington, D.C. The best job in our company right now is publisher of our Guam paper. Next best is Honolulu. The further removed from company headquarters, the more independence you have, the more fun you have.

"Also, think about this: These other people are not only right here, but they think they know something about what you're going to try to do. We're not here, and we don't know anything about it.

"They'll not only give you a home. They'll be looking over your shoulder and second-guessing you every day. If you want a partner with money who won't meddle, we're it. Think about that."

That was our best shot, so we left.

Ten days later he called and said he'd like to be partners.

His financial people and ours worked out the details.

Those aspects of a deal are a necessary nuisance for me. I gave our bean counters the broad outlines and told them to work out what made sense. We were ready to commit up to $100 million. I knew Doug would protect our interests.

We weren't accustomed to committing $100 million without total control. But we had confidence in Tinker. We were betting on two things:

▷ Tinker had the hottest hand in the industry and could attract the creative talent to succeed once again.

▷ Television programming would ultimately bring Gannett big bucks.

Tinker, Curley, and I turned our attention to what to call our partnership and how to structure it.

We quickly agreed on GTG—Grant Tinker Gannett. I told him his name was the hot one and needed to be featured.

GTG would produce thirty-minute and one-hour shows for syndication with the networks or independent stations. Tinker would call the shots on what to produce and where to try to sell it.

Hooking the Nation on the Air

Then we focused on my primary interest in getting into show biz. I wanted to develop a *USA TODAY* television show, to try to hook the nation on the air the way we had in print.

Three other top TV executives had approached us about such a program:

▷ Van Gordon Sauter, when he was the CBS news division president, met with us to see if we'd join him in a new CBS morning show, with a *USA TODAY* flavor. We were not impressed and said no. Two weeks later, he was fired by CBS.

▷ Larry Grossman, NBC news president, asked me if we might join in a show he was planning with a *USA TODAY* flavor. I was leery and said no. That show, "American Almanac," with

Roger Mudd and Connie Chung hosting, failed. Grossman later was fired.

▷ Much earlier, when *USA TODAY* was only a year old, my Miami friend Derick Daniels, who had just left *Playboy,* and Jim Bellows, who was credited with making "Entertainment Tonight" a success, came to see me about joining in a *USA TODAY* TV show. I was impressed with their approach, but thought it was too early in the life of the newspaper to try a TV version.

When I pitched Tinker about a *USA TODAY* show, he said, "That's not my bag. That's reality programming." But later he suggested: "There's a guy who I think is terrific at that, whose contract is going to be up next year at NBC and who might be available. His name is Steve Friedman."

I knew the name and the reputation.

"Why would he leave NBC?" I asked.

"Because he's tired of doing the 'Today' show. He's done it for ten years. And he wants to get rich, like me. Steve can't get a piece of the action at NBC. All they can do is increase his salary by $50,000 or $100,000 a year and that's not what he wants."

I told Tinker to explore options with Friedman. Twenty minutes later, I was on the phone with my South Dakota pal Tom Brokaw at NBC.

"Tom, tell me about Steve Friedman."

"You son of a bitch! Don't you steal him, too!"

"Is he the guy that made you such a star on the 'Today' show?"

"No," Brokaw said. "I made me a star, but he sure is good."

"Seriously, how good is he?" I asked.

"He's the best. He's the best there is, but keep your mitts off him."

We met with Friedman the next week, again on the enclosed balcony of our Waldorf Towers suite—Tinker, Curley, McCorkindale, and I.

My first impressions of Steve:

▷ Cocksure and coarse.

▷ Sloppy in appearance.

▷ The exact opposite of Tinker.

But Friedman was exuberant about a deal. "A great newspaper. We'll put it on the air and hit the moon. We'll revolutionize television the way you revolutionized the newspaper industry," he screeched in his high voice.

I insisted on an important distinction between what GTG might do in the East and what it would do in the West.

"Out West, anything Grant does on sitcoms is fine with us. But here, if we do a *USA TODAY* on the air, the show will have to fit with the newspaper in style and approach. We don't want the show to hurt the reputation of our well-established newspaper."

Steve's retort: "I wouldn't want the newspaper to hurt my reputation either." His ego was even bigger than I had been warned. That turned out to be a big problem.

My instincts said not to hire him. Too much sound, not enough substance. But I respected the judgment of Tinker and Brokaw. And I thought Grant could harness him. So we made a deal.

My Last Big Mistake

Now we were in big-time show biz.

Two highly respected, high profile partners. Tinker and his creative crew in our own studios in glamorous Culver City. Friedman with *USA TODAY* and other reality programming in the East. And a lot of publicity ink about Gannett's reach into the TV programming world.

For fifteen months I minded my own business and maintained a hands-off policy. This never was my style on any new venture and it certainly should not have been on one so closely linked to *USA TODAY.* It was my last major management mistake as chairman.

But I had promised money without meddling. I put too much confidence in Grant's management skills, too much confidence in Steve's reputation.

The promotion and selling of the TV show was sensational. Before it went on the air, 156 TV stations were signed up, the most ever for the start-up of a first-run syndication show.

On September 12, 1988, the whole nation was waiting for *USA TODAY, The Television Show.*

It bombed, panned by critics from coast to coast.

Tom Shales, *The Washington Post*'s syndicated critic wrote:

"As it turns out, the most ballyhooed infotainment program in TV history has neither enough info nor sufficient tainment.

. . . There are sound bites, light bites, news bites, everything but mosquito bites. This is a show that tends to nibble itself to death."

I was accustomed to seeing savage attacks on Gannett and *USA TODAY* in the *Post*. But this one was different. It was on target and I agreed with it.

The day after the show opened, I had Tinker and Friedman join Curley and me for lunch. Steve was startled by the universally negative reviews. For an hour or so he bordered on humility.

Grant urged Steve to pay attention to the critics. Slow the show down, give it more substance. It was the first time Tinker really got into the content of the show. He, too, had been willing to let Steve do his thing.

For the next two weeks, I watched every 4:30 P.M. feed of the show from its Arlington, Virginia, studios to the stations. Afterward, I'd meet with Friedman and offer reactions. He listened to me, but then did as he pleased.

Finally, I abandoned my soft, suggestive approach and reverted to form. On September 28, the third week of the show, I wrote Friedman this Love Letter:

"Steve:

"Furchrissakes! You really blew tonight's show. Your lousy editorial judgment on how to sequence the thing made a weak 'B' out of what could have been a strong 'A.'

"I've gently told you several times in the past two weeks that the show needs some currency, immediacy, newsiness.

"[No more] gentleness. After tonight, you need to be hit over the head with your baseball bat (which he always kept on his desk) or my sledgehammer. . . ."

I sent a marked copy to Grant Tinker.

When Steve got the memo, he called. "Hey, maybe you're right. But I wish you'd address me as Mr. Friedman, rather than Steve." Always the wisecracker. Always playing on his ego. Never able to understand.

Friedman obviously was better at running something already in existence than something new. Because of his NBC "Today" show successes, he believed he was as good as his reputation. He wasn't.

Goodbye, Steve

Finally, Tinker sent Friedman and his free-form management style packing. We parted for a price—about $1 million—and Steve was free to do whatever it is he is a genius at.

With a little egg on our faces, Tinker, Curley and I agreed that Gannett would take control of the *USA TODAY* TV show. John Quinn, then editor-in-chief of the newspaper, quarterbacked the salvage effort.

That left Tinker free to devote his full time and attention to GTG in the West.

While GTG's first three sitcoms on CBS bombed, a fourth—"Baywatch"—got good notices and was moved to a choice prime-time spot on NBC for the 1989 season.

In TV production, it takes only one hit out of every five or so shows for the owners to get well. So there's plenty of time for the Tinker touch to pay off.

The *USA TODAY* TV show has survived Steve, management chaos, and the sleaze factor that threatened to kill it in its early months. It more nearly reflects the bright, breezy, upbeat approach of the newspaper.

Win or lose, the new leadership of the show seems to be operating under the dictum of my belated and one of my last edicts before retiring as chairman:

"It would be far better to fail with a show we can be proud of than to win the ratings game with a show we'd be ashamed of."

Meanwhile, the Gannett board and its new leadership have demonstrated that they have patience as well as deep pockets. That's usually a winning combination.

PLAIN TALK:

Cutting your losses too soon on new ventures is like cutting your own throat.

VIII

BEATING BIAS AND BIGOTRY

"As there were no black Founding Fathers, there were no Founding Mothers . . . a great pity on both counts."

FORMER U.S. REPRESENTATIVE SHIRLEY CHISHOLM OF NEW YORK

Our childhood makes us what we are, if we pay attention.

Its joys and its hurts. Its battles and its battle scars. Its loves and its labors. Its wins and its losses.

All are woven into the fabric of our adult character.

They form the secrets of our success—or our failure.

They shape the philosophies of our practices.

I learned my lessons of bias and bigotry early.

At age twelve, I began to understand the great pain and injustice of discrimination.

I watched my mother work longer and harder for less money to support her two sons than the heads of households who happened to be men.

That adolescent fury of a defensive son matured into a lifelong battle against prejudice of all kinds. And a commitment that equality must be for all, not just those who can control it.

As a smart-aleck student, I learned another lifelong lesson the hard way.

I indulged in, and enjoyed, the ancient and once honorable art of using the power of the press to favor my friends and get my enemies.

It was fun. It was stimulating. It was totally unfair.

I learned that early enough to mend my ways, triggering a career-long campaign against the very biased kind of journalism I practiced as a kid.

I am still trying to teach that lesson to some of my colleagues in the "Holy Shit" journalism establishment.

Some day they may grow up, too.

"I hope we never live to see the day when a thing is as bad as some of our newspapers make it."

WILL ROGERS

MANAGING WOMEN AND MINORITIES

"Al Neuharth has brought new meaning to the word 'opportunity' in the 1980s."

ROSALYNN CARTER
Former First Lady
of the United States

When I was a kid growing up in South Dakota, discrimination by sex was so shameless even the federal government practiced it openly.

The WPA (Works Progress Administration), which President Franklin Delano Roosevelt established to provide bread money for those who could not get private employment during the Depression, had these publicly posted pay standards:

▷ Men—$5 per day.

▷ Women—$3 per day.

WPA bosses in my part of South Dakota carried it a step further. They didn't hire any women.

My mother was the first victim of discrimination I knew.

While I watched sometimes shiftless men lean on their WPA shovels and collect $5 per day, my mother worked as a dishwasher six days a week from 6 A.M. to 5 P.M. for a dollar a day—and after supper did other people's laundry.

South Dakota may seem an unlikely seat of sexism or racism. But, in the 1930s and '40s it was both. It didn't get the attention the then racist South got because the population was small and the victims were different.

In the South, the vow of many whites was to keep the "coloreds" down on the plantation. In South Dakota, it was to keep the Indians down on the reservation.

And a woman's place was in the home.

Those lives and times instilled in me a commitment to try to wipe out sexism and racism, some day, some way. And so I became:

▷ A believer as a kid in South Dakota.

▷ A preacher as a journalist in my twenties and thirties.

▷ A disciple for two decades, from my mid-forties to my mid-sixties, as the head of Gannett and *USA TODAY.*

Gannett and I received repeated recognition in the 1970s and '80s as media leaders in hiring, training, and promoting women and minorities.

Before my mother died at age eighty-six, I told her all those awards belonged to her.

No organization, private or public, can implement equal opportunity programs unless the boss believes in it, preaches it, and practices it.

In the beginning, even just preaching equal opportunity met resistance from the white male establishment in the media.

Even now, practicing it continues to run into roadblocks from some male media decision makers. And, unfortunately, from a few female executives who would rather be token stars than help other women to the top.

My preaching began in earnest soon after I joined Gannett and declared war on the good old boys in our business. Inside and outside Gannett, my pitch was that "our leadership must reflect our readership."

This was my message to a national audience of women journalists at the University of Missouri in 1969:

"Why do so many of you with so much talent allow the sex gap between yourselves and the top jobs in your profession to continue?

"Why don't more of you prepare yourselves and set your sights on such positions as publisher, editor, broadcasting station manager? Those are jobs on which the 'for men only' sign should come down."

Higher Aims, Lower Voices

In 1970, my call to the National Federation of Press Women at their convention in New Orleans was this: "The press is overmanned at the top and some of you are to blame for that. Here is a picture of three categories of women in the media:

▷ "Modern and moderate feminists who want to be a part of society on an equal basis with men. That's good and you must lead the way.

▷ "Radical extremists who want to escape from woman-hood and society. That's bad and you ought to lower your voices and raise your aim.

▷ "Women who really don't want to reach the top. They often put down other women leaders by charging 'She got there through the bedroom.' That category should stay in the bed-room—or the kitchen."

I provided opportunities for others to preach the cause, too.

In 1970, as president of the New York State Publishers Association, I invited feminist Gloria Steinem to be our keynote speaker at Lake Placid and urged her to lay it on the line. She did. With humor and a sledgehammer.

During the Q and A, the publisher of the *Rome* (New York) *Daily Sentinel,* George Waters, expressed the feelings of many in the old boys' club when he belligerently challenged Steinem: "Why should white male publishers like myself support your feminist movement?"

Fired back Steinem: "Because you'll screw more and enjoy it more!"

The boys snickered. But the barroom talk later clearly indicated they preferred submissiveness to aggressiveness—in the office and in the bedroom.

Eighteen years later, when I spoke to that same New York Publishers group, the same George Waters rose to ask a ques-tion. I interrupted him. "George, did you ever take the advice Gloria Steinem gave you here?"

This time he snickered, nervously. Afterwards his wife, Shirley, told a group triumphantly: "Yes, he did. And he does enjoy it more!"

In 1973, the year I became CEO, I named Gannett's first woman publisher.

Gloria Biggs, a highly regarded feature and women's editor in Palm Beach and St. Petersburg, joined Gannett when we started *TODAY* in Florida. When I named her publisher of our *Melbourne* (Florida) *Times,* she was recognized as the first woman from newsroom ranks to earn that title. She became a newspaper celebrity and we all encouraged her to accept many of the speaking invitations she got.

Biggs has a quick wit and keen sense of humor. When she spoke to a meeting of New York State editors in Binghamton, a conservative Gannett editor opened the Q and A with this question:

"Do you think a woman is as good as, better, or worse than a man?"

"At what?" quipped Gloria. That brought the house down, but it didn't win many converts.

After her appearance, editor David Bernstein of the *Binghamton Sun-Bulletin,* one of the early enlightened male journalists, wrote:

"The catty remarks revealed a male insecurity among the editors . . . behaving like clever maiden aunts whose powder room had just been invaded by Burt Lancaster.'"

Even after I broke the ice with Biggs as our first woman publisher, there were no Gannett females lining up at my office door seeking promotions. That disappointed me. But I pushed on.

You're Never Ready for a Promotion

In 1974, I asked *Rochester Times-Union* editorial writer Christy Bulkeley to become publisher of our *Saratoga Springs Saratogian.* She was shocked.

I told her: "You think you are not ready. Well, you're right. You're not. But you're as ready as I've ever been for any of my promotions and you'll grow into it." She did.

In 1977, I asked the editor of our *Niagara Falls Gazette,* Sue Clark, to become publisher as well. By then she was the fifth woman to be a Gannett publisher, the top job on our newspapers.

"There'll be a lot of pressure," she told me.

I agreed, but joked, "But the pressure will be on you, not

on me. Now we have enough women publishers so that I can afford to fire one of you if you don't measure up."

She got the point: She would be treated the same as any man in her new job. She not only measured up, she excelled. Today she is one of four Gannett regional presidents, supervising sixteen newspapers in the West.

In spite of promoting a woman here and there, Gannett needed a broad-based program for both women and minorities throughout the company.

Many male managers of our newspapers and broadcast stations were giving lip service only. They took their cue from my predecessor, Paul Miller. His attitude especially permeated the Rochester newspaper plant, where he had been the boss for sixteen years.

When I asked Tony Powderly, classified ad manager, why all the women taking want-ad telephone calls were white—most of them were girlfriends of Powderly's pals—he said:

"We hired a black once. But purses began disappearing and so we never hired another."

Powderly and others got the message after I hired a black, Doris Ingram, as one of my two secretaries. We plotted to hold up all of Powderly's staff change requests and other pet requisitions at her desk. Then, when he inquired of me about them, I'd smile and say:

"Apparently Doris hasn't approved them yet."

After Powderly had to retrieve several such from my black secretary, his want-ad staff became integrated.

My two key allies on people progress in Gannett executives ranks in the 1970s were:

John E. (Jack) Heselden, senior vice president/personnel, who firmly believed in equal opportunity programs, and John C. Quinn, then senior vice president/news, a totally people-sensitive person.

Quinn, Heselden, and I fashioned a program that tied a sizable portion of every executive's annual bonus to the EEO programs. Even the most chauvinistic of our male managers got the message when it hit their pocketbooks.

My Spouse Snoops Around

To encourage and monitor EEO programs, we recruited two highly visible white/black and female/male teams. The first two were temporary consultants. The next two became permanent corporate executives.

As consultants:

▷ Bob Maynard, a black journalist who had worked at *The New York Times, The Washington Post,* and later for Gannett. He headed the Institute for Journalism Education, which trained minority candidates for journalism at the entry level and groomed them to move up.

▷ Lori Wilson, a white female who was then married to me. She had been the prime sponsor of the ERA amendment when she served in the Florida State Senate, and had a strong record of EEO support.

Maynard and Wilson made the rounds of the Gannett newspapers, looking and listening. Maynard reported most of his findings to Quinn. Wilson told me.

Having my spouse check on male managers pissed off many of them. But it gave hope and encouragement to ambitious women who realized they now had a direct pipeline to me through Lori and our pillow talk.

At the annual meeting of all Gannett executives after the Maynard/Wilson program began, my usual State of the Company address praised the group for product and profit improvement. Then it turned to the subject of people and our EEO programs.

Deliberately, firmly, I told the roomful of more than two hundred executives: "Some of you are doing a good job in this area. Some of you are not." Then I scanned the room slowly and said: "And, I know who you are."

The guilty dropped their heads or shifted in their seats. My dramatics even smoked out some who I thought had been doing okay.

Now that they knew I was serious, it was time to follow up the Maynard/Wilson, consultants' effort with a permanent program.

To do that:

▷ Madelyn P. Jennings, formerly an executive at Standard Brands and General Electric, a white female, was named our vice president/personnel. She is now senior vice president.

▷ Jimmy Jones, a black former New York Jets football player and the personnel manager at Jersey Central Power and Light, became our director of affirmative action. He is now vice president/employee relations.

The "Partnership in Progress" personnel program was formalized and, for most of the 1980s, the Jennings/Jones team planned and policed that program.

Slowly, but steadily, results improved. Women and minorities inside Gannett began aggressively preparing for and seeking promotions. The word spread. Many of the best and the brightest young women and nonwhites on college campuses and at other media companies came to Gannett.

Wiping Out the Minority Myth

Staffing *USA TODAY* from scratch offered a unique opportunity to prove that it could be done—and to discard the off-repeated myth that "we can't find any minority recruits."

All that was needed was a decree from the top that all recruiting would bring together the right mix of sexes and race, as well as talent and experience, to do the job.

Paced by the news staff, *USA TODAY*'s equal opportunity percentages from its very beginning are reflected in its 1988 EEO scorecard:

▷ Overall employees: 51 percent women, 24 percent minorities.

▷ Professionals, managers: 41 percent women, 14 percent minorities.

By the time I retired as chairman in 1989, this was the total people picture at Gannett:

▷ 37,000 employees; 40 percent women, 21 percent nonwhites.

▷ In the top four job categories—managers, professionals, sales, technicians—41 percent women, 16 percent minorities.

▷ Among Gannett newspapers, 22 percent of our publishers were women. The women publishers in Gannett represented one fourth of the eighty-four women newspaper publishers in the entire USA.

▷ Five Gannett publishers were black. Two Hispanic. Two Asian.

▷ On the broadcast side, 30 percent of the radio station

general managers were female and 20 percent are minority; 18 percent of the television station general managers were minority and 9 percent female.

People progress among the rank and file and at the executive level would not have been possible without the example of the top level—the board of directors.

When I became CEO in 1973, Gannett had an all white, all male board of twelve directors.

When I left in 1989, the board membership had:

▷ Four females, including one black.

▷ One black male.

▷ One Asian male.

They, along with the white males, represent a rewarding diversity of experience and expertise, philosophy and geography. The leadership of Gannett now more nearly reflects its readership and viewership.

Notwithstanding some success in erasing color and sex lines at Gannett, I had far less influence on other media moguls.

For fourteen years I served as a director, then chairman and president, of the American Newspaper Publishers Association, the granddaddy of the industry's trade organizations.

When I joined that board in 1968, it, too, was all white and male. When I moved into the officer ranks and influenced or controlled the nominating process, three women publishers were elected ANPA directors.

The first was Kay Graham of *The Washington Post.* I maneuvered her into a position to become ANPA's first female chairman and president.

Yet, despite the good job Kay did as head of ANPA, she should have pushed harder for other women. Her example of leadership should have been enough. It wasn't. Her male colleagues reverted to tradition. She let them get away with it. ANPA hasn't had another top female officer since.

Journalists and editorialists generally are much better at preaching than practicing proper behavior. That certainly is true in the EEO area. Much of the people progress that has been made is the result of court action, rather than enlightened leadership.

Shame on the Preachers

In recent years, some of the biggest and most highly visible media operations have been sued and shamed into doing the right thing.

▷ The New York *Daily News* was found guilty of discrimination against black reporters and editors. The settlement: a reported $3.1 million.

▷ The Associated Press made a $2 million back-pay settlement on charges of discrimination against blacks, Hispanics, and women.

▷ *The New York Times* paid $650,000 to settle a racial discrimination case.

▷ NBC paid $1.4 million to women employees after they sued the network in 1975.

▷ *The Washington Post* was charged by the Guild with "pay discrimination by race and sex." At the time of this writing, that case is pending before the Washington, D.C., office of human rights.

It blows my mind that some of those in the media who preach most liberally practice most conservatively when it comes to their own staffs.

As recently as the spring of 1989, executive editor Ben Bradlee of *The Washington Post* and his former protege and then editor of the *Los Angeles Times,* Shelby Coffey, infuriated a conference on "Women, Men, and the Media" by their "so what's wrong?" attitudes.

That same evening, the conference program pitted Betty Friedan and me in what was supposed to be a point/counterpoint discussion. It turned into a love feast. In response to questions, I was able to contrast sharply with Bradlee's chauvanistic arrogance earlier in the day.

Shortly thereafter, an enraged Bradlee told *USA TODAY* editorial director John Seigenthaler: "I'm going to get Neuharth for that. I'm going to get him!"

So, what else is new? I've shaken that S.O.B. off my back before and I will again.

Credit for Gannett's EEO record belongs to many of my associates, who believed in it as much as I did. They practiced it up and down the line.

But when it came to going after the biggest targets, I turned headhunter myself. Two of my key catches were:

▷ Former First Lady Rosalynn Carter, as a member of our board of directors.

▷ Cathie Black, former publisher of Rupert Murdoch's *New York* magazine, as publisher of *USA TODAY* and a member of our board of directors.

I started courting Rosalynn Carter shortly after she and President Jimmy left the White House.

After a first visit to the Carter home in Plains, Georgia, I invited both President Jimmy and Rosalynn as guests of honor at a luncheon in Atlanta with our Gannett board of directors. She was impressed with the other directors.

After my second visit to the Carter home in August 1983, she was still stalling me.

President Jimmy said he would be pleased if she decided to join our board, but that it was strictly her decision.

Someone else was needed to lobby in Gannett's behalf. That night I called Bert Lance, Carter's former budget director and still close friend of the family, and I urged him to urge Rosalynn to accept: "This is a chance for one of your Carter crowd who has been on the other side of the press perspective to bring her views to our side of the table."

Lance bought the idea enthusiastically.

"I'll call her tonight. I'll tell her that if this were *The New York Times* or *The Washington Post,* I wouldn't ask her to do it. But this here Gannett is an all-American company, an all-American company."

The next day President Jimmy called my New York office.

"This is Rosalynn Carter's secretary," President Jimmy said. "She'd like to talk to you."

She accepted. She's been a hardworking, participating director of Gannett ever since. Her business perspectives as the former bookkeeper of the Carter family peanut farm and her political and pillow talk perspective from the White House are great assets.

When her appointment was announced, a reporter from *The Washington Post* asked: "Why didn't you invite President Carter himself?"

"Because he would have been just another white male on the board. We have plenty of those," I quipped.

Macho Messenger Misfires

The conquest of Cathie Black was equally challenging.

Black had a reputation on Madison Avenue as one of the best female hucksters in the publishing business. Most on Madison Avenue still insisted on distinguishing between males and females. I thought she was one of the best—period.

She had started in advertising at *Holiday* magazine, then joined *Ms.* magazine when it was founded. After a sojourn on *San Francisco* magazine, she joined *New York* magazine, worked her way up to publisher after Rupert Murdoch bought it.

We had made our first pitch to Black in the summer of 1982, when we were putting together the staff for *USA TODAY.* But I made the mistake of sending a macho man to see her— *USA TODAY*'s president Phil Gialanella, along with executive veep Vince Spezzano.

They sounded her out about the job of vice president/ advertising. They reported back that she wasn't interested. Indeed she wasn't. She thought she was better than either of them and wouldn't consider working for them.

Actually, she underrated both of them and they underrated her. Spezzano, particularly, is many-talented and worked well with both males and females.

Gialanella, who was then president of *USA TODAY,* is uncomfortable working with top-level women. Like many men, he simply doesn't know how to treat them. As a result, he generally makes one of the two mistakes most men business executives make:

▷ Coddling or pampering women.
▷ Treating them as serfs.

The answer, of course, is so simple. Male executives should treat female co-workers as people. Provide them the same opportunities. Demand the same results. Give them the same rewards. Compliment them when they do well. Kick their asses when they don't.

That's how I promised Cathie Black she would be treated a year later, when I realized how much we needed her and went after her myself. And that is how I did treat her—somewhat to her dismay after a couple of ass-kicking incidents.

Madelyn Jennings arranged my first meeting with Black.

Before we met, I learned all I could about her, professionally and personally.

She makes forceful sales presentations and has a positive outlook. A good personal impression. A good-looking blonde. A bit flashy. She'd just married again. Her new husband, Tom Harvey, was a lawyer working for the federal government. They had a commuter marriage between New York and Washington and each had his/her own home in those two cities.

At *New York* magazine, Black had reached the top and felt stymied. Murdoch did not hold out hope for anything bigger. A major Madison Avenue advertising agency had talked to her about a top job and she was thinking about taking it.

In short, personally and professionally, she was reassessing her life, the ideal time for a suitor to make a pitch.

At first we sized up each other in a low-key way.

Dinner at Four Seasons, cocktails in our Waldorf Towers suite. General talk about a top sales executive job in a growing Gannett company and assurance that if we made a deal the compensation would be well above her then take in the low six figures.

At our third meeting, she said she and Tom were going to take the weekend to hide out at their Lakeville, Connecticut, cottage and talk about their futures.

After that meeting I asked Madelyn, "What can I do to keep Gannett uppermost in Cathie's mind over the weekend?"

Madelyn had learned from conversations with Cathie that she loved cooking when they were at their country home. And that Cathie did her grocery shopping at a chic gourmet place in SoHo.

Bushel Basket by Limo

We arranged for that shop to prepare a huge basket of herbs and other fancy condiments that they said were Cathie's favorites, plopped a bottle of Dom Perignon champagne in the middle. On Saturday morning, my New York chauffeur delivered it by limo to the Connecticut cottage.

A personal note read: "Enjoy your time with your guy. I hope you will be thinking about Gannett. Let's talk again next week."

I sensed by then Black could be had by us if we made her

the right offer. But we'd have to aim higher than we had a year earlier.

We met again the following Friday in the Waldorf Towers suite— Jennings, Heselden, Black, and I.

"Can I assume you've now seen the light and are interested in Gannett?" I asked.

"Yes, under the right circumstances," she replied.

"Is it also true we haven't yet been smart enough to figure out the right job for you?"

"Yes," again her response.

"How would you like to be president of *USA TODAY?*"

Her eyes lit up. She beamed. She would be the advertising sales guru of The Nation's Newspaper with an impressive title. I had hit the target. The game was over.

"You could have saved yourself a lot of fancy dinners if you'd talked about that in the beginning," Black quipped.

She didn't say yes immediately. But I knew she would on Monday morning. And she did.

Over the weekend, Vince Spezzano was promoted to senior vice president/communications for Gannett, so that he would vacate the *USA TODAY* president's title and make way for Black. Phil Gialanella had already left *USA TODAY* to return to our Honolulu newspaper.

Before we made the public announcement on Black, I called her employer, Rupert Murdoch, then at the *New York Post,* as a courtesy. He was at his Australian/British gentlemanly best.

"Congratulations. She's very good," he said. "I was afraid I might lose her but I didn't know what to do about it."

When she was interviewed about her job changing decision, Black said:

"Al's a maverick who wants change. He wanted to change the front page of American journalism. He was also willing to go out on the edge to change fundamentally how society and business work. I don't think Rupert cared about any of that."

Five years later, Murdoch seemed to have learned his lesson, then forgot it.

Just months after paying $3 billion for Walter Annenberg's publishing empire, Murdoch turned to Gannett and a woman to run his new flagship, *TV Guide.*

Valerie Salembier, senior vice president/advertising for *USA TODAY,* was one of many women in Gannett who have achieved national reputations by doing their jobs well. Murdoch tapped Salembier to be publisher of *TV Guide*. But they lasted only five months together. Murdoch made the mistake of leaving her to report to an executive who did not know how to manage her. Salembier moved on quickly to president of the *New York Post*.

USA TODAY hiring policies gave it another strong woman on its ad sales team to succeed Salembier. Pat Haegle, first with *USA TODAY,* then publisher of *USA Weekend,* became senior vice president/advertising.

Cathie Black's rapid rise at Gannett is an example for all employees, regardless of sex or race. A year after joining us, Black was promoted from president to publisher. A year later we put her on the Gannett board of directors. She's now the most highly visible female publisher in the USA. And one of the best.

Her compensation is public information because the SEC requires that salaries of Gannett's five highest paid employees be published in the annual proxy statement.

In 1988, she collected $585,000 in cash, plus substantial Gannett stock awards and other perks. Her total annual take approaches a million dollars.

A pretty big jump from my mother's dollar a day. But my mother would have been the first to say Cathie's worth every penny of it.

PLAIN TALK:

The secret to managing women or minorities: Treat them the same as you do all other people.

"HOLY SHIT" JOURNALISM

"Neuharth likes young journalists because they are not cynical like the veterans."

PEOPLE MAGAZINE
September 28, 1987

How good—or how bad—is your daily newspaper?

Does it hold out hope for a better tomorrow?

Does it give you a diet of despair?

Or does it keep you off balance with what a top editor in the nation's capital calls "Holy Shit" journalism?

How does your newspaper rate with others across the USA?

There were 1,643 daily newspapers in this country as we entered 1989.

I have looked at or read most of them, many very carefully. I read a dozen or more regularly, many more of them frequently.

At Gannett, we have done reader research in most markets to find out what you like or don't like about your newspaper. Here's what most of you say:

▷ You want your newspaper to inform and entertain you.

▷ You want it to debate issues, but not dictate answers.

▷ You want your news to be balanced, not biased.

▷ Most of all, you want it to reflect truly the world in which you live—the good and the bad, the glad and the sad.

Many of you have a love/hate relationship with your newspaper. But even when you criticize it, you call it "my newspaper." Even though most of you spend more time watching television than reading, you still consider your newspaper an indispensable part of your daily lifestyle.

When our daughter Jan's third grade teacher at Allen Creek School in Rochester, New York, asked her to tell the class what her father did for a living, she said: "He reads newspapers."

I've been reading and running newspapers for fifty years and getting paid to do it.

Report Cards for the Media

Does that half century of newspapering across the USA qualify me to pass judgment on the nation's newspapers, or the schools which train our journalists?

Actually, you the readers are the best judges of your own newspaper. But I'm a much better judge than the fraternity of journalism professors and insiders who regularly pick the best or the worst from the isolation and insulation of their ivory towers.

The best newspapers are those that do the best job for the particular audience they are trying to serve. That may be a single community, a region, a state, the nation, or a specialized readership.

I'll share with you my purely personal perceptions about some of the best—and some of the most overrated—newspapers in our business. And, the reasons why.

My "best" list is limited to newspapers with circulation of 100,000 or more, although some smaller ones are every bit as good in their league.

Of course, I agree with the 6,300,000 daily readers across the USA who say *USA TODAY* is number one. But I disqualified my baby from this list because I didn't want to be accused of prejudice in a chapter on fairness.

Top Ten Newspapers

1. *Chicago Tribune*
2. *Los Angeles Times*
3. *The New York Times*
4. *Dallas Morning News*
5. *The Wall Street Journal*
6. *Boston Globe*
7. *Detroit News* (Gannett)
8. *Orlando Sentinel*
9. *Charlotte Observer*
10. *Atlanta Journal and Constitution*

That list will deeply offend some of my journalist colleagues in the East. That's because many of them have blinders on. They can't see as far as Chicago or Dallas, let alone all the way to Los Angeles.

The *Chicago Tribune* tops my list because it offers a balanced combination of news from the Midwest and the world. It covers its hometown as well as or better than any other on my list. And it does it interestingly, colorfully, fairly.

Twenty years ago the *Tribune* would not have made my list at all. James Squires, who became editor in 1981, deserves much of the credit. He's so smart he even stole *USA TODAY*'s blue color for his own Page One nameplate.

The *Los Angeles Times* was a second-rate rag until Otis Chandler took over from his father Norman in 1960. It might edge the Tribune as number one if the Times's editors could control the endless prose of many of its so-called stars. The gross overwriting and jumping of stories from page to page to page turns off many readers.

Present publisher Tom Johnson and editor Shelby Coffey are topnotch pros, building on the base Otis Chandler gave them.

The New York Times makes both my Ten Best and Ten Most Overrated lists because it is both.

It overcovers the world, especially third-world countries, and badly undercovers its hometown. The intellectual snobbery of Abe Rosenthal, while he was executive editor for nine years, kept the *Times* from reaching its potential. Editor Max Frankel has made some meaningful improvements since he took over in 1986, including mimicking *USA TODAY* in some reader-oriented techniques.

It would not surprise me if *The New York Times* finally lives up to its overrated reputation in the next decade.

Some of the best, and some of the worst, journalism in the USA is practiced in the nation's capital. But the pompousness east of the Potomac is so prevalent that those who practice both the best and the worst often are not aware of the difference.

That aura of arrogance and the erratic performance it produces makes *The Washington Post* the most overrated newspaper in the USA. Not the worst, by any means. But certainly not among the ten best.

The *Post* has company. Other newspapers through the years have gotten on many dean's lists without belonging there.

Ten Most Overrated Newspapers

1. *The Washington Post*
2. *Miami Herald*
3. *St. Petersburg Times*
4. *Louisville Courier-Journal* (Gannett)
5. *Philadelphia Inquirer*
6. *Denver Post*
7. *Des Moines Register* (Gannett)
8. *The New York Times*
9. *Baltimore Sun*
10. *St. Louis Post-Dispatch*

Most of the overrated newspapers got that way by making prizes, rather than their news product, their primary purpose.

For newspapers, the Pulitzers are considered the prime prize of them all. Many editors of overrated newspapers would kill for a Pulitzer. And they have.

They kill news that their readers want or need in order to spend time, money, and space on news that might win a Pulitzer.

Most Pulitzers are won for news that's bad and sad. The good or the glad seldom makes the cutoff when Pulitzer juries meet in the Cimmerian climate at Columbia University in New York City.

The New York Times' media writer Albert Scardino put the Pulitzers in perspective: "The prestige and influence that a Pulitzer bestows can improve the morale and profits of a once undistinguished newspaper like the *Philadelphia Inquirer.*"

Philly's prize-prone editor Eugene L. Roberts, Jr., did just that, with abandon. When he arrived on the scene in 1973, the *Inquirer* was doing a good job of covering local news, but it didn't get much attention beyond the Pennsylvania border.

Roberts decided the way to move out of the shadow of *The New York Times* was to target the Pulitzers by covering Afghanistan and Africa.

It worked. Since Roberts arrived, the *Inquirer* has won fourteen Pulitzers. The job it does for its total reader audience is not as good as before. But he has captured the audience he was after, the Pulitzer judges.

"The prizes probably did a great deal to restore self-respect to the staff and to the paper," Roberts says. Self-respect. Never mind the respect of readers.

Lest you wonder, Gannett newspapers have won their share of Pulitzers. Thirty-seven in all. Some before they joined Gannett, some since.

The two Gannett newspapers on my most overrated list— Louisville and Des Moines—are those where interest in prizes prevailed over product. They're good newspapers and getting even better. Just not as good as their overall reputations.

Journalism of Despair

Inevitably, prize-prone editors practice a journalism of despair. The depth of that despair rests in the bowels of New York City and Washington, D.C.

If the cynicism of those journalists were confined east of the Hudson and east of the Potomac, it would simply be an unfortunate local problem. But because the thoughts from those so-called thought centers are beamed across the USA and around the world, the problem is global.

When I was doing my newspapering in South Dakota, Florida, and Michigan, I was not fully aware of the magnitude of the media misanthropy in New York and Washington. When I moved to Rochester and read newspapers from the Big Apple regularly I was appalled.

This column by Bill Reel in the New York Daily News reads like a cynics' handbook:

"Good news is no news. . . .

"A happy headline always elicits a derisive, disbelieving snort from New Yorkers who know that any hopeful development is too good to be true. New Yorkers—and I assume folks elsewhere are no different—want to read stories that make them mad and indignant.

"A good newsman can find a depressing angle to any story."

When I spent more time in Washington, D.C., and saw the perniciousness with which the *Post* approached the news, I decided to speak out about this Journalism of Despair.

My forum was the Overseas Press Club in New York City. October 24, 1983. It was my second appearance. On March 21, 1979, I had spoken to the same group.

Then the title of my speech was *"Preserving* Freedom of the Press."

This time, the title was *"Deserving* Freedom of the Press."

I said: "The best journalists are skeptics.

"They don't accept things at face value. They ask tough questions, dig deep for the truth. They weigh all sides, ignore public relations pitches, and write a fair story.

"But there's a fine line between skepticism and cynicism.

"The cynics assume the worst and publish it. They think their mission is to indict and convict, rather than inform and educate. They believe they're drawing in readers with negative coverage, but instead are driving them away.

"Cynics practice the Journalism of Despair.

"The issue, very simply is:

"Whether the old Journalism of Despair, this derisive technique of usually leaving readers discouraged, or mad, or indignant, can/should survive or thrive in the 1980s and '90s.

"[Or] whether a new Journalism of Hope, a technique that chronicles the good and the bad, the glad and the sad, and leaves readers fully informed and equipped to judge what deserves their attention and support, can and will prevail in the decades ahead."

Those comments got only polite and light applause from my New York audience, as I had expected.

Journalists of Hope

Across the USA, the reaction was different. Editorialists and columnists approved. Some said they'd been practicing a Journalism of Hope all along without having labeled it. Others vowed to begin doing so.

Publisher Robert Rawlings of the *Pueblo* (Colorado) *Chieftain* sent a copy of my speech to every member of his staff with a note that said: "Read and heed."

Chairman Dolph Simons, Sr., of the *Lawrence* (Kansas) *Journal-World* applauded my approach and that of *USA TODAY*. He explained the difference between journalism of hope and despair to a group of community leaders.

"There's media and there's media. Network television and a few major newspapers do one thing. Most newspapers throughout the country use an entirely different and responsible approach."

My light spanking and the Journalism of Despair label hurt most where it hit closest to home—at *The Washington Post.* Columnists began deriding what they termed my Happy News formula—their interpretation of my Journalism of Hope.

Because *The Washington Post* is the most overrated newspaper in the country—and because it's read by most of our leaders in the nation's capital every day—its brand of journalism is worth a brief case study.

"Holy Shit" journalism is what *Post* executive editor Ben Bradlee calls it.

He teaches his disciples that when a reader picks up page one of the *Post* at breakfast, he wants him to say "Holy shit!"

More often than not, the *Post* gets that desired reader reaction. Often the reaction is: Holy shit! Can I believe this?

Sometimes they can. Sometimes they cannot, or should not.

Fact and fiction can be comfortable bedmates in the *Post*'s Palace of Malice, the home of "Holy Shit" journalism. Anonymous or unnamed news sources are the key to the *Post*'s brand of journalism.

That policy of unnamed sources openly invites two violations of journalistic ethics:

▷ The anonymous source often tells more than he or she knows.

▷ The reporter often writes more than he or she hears.

The only sure way to separate fact from fiction in newspapers is to ban anonymous sources. A less effective alternative is to require reporters to reveal to their editors the identity of such sources and make the editors decide whether the material should be used.

USA TODAY has a firm policy banning all anonymous sources. It has taught our reporters responsibility and has given the newspaper unprecedented credibility with sources and readers.

Most newspapers other than *The Washington Post* have tightened up on their use of unnamed sources. Retired Executive Editor Abe Rosenthal of *The New York Times* defends such sources only if used "decently."

But Rosenthal adds, "Sickeningly often the anonymous source simply provides a mask for unprovable and unanswerable attacks and defamation."

Because *The Washington Post* publishes so many unprovable, unanswerable, and unethical stories based on anonymous sources, examples could easily fill an entire book. A couple concerned some well-known and an unknown.

The *Post* reported that President Jimmy Carter and his wife Rosalynn had bugged the Reagans while the President-elect and his wife Nancy were staying at Blair House across the street from the White House before the inauguration.

Carter angrily denied the report and called for an immediate retraction and apology.

A Bare-Assed Bradlee

Three days later Bradlee was quoted: "How do you make a public apology—run up and down Pennsylvania Avenue bare-bottomed shouting 'I'm sorry'?"

Bradlee missed a real opportunity by not doing just that. Such a personal example of his "Holy Shit" journalism, with his bare-assed picture on Page One of the *Post* would have given breakfast table readers a real treat.

Instead, the *Post* waited six days and then published a weak editorial saying the Blair House bugging story was just rumor.

Carter wasn't satisfied. He pressed for an apology and threatened to sue.

Finally, eighteen days after the *Post* ran the blatantly untrue rumor about a former president, it printed a brief retraction and apology.

Carter then announced he would not sue and issued this statement, which should be required reading in every journalism school in the USA and should be engraved on the newsroom walls of *The Washington Post:*

"Fortunately, because of my previous position, I had access to the public news media and could draw attention to my problem. Many victims of similarly false allegations do not enjoy this opportunity, but suffer just as severely."

Washington Post publisher Donald Graham, who probably chafes more with Bradlee than with his mother, Kay, sent Carter a letter of apology. I sent both Grahams notes congratulating them on the apologies even if it meant crossing Bradlee, who thinks he's the real *Post* boss.

"Your letter to Carter was probably the most important decision you made as publisher of the *Post,* not just for the *Post* but for all of us in this business," I wrote to Don Graham.

"You (we) were in deep trouble, not just with the politicians, but with the vast public out there. They will occasionally forgive us for making a big mistake in judgment, but they will not forgive us when we fail to admit it. I salute you."

I took a jab at Bradlee in a postscript to Kay Graham: "Congratulations for properly asserting your influence as the distinguished and wise elder statesman of the *Post.*"

Post reporter Diana McLellan embarrassed the Carters with her hearsay about the bugging. *Post* reporter Janet Cooke embarrassed a police department, a city, her newspaper, and her profession with a story she made up.

Cooke wrote a compelling series about an eight-year-old inner-city heroin addict she identified only as Jimmy. The stories, designed to dramatize the District of Columbia's drug problem, read so well that the *Post* nominated them for a Pulitzer Prize. And won.

Trouble was that there was no Jimmy. After the prize was awarded, the stories were exposed as fiction and the *Post* had to give back the Pulitzer.

"Holy shit!" exclaimed the whole journalism fraternity at this embarrassment to us all.

"Deep Throat" Lives

To the *Post*'s credit, it has sometimes used anonymous sources to protect whistle blowers who were not just whistling "Dixie."

Watergate is an example. The *Post* led the pack that knocked off the Nixon administration. That also won it a Pulitzer. It deserved that one and got to keep it.

Post publisher Kay Graham was a key player on Watergate. She took an active part in reviewing many of the Watergate stories and in general kept an eye on Bradlee during that period.

Left to their own judgment on the Janet Cooke stories, Bradlee and his team misused their authority and abused their readers.

But the *Post* ghosts involved in the Watergate coverage raised some questions that remain to this day.

Reporters Bob Woodward and Carl Bernstein claim their main source was Deep Throat—an unnamed government employee who allegedly would pop up in parking garages and provide information on deep background—meaning he/she could not be quoted directly.

I felt then and believe even more firmly now that Deep Throat was none other than Ben Bradlee himself.

You might ask, how could that be?

Easy. Bradlee has hundreds of political and social contacts in Washington. Many of them comfortably pass tips to Bradlee at cocktail parties or in phone calls. Many or most of them would not do so directly to reporters.

So, my hunch is that Bradlee himself is the legendary Deep Throat. We probably won't know until Ben retires and writes his own autobiography. His book's title should be: "Holy Shit!"

Most newspapers in the USA have a fairly distinctive style. The *Washington Post* is one of a kind with its erratic best and worst behavior. Most others practice the journalism of hope, but some still offer a heavy fare of journalism of despair.

Former *USA TODAY* Editor John C. Quinn put some of those styles in perspective when he was named Editor of the Year by the National Press Foundation in Washington. In accepting the award, Quinn said you can tell a lot about a newspaper by how it would headline the ultimate story—the end of the world.

Quinn's predictions:

▷ *New York Times*—"World Ends. Third World Countries Hardest Hit."

▷ *Washington Post*—"World Ends. White House Ignored Early Warnings, Unnamed Sources Say."

▷ *USA TODAY*—"We're Dead! State-by-state demise, page 8A. Final-final sports results, page 10C."

Journalism educators help set the tone—either positively or negatively—for the media because they train most aspiring journalists.

I have observed four decades of students graduating from journalism schools. We have hired hundreds from dozens of different schools. The quality of students graduated is the most meaningful measure of the best journalism schools. Using that criteria, these are my ratings for the decade of the 1980s.

Top Ten Journalism Schools

1. North Carolina
2. Kansas
3. Northwestern
4. Southern California
5. Indiana
6. Nebraska
7. Florida
8. Missouri
9. Texas
10. Maryland

Some journalism schools are not nearly as good in the 1980s as their reputations. That does not mean they are bad—just overrated. Generally such reputations are based on history and/or zealous deans or department heads. That's why Missouri makes both the best and the most overrated lists.

Five Most Overrated Journalism Schools

1. Columbia
2. University of California at Berkeley
3. Missouri
4. Ohio State
5. Penn State

Hope and Despair on the Air

Since I've spent a half century in newspapering and only a decade learning the business of broadcasting, I'm less sure of myself in that arena.

That's true in running broadcast operations or rating the performance of broadcasters.

But the Journalism of Despair and of Hope—and certainly "Holy Shit" journalism—are all available on the air with a flip of your dial.

Geraldo Rivera and Morton Downey serve up a plate full of "Holy Shit" only. Too much. Sooner or later, most viewers will throw up and tune out.

Phil Donahue, Oprah Winfrey, and Larry King offer a marvelous mix of Hope and "Holy Shit." They talk with their viewers, rather than to them. They'll be around a long time.

"60 Minutes" is despair on the air. But it's so entertaining that even those who are turned off by print journalism of despair will keep turning on Wallace and Bradley and Reasoner and Safer.

I still tune in, even though they tuned me out of an appearance on the show after having spent hundreds of hours and thousands of dollars preparing to do me.

I remember well when "60 Minutes" producer Don Hewitt told me, in the presence of Bryant Gumbel of NBC's *TODAY,* that they were going to "do you."

We were aboard Malcolm Forbes's *Highlander II* cruising around Manhattan with the Trumps and other towers of the Big Apple. *USA TODAY* was approaching its fifth anniversary and Hewitt thought the success of my baby made me a candidate to appear on his baby.

I was leery, because I knew the "60 Minutes" goal is to get you. But I agreed to cooperate because I thought the huge audience would help highlight my newspaper's fifth anniversary.

For weeks, "60 Minutes" crews followed me and filmed me from New York to Los Angeles and in between.

Finally, we sat down to tape a one-on-one interview—Harry Reasoner and I. Producer Sandy Socolow hovered over us.

An hour into the interview, we took a break and both Reasoner and Socolow urged me to come on stronger. "Show us your famous temper," they said.

When we resumed, Reasoner became rude and tried to rile me about *USA TODAY,* "McPaper, the fast food of journalism."

But I'd heard it all before. I stayed cool, smiled, answered the toughest questions politely.

The profile never ran. They told me I'd been too nice a guy. They hadn't been able to draw out their version of the S.O.B. in me.

Speaking of S.O.B.s, Ted Turner deserves much more credit than he gets for the success of his Cable News Network. CNN brings television's most comprehensive news reports into 49.6 million homes around the clock. It has provided the impetus for the three major networks to upgrade and expand their news programs and we all benefit.

ABC, CBS, and NBC offer a pretty good balance of hope and despair, from their morning shows to their nightly newscasts.

I'm a dial flipper. In my offices and in my home, I have four or more screens side by side. All pictures are all always on. I select the audio that interests me at the moment.

I learned that from President Lyndon Baines Johnson. In 1966, after the president had undergone surgery, my boss Paul Miller and I had lunch with LBJ and his aide Jack Valenti, now president of the Motion Picture Association of America, at the White House. Afterward, LBJ invited us to the presidential bedroom while he undressed for a nap. He wanted to show off the lineup of three TV sets at the foot of his bed.

Remote controls were fairly new then. He had one under his pillow.

"I keep all three pictures on all the time. But I only turn on the sound when I'm on the picture so I can listen to me," LBJ said.

Analyzing the Anchors

I watch Peter Jennings on ABC, Dan Rather on CBS, Bernard Shaw on CNN, and Tom Brokaw on NBC. I turn on the sound based on the subject matter they're dealing with.

All four are pretty good. Not yet as good as Walter Cronkite was, but pretty good.

Each offers a mix of hope and despair. Usually tilted toward despair—and available film footage—but not a bad balance.

How do they compare?

When we at Gannett were trying to acquire CBS, I thought we'd end up with the fourth best.

Here's how I rate the anchors:

1. Tom Brokaw
2. Peter Jennings
3. Bernard Shaw
4. Dan Rather

I admit I'm partial, because I identify more with Brokaw. He's a South Dakota buddy, and his wife, Meredith, is on the Gannett board. But Brokaw is the All-American, or All-USA, kid even though he's facing the big fifty. He plays well in Peoria and across the heartland of the country. Would do even better if he had someone else select his neckties.

Jennings is the sophisticated foreigner, who appeals most to the Eastern Seaboard. He's very smart and handles news substance superbly. But mucking stalls or milking cows on a Midwestern farm for a weekend would help his perspective.

Shaw gets more air time on CNN than the other networks give their anchors. He takes full advantage of it by being steady and ready with straightforward, no-frills news reports. But he needs to learn to smile.

Rather is the Ben Bradlee of broadcasting. Good, but not nearly as good as he thinks he is. As Cronkite said when Rather disappeared from the CBS screen in a snit for seven minutes in 1987, "I would have fired him." Me too.

These four anchors and all of television could learn from listening to Charles Kuralt, of "On the Road" at CBS.

Kuralt has a message for all of us in print or on the air:

"The country I see on my television screens and on my newspaper front pages is not quite the country I see with my eyes and hear with my ears or feel in my bones."

PLAIN TALK:

The First Amendment guarantees a free press; the press itself must guarantee a fair one.

IX

EYEBALLING THE POWERFUL

"A leader has to lead, or otherwise he has no business in politics."

FORMER PRESIDENT HARRY S. TRUMAN

A successful CEO, who is likely to be a smart S.O.B., is a good judge of leadership talent. Of the skills and stamina needed for success in any field of endeavor.

In running a business in corporate USA.

In running a state, any of the fifty in the USA.

In running a nation, the USA or any other.

The experience of building and managing a successful business enterprise in the private world gives special credentials for appraising the strength of leadership in the public world.

Especially if the appraisal is built upon eyeball-to-eyeball conversations across the desk or coffee table of the public leaders on their home turf.

I had the unique chance to do that—firsthand talks with the governors of all fifty USA states, with the leaders of thirty-two foreign countries, and with the President of the United States, all within an eighteen month period.

As a lifelong journalist, I have had a window on the nation and the world in different jobs, with different views. But always as a reporter, always on the run. Always with just a fleeting glimpse through the window.

Finally, I had the opportunity to take a closer and longer look. And I did.

As the chairman of a major media company and as a working reporter I stayed clear of casting judgments on the politics, policies, and personalities of our leaders for nearly a half century.

Then, I presented news, not views.

Now, as a retired executive and a columnist and author, I feel free to air my opinions. Here, then, is my report card on leadership, at home and abroad.

"If you want to understand democracy, spend less time in the library with Plato, and more time on the bus with people."

SIMEON STRUNKSY
former editorial page editor of
The New York Times

RATING THE USA'S GOVERNORS

"The chairman of the nation's largest newspaper group, Al Neuharth, came to Boise on Monday. . . . he learned just how the governor likes his spuds."

IDAHO STATESMAN
Boise, Idaho, June 9, 1987

Our fifty USA governors are a dynamic and diverse bunch of leaders.

▷ Some show potential for higher office.

▷ Most fit nicely into their statehouse roles.

▷ Many bring distinctive styles to their jobs.

▷ A few ought to be voted out of office and into new careers.

▷ As a group, they are the most underrated and least understood public officials in the nation.

And generally they are the most undercovered by the national media, unless they are in trouble. Governors have, and former governors have had, great impact on the destiny of this nation. Yet much of the innovative leadership in states like Illinois and Iowa and Idaho are state secrets.

That no longer should be the way the media covers the country.

State boundaries have become blurred, as we have become truly one nation. Our focus on state leaders needs to be sharpened.

Our 34,905-mile BusCapade journey crisscrossing the USA confirmed our closeness on every highway and byway, at every stop from hamlet intersections to statehouse grounds.

Modern mobility has brought us together.

Media technology can help us know each other better.

Traveling lifestyles mean we can care more and share more. So we all must understand each other better.

Our talks with each governor reached particularly for better understanding of life and times in each state—the dreams and the difficulties, the highs and the lows, the problems and the hoped-for solutions.

Incidentally, through the years I have been registered variously as Democrat, Republican, and independent. When George Wallace began mounting a campaign for president as an Independent, I changed my Florida voter party registration from independent to "none." So my report card on each governor is without regard for party politics.

Now, based on my appraisal of the job each was doing for that state, here is my rating of the best, in alphabetical order.

Top Ten Governors

Jim Blanchard, 47, Michigan (D)
Bill Clinton, 43, Arkansas (D)
Steve Cowper, 51, Alaska (D)
Mario Cuomo, 57, New York (D)
George Deukmejian, 61, California (R)
Tom Kean, 54, New Jersey (R)
Kay Orr, 50, Nebraska (R)
William Donald Schaefer, 67, Maryland (D)
John Sununu, 50, New Hampshire (R)
Jim Thompson, 53, Illinois (R)

Seventeen of our governors have gone on to become president of the USA. In our early years, the governor's job was most often the stepping stone to the presidency. In recent times, both former presidents Carter and Reagan came to the White House via the statehouse.

When I asked Ronald Reagan about that background, he was emphatic:

"Being governor was the best training ground for this job."

It's likely that one or more of our present governors will find their way to the White House.

Several clearly are qualified to do so. But a number of considerations other than qualifications weigh heavily in our presidential process. Timing. Political party affiliation. Sex.

Weighing all factors, I consider these governors the most likely candidates to make a run for the White House someday, again in alphabetical order.

Presidential Possibilities

Bill Clinton, Arkansas (D)
Mario Cuomo, New York (D)
Tom Kean, New Jersey, (R)
Kay Orr, Nebraska (R)
Jim Thompson, Illinois (R)

The timetable: Clinton and Cuomo in the 1992 race. Kean, Orr, and Thompson in 1996.

If you brush off the reference to Kay Orr, you're probably either a sexist or politically uninformed.

Orr is now one of only three female governors. She's the first woman elected to statewide office in Nebraska—state treasurer in 1982. Elected first female governor in Nebraska, 1986. Named first female to chair the Republican Platform Committee at the 1988 GOP convention.

While the media focuses on females on the east or west coasts, Kay Orr is becoming a midwestern political power. I wouldn't bet the rent money on her becoming President, but at age fifty she's a female with a political future.

I would bet my rent money that a certain number of present governors will never end up in the Oval office. In fact, I'm amazed at how several of them got into the statehouse.

In Over Their Heads

With sympathy but sincerity, my list of those governors who aren't up to the job:

▷ Bill Clements, Jr., 72, Texas (R)

An old-style Texas governor with new-style Texas problems. He's on record as calling the state legislators a "bunch of idiots." Not the way a modern governor can solve Texas problems of illegal aliens, drug trafficking, the impact of the oil recession.

▷ Rose Mofford, 67, Arizona (D)

Probably few who voted for her for Secretary of State would have voted for her as governor. And, they're unlikely to do so if given a chance. A political accident who happened to be first in the line of succession as Secretary of State when Governor Evan Mecham was impeached.

▷ Rudy Perpich, 61, Minnesota (DFL)

A lot of governors told us why they weren't going to run for President. Perpich told us why he might. He thinks people across the USA would welcome another Minnesota presidential candidate, pointing to fellow Minnesotans Eugene McCarthy, Walter Mondale, and especially Hubert Humphrey. I know McCarthy and Mondale, and knew Humphrey very well. Perpich, a dental surgeon, is no Humphrey, or Mondale, or McCarthy.

Other Glimpses of Governors

▷ Most accessible: Governor Ted Schwinden, 64, of Montana lists his home phone number in the telephone book. "The average Montanan feels very little hesitation in picking up the phone and telling me exactly what they think or don't think about something I do," Schwinden told us. He likes getting those calls at home, night or day. His telephone number is (406) 442-1262. His term expired in 1989, but he still lists that number in the book and takes calls from friends and strangers alike.

▷ Most disarming: Governor Roy Romer, 60, of Colorado insists on sitting with visitors at a small table. Gesturing at the governor's desk, he said, "I don't like that big desk. It's an imposing barrier. It makes me feel separated from people."

▷ Most blunt: Governor William D. Schaefer of Maryland is a polished politician, but he says what he thinks. "I'm not loved by the media because if I don't like what they're saying, I don't mind telling them."

▷ Driest wit: Governor John Sununu of New Hampshire, now Chief of Staff to President Bush. When I asked him if it is fair for the New Hampshire primary to have such a tremendous impact on the presidential political process, he quipped, "I just assumed that's the way God intended it to be."

▷ Most casual: Governor Mike Sullivan, 50, of Wyoming met our news team at the door of the governor's residence wearing cowboy boots, a Western shirt and blue jeans. "We can do this interview anywhere you want to," he said. "We can sit around this coffee table in here. Or we can go outside, sit in the sun with the dog, and do it out there." We went for the sun and the dog.

▷ Lowest-key: Swiss-born Governor Madeleine Kunin, 56, of Vermont has a style that quickly turns an interview into a quiet, candid conversation. The picture of calm, classy competence.

▷ Most outspoken: Former Governor Evan Mecham, 65, of Arizona got into hot water with the public when he rescinded the state holiday for the Reverend Martin Luther King's birthday. He later said he considered "pickaninny" for black children "a term of endearment."

Was that controversy hurting Arizona? I asked. "Not in the least," he said. "There isn't one person in 10,000 who cares what our politics are who wants to come to Arizona."

▷ Most outrageous: Former Governor Edwin Edwards, 62, of Louisiana was the picture of confidence when he entertained us at a lunch of cajun food at the mansion.

He loved his notoriety: "Call me colorful, controversial, brash—anything but modest," Edwards told us. "The only way I could lose the next election is if I was caught in bed with a dead woman or a live boy." He did lose the next election with a dismal primary showing.

That brings me to my report card on the USA and its people.

A-plus.

No one could feel otherwise after a trip that covered so much of the USA, talked with so many of our people, heard so much hope, saw so much ability, sensed so much spirit.

The USA of the late 1980s is still the same land of hope and opportunity it was fifty years ago when I was growing up during the Dustbowl Days in South Dakota.

Even more so. And more and more people all across the USA realize the entire country is still a frontier, with unlimited opportunity for individual and collective achievement.

That's true for those who run our statehouses and it's true in every house across the land.

Of course, we are a nation of different problems, different solutions, different goals.

But as a people, we are truly one nation.

PLAIN TALK:

Political potential thrives beyond the Potomac.

THE WHOLE WORLD IN OUR HANDS

"His jet aircraft, famous name, and persistence opened the doors for Neuharth around the globe . . . to the poorest quarters and to the presidential palaces."

LITERATURNAYA GAZETA
Moscow, August 31, 1988

Judging the job that a foreign head of state is doing is more difficult than appraising the performance of a governor or president in the USA.

Leaders, and their followers, on different continents have different mindsets and morals, histories and traditions, ideas and ambitions.

Prime Minister Lee Kuan Yew of Singapore gave me this caution:

"This is a plea. Don't believe that what has worked in America must work elsewhere. Yes, we are all human beings. But we are different kinds of human beings. The more you judge others by your own standards, the more you show total disregard for their circumstances."

Lee's warning was echoed in many ways by many around the world.

I also kept in mind, as a USA citizen and as a journalist, our nation's historic commitment to the right of self-determination and human rights. We can never turn our backs on violations of these.

So all of us writing about and working on our global concerns must stand up for the principles of a free people in a free world.

But we cannot let ourselves mix our dream world with the

real world. We must stand on our principles, but also understand the practical realities.

Accordingly, I kept an open mind to the problems and achievements of each head of state. I observed the mood as well as the messages from people in the street and those in the palaces of power.

The true test of any political leader is what kind of job he or she is doing for the country and its people. The question frequently heard in USA presidential elections offered a good standard around the world: "Are you better off today than you were?"

The range of report cards for foreign leaders is wider than that for those in the USA. A handful or two are truly outstanding. A small number hopelessly in over their heads. A much larger number of adequate or average performers.

Based on what I have seen, heard and felt, this is my list of the 10 leaders outside the USA who deserve the best report cards, in alphabetical order by country.

Top Ten Heads of State

Australian Prime Minister Bob Hawke, 59.
Canadian Prime Minister Brian Mulroney, 50.
Egyptian President Hosni Mubarak, 61.
French President François Mitterrand, 72.
Singapore Prime Minister Lee Kuan Yew, 66.
Spanish Prime Minister Felipe Gonzalez, 47.
USSR General Secretary Mikhail Gorbachev, 58.
UK Prime Minister Margaret Thatcher, 64.
Vatican Pope John Paul II, 69.
West German Chancellor Helmut Kohl, 59.

China's Communist Party General Secretary Zhao Ziyang was on that list until he was unseated following the 1989 uprisings and martial law in Beijing.

Now China must stabilize its leadership at home before it can play on the world stage. Not likely in this century.

Since no leader of the whole world will be elected—at least in your lifetime or mine—listing the kind of presidential material I did with the governors would serve no purpose.

But more regional powers will emerge. The area to watch

is Western Europe. A new world power broker could surface there in the nineties.

When the twelve-country European Community is officially in place by 1992, it could have economic and political clout about equal to these regional neighbors:

▷ The USA and Canada combined.

▷ The USSR and entire Eastern European bloc.

▷ Japan and all of the Pacific.

Small wonder that three of Western Europe's leaders now have one eye on running their country, the other on unofficially running for unofficial "President of Europe." They don't use that title, but that's their goal.

France's President François Mitterrand expressed it this way when I helicoptered with him from Paris to Normandy on the forty-fourth anniversary of D-Day, June 6, 1988:

"We must use the might Europe will derive from its independence and unity—the European Community—in 1992. Many think the Community is just an economic union. It goes much further. It will enable Europe to speak with a single voice on world affairs."

Mitterrand wants that voice to be his. West German Chancellor Helmut Kohl would nominate himself. And Britain's Prime Minister Margaret Thatcher thinks she's the one.

Listen to what they told me:

Thatcher: "We're coming up to a time when I hope my cumulative experience will help the whole of the free world. I hope that doesn't sound pretentious—it's not meant that way."

Kohl: "President Mitterrand and I are of the opinion we would like to bring about political integration. There are some differences when we talk with Margaret Thatcher about political unity. Right now I aim at 1992."

Whether, or when, an undisputed champion for all of Europe emerges is questionable. But if that happens, here's my early line on the candidates:

▷ Mitterrand is likely to be too old. He's seventy-two at the time of this writing (1989).

▷ Kohl's German heritage precludes his ever being totally trusted by the rest of Europe.

▷ Thatcher might make it, despite her present differences with Mitterrand, Kohl, and others over NATO and some economic and political issues.

The sharp and steely lady has ten years of infighting experience as Britain's longest-reigning prime minister of this century. She's every bit as smart as and probably tougher than either Kohl or Mitterrand.

"You need a thug to fight her," warns former Prime Minister Harold Wilson.

Now sixty-four, Thatcher has her eyes on the future. "I'm always looking ahead. I'll be looking ahead until the day I die," she told me in her No. 10 Downing Street office.

Despite the ambitions of this trio, a single European leader with the worldwide clout of the head of the USA or the USSR seems doubtful in this century.

It's much easier to forecast the future for a handful of heads of state who are more likely to go down or out than up.

I put some on that list with sympathy, because they inherited seemingly ungovernable countries or insurmountable problems. Others won't make it because of problems of their own creation.

In over Their Heads

Greek Prime Minister Andreas Papandreou, 70.
India Prime Minister Rajiv Gandhi, 45.
Israel Prime Minister Yitzhak Shamir, 74.
Japan Prime Minister Noboru Takeshita, 65.
Philippine President Corazon Aquino, 56.

One judgment became apparent in Japan in April of 1989 when Takeshita announced his resignation. Another when Papandreou's party lost the June 1989 elections in Greece.

I wish the other three people on that list hadn't made it, because I have very positive personal feelings for them. I just don't think they can do the job. Two of them don't have enough S.O.B. in them. One has too much. The three:

▷ President Aquino is a bubbly, bouncy five-foot-two-inch mother of five. To know her is to like her. Her husband's assassination was the key to her ascending to a job that is too big for her.

She simply is not prepared by either experience or expertise to lead the Philippines out of the morass in which predecessor Ferdinand Marcos left it.

▷ India's Gandhi is Aquino's male counterpart. Courteous, soft-spoken gentleman. He didn't want his job. His love is flying airplanes. Was propelled into the prime minister's post in 1984 when his mother, Indira Gandhi, was assassinated by her own guards.

When I asked him how he stands the pressure of trying to govern 800 million people—nearly 40 percent of whom are below the poverty line—he replied: "I don't think of myself as prime minister." That may explain his problem in trying to govern.

▷ Israel's Shamir is the toughest foreign leader I met. His thinking reflects his years as one of three leaders of the Stern Gang, the underground terrorist organization seeking the ouster of the British occupiers of Palestine four decades ago.

If I were looking for a steely S.O.B. to lead me in battle, I'd pick a younger Shamir. But at age seventy-four, he can't adjust to a Middle East situation where diplomacy is the solution.

Two Fascinating S.O.B.s

Other glimpses of global leaders must include two who don't make either list. But they're the most fascinating because they represent the extremes of the communist left and of the fascist right.

▷ Cuba's President Fidel Castro, 62.

▷ South Africa's President Pieter Willem Botha, 73.

The way they run their offices and schedules tells you a lot about both of these S.O.B.s.

Most of my meetings with heads of state were scheduled well in advance, at a particular time and place, to fit their busy schedules and my globe-hopping agenda.

Not Castro and Botha.

We had crisscrossed Cuba, quite freely, for days before we knew whether Castro would see us. At 9:50 P.M. the night before our scheduled departure, the telephone call came to La Habana Libre, formerly the Hilton Hotel, in the heart of Havana.

"The President has granted your request for an interview. Be downstairs in the lobby in five minutes."

Castro greeted us in his familiar military fatigues. We didn't know whether it would be a five-minute courtesy call or a substantive interview session. Neither did he, until he sized us up.

He clearly had been well briefed.

"I hear your newspaper *USA TODAY* lost money for five years. How did you pay the bill?" he asked.

I told him that for more than four years *USA TODAY* was subsidized by other profitable Gannett operations.

"Aha!" Castro laughed. "So your company and my country are both socialistic!"

If I'd argued the point, I think the interview would have been over. But I laughed with him.

Six hours later, at 4 A.M., after listening to a fascinating mix of lies and truths, sharing Cuban coffee and rum, we said goodbye.

He answered every question I asked except this one:

"Was it your idea or Khrushchev's to have Soviet missiles in Cuba?"

Castro paused. "I'm saving that for my memoirs."

Botha kept us dangling as Castro had, but even longer. Months of requests for visas to enter South Africa and for the interview were stonewalled.

We pressed hardest when we were in Kenya for a week's tour—only a three and a half hour flight to South Africa. No luck.

A month later, when we were enjoying a two day break on the beaches and among the beauties of Tahiti in the South Pacific, the call came through at 3 A.M. Tahiti time.

"President Botha will see you if you can be in Cape Town at 2 P.M. the day after tomorrow."

We made it. After a 13,778-mile trip.

Botha opened the door to his office at exactly 2 P.M. He posed with us for pictures for two minutes, then asked our photographer to leave.

His principal message in an hour's interview:

"Most of the politicians and press from the United States are mere mischief makers when it comes to my country."

Not only did we visit with heads of state, but also heads of households, bankers and beggars, lawmakers and lawbreakers, young and old, rich and poor.

Inescapable impressions from JetCapading thirty-two countries on six continents:

▷ The world has indeed become a huge global village, as Marshal McLuhan predicted in 1964.

▷ There are few mysteries, even in the most remote gullies of the globe.

▷ We are linked electronically, economically, sometimes emotionally, country to country and continent to continent.

▷ Pragmatism is the politics that pilots today's world, prevailing over both capitalism and communism.

▷ Materialism is the medium of the rich and poor, the young and old, mastering most spiritual and intellectual values.

▷ The media, thanks to instant satellite communication, is the harness that hitches it all together.

Political leaders of most of these countries once had impact on only the citizens of their country. Now most of them are players on the global stage.

The good guys and the bad guys and the in-between differ in style and approach. But where and when it really counts, the goals are pretty much the same. Peace and prosperity.

We are *nearly* one world.

PLAIN TALK:

In today's world, we're all neighbors, not foreigners.

X

THE SUBSTANCE OF STYLE

"The style is the man."

ROBERT FROST
USA poet

Style is an often overlooked part of leadership and living.

I always use my own style to dramatize my ideas, my plans, my expectations.

Whether I am writing a memo or traveling the globe, I expect my style to help communicate my ideas.

People remember style as much as substance.

Plain talk and clear writing are part of my style. So is first class living and traveling. I've never left either to chance.

Most people hear selectively. Remembering what they like. Forgetting what they don't. And then saying "I don't remember your saying that."

Nobody can tell me that. Because if it is important, I put it in writing. And in the files. Nothing can replace a straight, blunt memo.

During my years as a boss, I wrote a steady stream of memos and letters. I averaged an hour or more daily on these notes. Probably my most important task each day. They worked in special ways:

▷ Most were short, less than a page.
▷ They dealt with big deals and small details.

▷ They applauded and kicked ass with equal vigor.

Recipients showed off the congratulatory ones, took them home, saved them. Many tore up the critical ones or stuffed them in a drawer. Either way, they remembered them. And so did I.

All my internal memos are on distinctive peach-colored paper and in peach envelopes. The color is not important, but the distinctive look lets the memo from the boss get noticed quickly.

I'm as open about my personal preferences as I am about the professional. Fun and business can go together if they are planned properly. Leaving things to chance produces unnecessarily uneven results at work or play.

"Good communication is as stimulating as black coffee, and just as hard to sleep after."

ANNE MORROW LINDBERGH
USA author

FIRST CLASS IS
MORE FUN

*"If Al Neuharth really ever does retire, I
have a stock tip. If you own any Cristal
champagne stock, sell it short."*

TOM BROKAW
NBC news anchor

Up-tight managements run no-fun and no-win businesses.

CEOs who try to run a company on the cheap end up
having a cheap company.

Dull people lead unhappy lives.

All my life, I've insisted on having fun. Even as a poor kid
growing up in South Dakota. I couldn't afford much else, but I
could afford to laugh. And I did. A lot.

Fun doesn't require wealth. It depends on an outlook—
taking what comes your way and making the most of it. Enjoying
it.

If you learn to have fun when you're going second class,
you can have a helluva lot more of it in first class. And, that's
what I've been doing most of my adult life.

I've caught a lot of flak for my first-class tastes from my
critics and even from some cheapskate co-workers. They didn't
understand what my perks and privileges as a CEO meant,
professionally and personally:

▷ A $17 million Gulfstream IV jet, equipped with typewriters, television sets, and a shower, to fly me where I needed to
go on business anywhere in the world.

▷ Limousines and drivers at every destination to allow me
to work or visit with colleagues while on the move.

▷ A $360,000-a-year nine-room hotel suite in the Waldorf
Towers in New York City and a $160,000 suite at the Capital
Hilton in Washington, in which to do business with pleasure.

My philosophy, policy, and style always have been that first class only costs a few dollars more and is a smart investment for a smart company on the climb.

Some critics also have preached at me to quit playing practical jokes and to be more properly serious.

I've laughed at them all. Sooner or later, most have laughed with me.

We never could have made it through the toughest days of starting *USA TODAY* if we hadn't learned to laugh, usually at ourselves.

If you don't know how to loosen up, you're much more likely to choke up under pressure.

The key to staying loose, having fun, and being effective at work or play is to start your day right and bright.

Working hours may vary. But whenever your day begins, how you start it is important.

Here's how I started most of my days during the thirteen years I was CEO of Gannett:

▷ 4:45 to 5 A.M.—Wakeup.

▷ 5 to 6:30 A.M.—Reading newspapers, with orange juice and decaf coffee.

▷ 6:30 to 7:30 A.M.—Exercise and jogging. Preceded by a stop at my beachside chapel when I'm at Pumpkin Center.

▷ 7:30 to 8:15 A.M.—Shower, shave, dress, light breakfast, while watching TV news.

By 8:30 or so I was at my desk—at Pumpkin Center, Washington, New York, or anywhere on the globe. My mind was working, my blood pumping—feeling great, mentally and physically.

That put me at an advantage over most of my coworkers or competitors.

There weren't many Dagwood Bumsteads in Gannett. But that comic strip can teach you a lot about how not to get ahead in the business world.

Blondie has to pull Dagwood out of bed. Help him dress. Feed him with his eyes still closed. Shove him out the door to catch his bus. And that's why he's never amounted to much.

If you dread going to work in the morning, you're in the wrong job.

I've never had a job I didn't want to get up for and get at.

Even in Army training during World War II, I welcomed reveille every morning. I wasn't all that crazy about combat later in Europe. But I wanted to get that job over with also.

Even though I always welcome going to work, I play as hard as I work. Often, the two go hand in hand.

Regular exercise, like my daily jogging, is considered monotonous work by some. I consider it playing at very worthwhile work.

I've been a bit of a fitness nut ever since I left the Army at age 22 in 1946. But I got really serious—some say obsessed—at age 47. That year doctors discovered during my annual physical that I had developed a heart irregularity. Atrial fibrillation. They tried an electric conversion but it didn't work.

"You're going to have to live with it," the doctor said. "And you could live with it for another fifty years if you really take care of yourself. That means especially watching your diet and regular exercise."

My daily jog became a must. I increased my normal distance gradually from three miles to five. Reduced the speed, but increased the distance.

As a result, I've felt better physically in my fifties and sixties than I did in my forties.

Feeling good physically is important to your mental well-being, as well as your productiveness and happiness.

Sluggish Body, Sluggish Mind

I've never hired or promoted anyone in an important position who was grossly overweight. A sluggish body usually supports a sluggish mind. It also indicates a lack of self-discipline.

Most people want weight control made easy for them. There is no easy way, long-term. You have to work hard and play hard at it.

At Gannett and *USA TODAY* headquarters in Washington, we encourage fitness with a Health/Works center for all employees. Corporations that invest in health centers for employees and day-care centers for children of employees are making a smart investment in physical and mental well-being.

At Gannett, because we do business in all fifty states and our executives travel a lot, I encouraged everyone to take care of their bodies both at home and away.

I set the example. Most people, when they travel a lot, gain weight because they eat and drink more and exercise less.

During my six-month BusCapade visit to all fifty states in 1987, I lost two pounds. In 1988, during my eight-month Jet-Capade to thirty-two countries covering 148,261 airmiles, I lost five pounds.

A rigid exercise routine does not mean you can't enjoy the good life. Just the opposite. You can indulge in the best, occasionally rich food, and drink the best wines if you counteract that by burning up the calories you've consumed.

That's important to me. First-class restaurants, suites in first-class hotels, are as important to me as the limousines or jets that get me there.

Some of my critics keep pointing to that as unnecessary Neuharth indulgences. Indulgences, yes. But not unnecessary. They help me do a better job.

What they don't understand is that I work while I'm enjoying those indulgences. My limos have a typewriter, a telephone, a TV set to keep up with news developments.

The minute I walk into a hotel suite, I check my office arrangement. My secretaries plan ahead with hotel management to make sure one of the rooms is set up with a big desk, proper lighting, television, and telephones properly located. The minute we arrive, my secretary adds my typewriter, copy paper, paper clips, rubber bands.

Whether I arrive at 3 A.M. in Singapore or 3 P.M. in Paris, I have an instant office. I hurry to get my work out of the way, so that I can play.

I've stayed in hundreds of hotels and motels across the USA and around the world. My list of best hotels is based on hospitality, facilities, services they offered, and how they reacted to my special requests.

World's Top Ten Hotels

1. Dolder Grand, Zürich, Switzerland.
2. Plaza Athenee, Paris.
3. L'Ermitage, Beverly Hills.
4. The Mansion on Turtle Creek, Dallas.
5. Las Brisas, Acapulco, Mexico.
6. Kahala Hilton, Honolulu.
7. The Grand Hotel, Stockholm.
8. Harrah's, Lake Tahoe, Nevada.
9. Mount Nelson, Cape Town, South Africa.
10. Sylvan Lake Lodge, in the Black Hills of South Dakota.

With Donald Trump's money and Ivana Trump's ingenuity and style, the Plaza in New York will likely be on that list soon.

Some hotels I've used fell far short of living up to their reputation. That doesn't mean they're bad, just not nearly as good as their billing, or their big bill.

World's Most Overrated Hotels

1. Claridge's, London.
2. The Waldorf, New York.
3. Caneel Bay, St. John, the U.S. Virgin Islands.
4. King David Hotel, Jerusalem.
5. The Ritz, Boston.

The Waldorf on my overrated list requires explanation, because I've referred often to the suite there at which a lot of major Gannett business took place.

That's the Waldorf Towers, which is part of, but distinctly different from, the Waldorf Hotel.

Even the Towers is not five-star in rooms and service. But our Gannett suite was totally remodeled and refurnished in a pretty fancy way by us at our expense for business office use and business entertaining. Because it's at a good location in New York, it served that purpose well.

While I prefer first-class accommodations,' I have often found myself in pretty crummy places and I've laughed and enjoyed them.

Two examples, one from my nationwide BusCapade in 1987 and one on my worldwide JetCapade in 1988:

▷ The Best Western motel in Gallup, New Mexico. A remote cowboy-and-Indian hangout. But I enjoyed the local flavor and kidded my coworkers to get into the spirit. Those who did had fun.

▷ The government guest house in Hanoi, Vietnam. Next to the Ngo Queyn presidential palace and Lake Hoan Kiem, this was a fly- and mosquito-infested, rundown, dormitory-style facility. But it was the best the Vietnamese government had to offer.

For three nights we slept under mosquito nets in steamy rooms. But I told my JetCapade associates this was a helluva lot better than conditions for the servicemen who fought in Vietnam for us. Most of my companions got in the right frame of mind and benefited from the experience.

How to Avoid Burnout

Whether at home or away, I take care of myself.

Executives who pride themselves on hard work but ignore fun and fitness are candidates for career burnout.

People ask me why I appear so relaxed after a long day of work or days of travel: It's simple. Be very particular about what you put into your body and how you use it. You too can feel great if you:

▷ Eat only when you're hungry.
▷ Drink only when you're thirsty.
▷ Sleep only when you're tired.
▷ Screw only when you're horny.

There may be more scientific ways to achieve fun and fitness in a first-class way, but I haven't found them yet.

PLAIN TALK:

Enjoy it all while you can.

LOVE LETTERS: PLAIN TALK

"Al wrote memos on little pieces of orange paper. They contained brief but powerful messages. 'Please fix,' many of them said. Others I have erased from my memory in order to preserve my self-esteem."

DICK DOUGHERTY
editor and columnist,
Gannett Rochester Newspapers

Too often CEOs act more like politicians than like bosses. Employees do not want to be wooed.

They don't want soft soap.

They like plain talk.

And as Gannett CEO I delivered plenty of it—in writing.

I called my memos on peach-colored paper Love Letters whether they were tender or tough.

Some of the irreverent recipients called them "Orange Meanies." I didn't consider them mean. They helped people do a better job. Sure, I sometimes used tough language and I got pretty personal.

I wasn't trying to win a popularity contest. What I wanted was results.

The memo system worked for me from my earliest days as a manager. And they became a badge of honor around Gannett. A peach-colored envelope on your desk meant the CEO had noticed you.

The tough tone of some notes had nothing to do with my personal feelings. My closest colleagues frequently received the severest notes.

The start-up and progress of *USA TODAY* required some of my strongest and most direct memos. More than a thousand people had to be pushed and pulled in the same direction every day. My notes established the goals and expectations so there could be no misunderstanding up or down the line.

I have great respect for the top players at *USA TODAY,* but it never kept me from berating them if I thought they did something stupid.

John C. Quinn, editor-in-chief of *USA TODAY* and my closest professional colleague, got the brunt of these notes. So did John Curley, founding editor and now Gannett CEO; Ron Martin, then executive editor; John Seigenthaler, editorial director; and Henry Freeman, managing editor/sports.

Editing the Editors

To John Quinn, Henry Freeman:
Dammit! After two years, can't we find someone on the Page One desk who can add and subtract? And can't we find someone in the sports department who can read and think and double-check things?!
Screwing up the World Series schedule as we did in Rudy Martzke's Page One story today is absolutely inexcusable.
Unless we can figure out a fool-proof system to have this sort of thing done right, you will find me back haunting all of you in the Sports Department and on the Page One desk every night, pretty damn soon.

To John Quinn:
Do you think you owe me either some quick results or a quick explanation on the continuing farting around with the weather map of the *USA TODAY* International edition!
I do!
If you're still in charge, I'll appreciate some reaction to my suggestions and some action.

To John Seigenthaler et al.:
I am tempted to propose a new category for Pulitzer Prizes—dumbest editorial judgment of the year.

In such a category, I would nominate today's *USA TODAY* editorial on the Philippine elections. Not just for this year—dumbest judgment in our three and a half years of publication.

We decided we would not endorse a candidate for president of the USA. So we endorse a candidate in the Philippine presidential election!

Of course, we should editorialize for fair and free elections in the Philippines. But for us to take sides as we did today makes me wonder if we're beginning to forget what *USA TODAY* is all about.

I'm not about to forget that. I hope this memo will jar you and your associates back on the right track.

To John Quinn, Ron Martin et al.:

I'll explain it one more time, Geography 101:

America is made up of Canada, the United States of America, Central America, South America, and more (see attached map).

The USA is made up of the United States of America. All fifty of them. And its territories. No more. No less.

Any poll, any news story (like today's Life section stuff) which refers broadly to Americans, when it really means the people of the United States of America, is a subterfuge. It represents inexcusably sloppy reporting and editing.

Perhaps equally important, it flies in the face of the philosophy, policy and style clearly spelled out by the founder of *USA TODAY* from day one. In our news columns, it is *never* appropriate to refer to America or Americans *unless* we mean *all* of the Americas or *all* Americans. It is *always* appropriate to refer to the USA when we mean the United States of America.

One more time, please make sure all editors understand. If anyone does not, I'll be happy to arrange a transfer for him/her to Calgary, or Cuzco, or Curitiba so that he/she can practice journalism for a different audience in the other Americas than that which we serve in the United States of America—the USA.

Motivating the Marketeers

Most of my notes were written because people did not do as well as I expected or they failed to follow through on plans. I monitored the advertising and circulation folks closely because they had a way of saying all the right things in a meeting but not always following up.

Two frequent recipients were publisher Cathie Black, who oversaw advertising, and Frank Vega, *USA TODAY*'s first vice president of circulation.

To Cathie Black:

I know you are busy, BUT I have had no response to my memo asking you how we are doing with Hilton and Procter & Gamble.

My Hilton question and the answer are important because I will be with Barron Hilton Saturday evening in Washington and I want to know what I am talking about.

In fact, all my memos and questions are important, or I wouldn't send them or ask them. Therefore, quick action by you is important and expected. Please fix.

To Cathie Black:

After my constant preaching about the importance of the presentation of our ads, and after your assuring me that you had allegedly fixed the alphabetizing of the lines in classified, how much longer am I going to have to wait before you get it done so that it will stay done?

Don't you care how often you screw things up?

To Frank Vega:

This morning, at 9:00 A.M., the vending machine kitty-corner across from the White House at Pennsylvania and Executive Avenue still had yesterday's *USA TODAY* in the window and in the box.

Directly across the street, the vending machine had its door ripped off, stashed along the side, and the machine was empty. This is the second consecutive day it has been in this condition. I did not report it yesterday because I wanted to see how quickly your efficient street crew would repair it.

This is one helluva impression to make on those hundreds who mill around the White House every day, and many of whom get their first impression of *USA TODAY* on those street corners.

Some swift and solid ass-kicking is necessary around here. I have started mine. Now it's your turn.

Spelling Out What's Expected

I make no apologies for my first-class lifestyle.

My colleagues understand that I expect my personal life to be as ordered and organized as my professional life. In fact, in my years as CEO and chairman, I didn't have a separate personal life.

I considered all of my activities an extension of the job. My daily routine required absolute efficiency to increase results for the company and me.

This meant devoting attention to details and standards. If colleagues couldn't get the little things associated with me right, how could they expect to do the big things?

The people with whom I worked the closest knew my expectations. But because I traveled extensively, I spelled out to Gannett publishers my requirements. It saved me a lot of time, helped get the details right and made me a better CEO and a more satisfied S.O.B.

To Gannett Publishers:

Based on our travels for regional or subsidiary meetings of recent weeks and in view all of us will be doing even more such in the future . . .

Here are some purely personal preferences and/ or prejudices which, if catered to, will make me even more charming and effective on these visits:

1. When arriving at local airport, I like to be met

by publisher himself or herself. That permits business talk enroute office or motel-hotel.

2. We should not waste time checking into and out of hotels. Preregistration, keys, billings, etc., should all be arranged.

3. A suite is essential for me so that I can have any desired business meetings without guests or associates sitting on bed or floor.

4. That suite should contain latest editions of local newspapers. Ice and fruit helps. Booze is not necessary, but a bottle of Montrachet or Pouilly-Fuissé wine never hurt anybody.

5. Enroute to office, I need list of names of persons I will be seeing first—starting with receptionist and/or publisher's secretary. This, of course, should include the department heads with whom we'll be meeting. Noting any recent important personal items about any of them helps.

6. The meeting room must include the last week's editions of the local newspaper.

7. *If,* in the infinite and autonomous wisdom of the local editor or publisher, an interview is desired with me, okay. But, it is a waste of time for all to have most recent recruit off the street do the interview. If it's worth doing, it's worth having reasonably intelligent reporter with some knowledge of Ganett [sic] and Newhart [sic] do the interviewing.

8. For social functions, advance list of attendees with first names is essential. A notation about babies, birthdays, anniversaries, girlfriends, boyfriends, etc., helps. Nametags are a must.

9. Breakfast meetings are a waste of time for me. I prefer those early morning hours for jogging, reading morning papers, telephone calls, and preparation for the day's meetings and/or travels.

10. Whether we publish a morning paper in that city or not, a copy of the nearest a.m. publication (including *The Wall Street Journal,* if possible) should be at the hotel room door before 6 A.M. No questions will be asked as to whether the publisher or circulation

manager delivered it on the way home from saloon or on the way to work.

Yours for even happier Holiday Inning . . .

To All Operating Committee Members:

Once upon a time, it was decided that certain high standards would be established and maintained at Gannett subsidiary meetings.

Included were morning newspaper delivery at everyone's door no later than 6 A.M., wherever we meet.

Also included was dining well. If there are local delicacies at meeting sites, those are to be served. If not, we are to stick to simple things like steaks.

In Olympia last week, no morning newspapers were delivered.

And in Olympia, the salmon capital of the world, Veal Parmesan (not very good Veal Parmesan) was served for dinner.

Please fix.

To Jack Gallagher [director of flight operations]:

Once again, our crew members have fallen into the pattern of concerning themselves only with what works in the cockpit, not what works for the passengers.

Examples:

▷ Last Thursday, on a flight from Washington to San Francisco when I needed to shower and get pretty for a dinner speech on arrival, there was only cold water in the rear compartment. Inexcusable.

▷ Last Friday, when we flew from Reno to Florida, the toilet in the rear compartment did not flush. Inexcusable.

▷ On Sunday, from Florida to Washington, the TV sets were all malfunctioning or not functioning at all. Inexcusable.

For the last time, I emphasize that the comfort and convenience of passengers on our airplanes is every bit as important as the comfort and operating ability of our crews.

You have run out of excuses. If you understand what I am saying, please fix. If you do not, please ask.

To John Curley:

Since the Gannett gals at Tower II objected to the two artistic partially nude female statues that were temporarily around the fountain in the dining room on the 30th floor and which are now hidden in a storeroom, I'm going to have those moved to the Gannett conference center at Pumpkin Center. There no one will object to their presence, especially next to my bathtub.

I've asked designer Barbara Whitney to get us a nice little boy statue to sit around the fountain in the Tower II dining room. I've told her to make sure the kid has some clothes on and that no ding dong or anything else offensive to our feminist friends is showing.

Parceling Out Praise

I wrote many positive, pleasant notes over the years. And those got noticed, too. Because I didn't overdo the praise, it had more impact as I parceled it out sparingly. The same *USA TODAY* people who got their share of orange meanies also remember bouquets along the way.

Former bosses like to be kept in mind. Despite our differences when he was still active, I often wrote or telephoned my predecessor Paul Miller after his retirement.

To John Quinn, Ron Martin:

Our coverage this morning of the presidential debate was unequaled by anyone else anywhere—in print or on the air. And that's not debatable.

The main story, the poll, the page 4 report, the entire package was superb both in concept and presentation.

Whoever wrote the page 1 headline "Who won? It's debatable" deserves a bonus.

To Cathie Black:

You done good this week!

Your preparation and participation in the Gannett year-end meetings were superb in every instance. You made many, many good impressions on many people.

I am more and more delighted that you are aboard and I am considering giving *myself* an additional year-end bonus for having hired you!

To Paul Miller
Palm Beach, Florida

Dear PM:

Over and over, I keep running into reminders of some of the really great moves you made when you were running this joint.

Not the least of which is the reminder this week that if you had not taken us into San Bernardino we would not have been in the great position we are in to launch *USA TODAY* in the Los Angeles market.

Just wanted you to know that we keep thinking about you and thanking you over and over. Cheers to you and Louise.

Back Talk

My daily dose of Love Letters provoked many in return. And in kind—both nasty and nice. But all good reading.

I read all my mail, thousands of letters through the years, mostly from readers criticizing or complimenting our newspapers. I replied myself or made sure an executive closer to the point of the letter made a personal response.

Some of the most meaningful mail came from colleagues, and even competitors, past and present. Kind comments from those with whom I have shared some rough times may surprise many as they did me.

▷ *From my favorite and frequently berated bean counter,*
Doug McCorkindale:

> Al:
> Your board resignation was a shock. Over the
> years, I think we made one of the best teams ever.
> I learned much from you, which can only help
> me in the future. But without you it will not be the
> same and maybe not as much fun. You're the best!

▷ *From Karl Eller, the S.O.B. who tried to steal my job:*

> Dear Al:
> It has been about a year and I know the dust has
> settled down, so I thought it would be wise for me to
> write you a little note to congratulate you on the recent
> stock split and the increase in the dividend. I really
> appreciate the performance of Gannett stock.

▷ *From Paul T. Miller II, son of the former boss I bested:*

> Dear Al:
> Your event for Dad (eightieth-birthday party)
> came off without a hitch, naturally, and Cass and I and
> my brothers and sisters will always be grateful, both
> for the Paul Miller fellowships and for your making it
> such a delightful evening.
> Also it was terrific sending us tapes of the evening.
> I think that's extremely important for Dad as it will
> help reinforce yours, and the others', comments.

Some of the best women in the newspaper business joined
Gannett for the equal opportunity to move up in management.
They also got equal treatment from me with their share of nasty
and nice notes. They took their battle scars in stride.

▷ *From Cathie Black,* USA TODAY *publisher:*

> Dear Al:
> The last five years have been very rewarding. You
> delivered on your promises and set a tone of leader-

ship and vision that will be a hard act to follow. I've enjoyed watching your style, determination, guts, and passion. I've learned an enormous amount from you and I've had a helluva lot of fun, too!

▷ *From Valerie Salembier, former senior vice president/ advertising for* USA TODAY *and later publisher of* TV Guide *and president of the* New York Post, *in a farewell note:*

Dear Al:
I have never been more challenged, pressed harder, or learned more than with this job. It is the most important career experience I have had and I will honor it always. Thanks for being an inspirational leader, a tough S.O.B., and a man who makes people dream bigger dreams.

Remembering your roots is important. And your former business associates. In the rush to get ahead, I tried to remember those who stayed behind. And it is gratifying to keep those contacts and to be remembered.

▷ *From Larry Berg of Huron, S.D., an investor in* SoDak Sports:

Dear Al:
There's no possible way I can begin to thank you for treating Michael and me the way you did at the Super Bowl. The Friday night party and your Sunday brunch were something we've never seen. Of course, the game itself was a treat we'll never forget. My small investment in *SoDak Sports* was the best thing I've ever done!

▷ *From Henry Clune, retired columnist, Rochester newspapers:*

Dear Al:
Among the larger tokens that came yesterday [his ninety-ninth birthday] was your delightful floral dis-

play. The florist who delivered it told Charlotte that to have a call on the telephone from you was the most exciting thing that had happened in Scottsville in months. I myself was pleased and honored to be so indulged by my old boss. My gratitude is profound.

The art of acquiring other people's newspapers can be touchy. But the right touch can lead to new warm relationships. Like this note from an acquiree.

▷ *From Mary Bingham, wife of Barry Bingham, Sr., of Louisville:*

> Dear Al,
> Thank you for all your kindness and thoughtfulness in making the final closing of the sale as easy and comfortable for Barry and me as it could be. The trip in your splendid jet, with its courteous, helpful crew, was an enormous convenience. Your sensitive awareness of the inevitable sadness for us of relinquishing the papers, your understanding of the wounding differences that exist between us and young Barry have made us feel that we have gained, in you, a true friend.

A little irreverence in the ranks never did a CEO any harm, especially if it helps build the blunt give-and-take necessary to get a tough job done.

▷ *From John Quinn, my most durable if not most diplomatic cohort:*

> AN—Thanks for your Merry Christmas orange meanie about this morning's page one.
> **BULLSHIT!**
> Happy New Year to you.

Author's Note: Quinn printed the **"BULLSHIT!"** with a rubber stamp, which I confiscated the next week. He also fixed Page One.

Sending Myself a Love Letter

One of my favorite love letters didn't even have my signature on it. I wrote it. To myself.

When I was traveling on BusCapade in 1987 in the upper Midwest, John Curley sent word that *USA TODAY* had turned a profit in May—earlier than we had projected.

I decided to have some fun with it.

I wrote myself a telegram and had Curley send it to me for receipt when BusCapade arrived in the Black Hills of my native South Dakota.

The orchestrated telegram allowed me to celebrate news of my biggest success on the sacred soil of South Dakota—33 years after fleeing there after my *SoDak Sports* failure.

> Al Neuharth
> BusCapade USA, Sylvan Lake Lodge
> Hill City, South Dakota
> Dear Al:
>
> McPaper has made it. *USA TODAY* broke into the black with a profit of $1,093,754 for the month of May, six months ahead of schedule. Staff betting you'll forgive us for ruining your prediction that we'd have to wait until the end of the year. Hope you'll fly back to Washington for a champagne celebration tomorrow.
>
> John Curley

That night, self-sent telegram in hand, I celebrated the success with my South Dakota friends, including some who were losing investors in SoDak Sports. The next day, I flew to Washington to drink toasts to those who helped me do it.

Baiting Your Adversaries

I enjoy corresponding with my friends at *The Washington Post*. Many people who have complaints about the *Post* worry about the reaction if they speak out. Most politicians are terrorized by the *Post* because they feel executive editor Ben Bradlee and his gang can "make" or "break" them.

Post chairman Kay Graham and her son Don Graham, the

publisher, and I trade compliments and barbs periodically and enjoy it.

But Ben Bradlee can't stand me. He loves to dish it out in the news columns, but he can't take criticism of any kind.

These exchanges indicate the differences in style.

Ms. Katharine Graham
Chair
The Washington Post Company
Dear Kay:

At the risk of being quite out of character, I must sincerely compliment you on the way you handled the Mauna Kea meetings.

Not only did I admire your deft touch, but the comments from those who lingered behind after you left were most complimentary.

You are taking giant steps for womankind at the ANPA helm. And, I am deeply grateful to you for doing it.

Dear Al,

Thank you for your hospitality the night of the Morton Forum.

Thank you, too, for all your help, both in going into (ANPA) office and being there. As I told you, I did enjoy it, and learned a lot—a combination I have come to enjoy.

Thanks, too, for the plug at the beginning of your Morton presentation.

Now that we have let down our guard for five minutes, we can safely go back to the tough shiv, and I have got my eye on you about your intentions with *USA TODAY* in our fair city, to say nothing about the hires you are making from our midst.

Please remember I would like to know from time to time when you are in town, and have a few extra moments for lunch or dinner, or in between.

Kay

Mr. Benjamin C. Bradlee
Executive Editor
The Washington Post
Dear Ben:

I've spent the last couple days, after returning from the San Francisco Demo bash, catching up on reading of old news and old *non*-news, published hereabouts while you and I were away.

In the latter category, I thought you might be interested in a factual review of circumstances re the attached *Washington Post* story about Gannett which appeared in your business section on July 20, under the headline "Gannett Cut from List of Stock Buys."

The story and headline were contrived from a Salomon Brothers report on Gannett, issued by Ed Dunleavy, a leading Wall Street analyst. What Dunleavy's report said, in fact, is that he was changing his designation for Gannett from O (expected to *Outperform* the S&P 500 market average for the next six to 12 months) to M (expected to *Match* the S&P during the same period).

As you may know (or perhaps you may not) reports and recommendations from stock analysts occur daily from many, many different sources. Most of them, like Dunleavy, are quite knowledgeable and respected.

To help you understand how Wall Street works, in the last few weeks analyst reports on public media companies have included, but probably not been limited to, the following:

On June 26, Salomon Brothers reported on the Chicago Tribune Company, changing its destination from O to M. (No story in *The Washington Post.*)

On June 28, Salomon Brothers changed its designation for Knight-Ridder from O to M. (No story in *The Washington Post.*)

On June 29, Salomon Brothers changed its designation for Times-Mirror from O to M. (No story in *The Washington Post.*)

On June 29, Donaldson, Lufkin & Jenrette issued a

report that recommended deferring further purchases of several media companies, including *The Washington Post Company,* but continued to recommend buying Gannett. (No story in *The Washington Post.*)

On July 9, Salomon Brothers changed its designation for Gannett from O to M (the basis for the story in *The Washington Post* eleven days later).

On July 10, Donaldson, Lufkin & Jenrette recommended the purchase of Gannett stock. (No story in *The Washington Post.*)

On July 11, Drexel Burnham Lambert issued a report on Gannett titled, "Strong Second Quarter/ Purchase Recommendation Reiterated." (No story in *The Washington Post.*)

On July 12, Donaldson, Lufkin & Jenrette issued another report recommending the purchase of Gannett stock. (No story in *The Washington Post.*)

On July 18, Drexel Burnham Lambert issued another report that said: "We continue to recommend strongly purchase of Gannett common stock." (No story in *The Washington Post.*)

Yet on July 20, *The Washington Post* weighed in with a 15-inch story that was misrepresentation of one analyst's eleven-day-old recommendation and failed even to explain what the recommendation was.

That story about Gannett didn't even get the day's stock closing price right. By-liner Michael Schrage reported that Gannett stock closed at 40⅜, down one quarter. Your own stock tables on following pages showed Gannett closed at 40, up one eighth.

Please do not misunderstand the purpose of this note. It is by no means a request for any retraction, correction or clarification. (Your clarification column already threatens to become the most rapidly growing section of your newspaper and I do not wish to add to that burden.)

This is not based on any worry that you folks might again pee on us poor people across the Potomac. It is prompted instead by my genuine concern about that unsuspecting public out there that doesn't under-

stand how a good newspaper can sometimes be so
bad.

Affectionately, if not admiringly.

Bradlee's reply:

Dear Al:

Thank you for your condescending and fundamentally unpleasant letter of July 24.

Now that you have moved your headquarters out
of Rochester, you must expect that we will cover you
as a major business in our area (the fifth largest
compared to ourselves, a tenuous tenth). You certainly
cannot expect to be covered as you were by the
Rochester papers. Nor can you expect our Business &
Finance section to run the stock-touting service that
we read in *USA TODAY*'s financial advice to the love-
lorn.

I have looked at all the points in your letter, and I
feel you are simply wrong about the Salomon recommendation. Dunleavy is the representative of one of
the largest, most prestigious investment houses in the
country. It is my understanding that he specifically told
Salomon Brothers clients not to buy Gannett stock. Not
because it was a bad, money-losing company, but
because the expected losses from *USA TODAY* were
such a drain on the Gannett operation that the company no longer warranted an "O" rating. This in turn
is newsworthy because they blamed the drain on the
losses created by the unusual experiment that is *USA
TODAY*. . . .

The Salomon Brothers report became newsworthy for precisely the reason you outline in your letter:
The other brokerages had been advising clients to buy,
and suddenly here comes a major investment house
that warns against such a purchase.

There is no way I can misunderstand the purpose
of your letter, what with its copies to Katharine Graham, Don Graham and Messrs. Dunleavy, Morton, and
Noble. I don't know how it will go over with them. It

grates in my craw. When I need help in Wall Street
Analysis 101, I can promise you I will turn to someone
other than yourself to arrange it.

P.S.: We did have one error. The stock did close at
40, up an eighth. And I can't tell you how much I
appreciated your cheap shot about our clarification
column. That is class.

Ben Bradlee

Dear Ben:

Ah shucks, I didn't mean to ignite your short fuse!

Your misguided missile of July 27, obviously hip-
fired in quick retaliation for my note of July 24, missed
all the marks.

Neither you nor I have the time to get involved in
a pen-pal relationship. Therefore, I won't prolong this
exchange by commenting specifically on your comments.

Suffice to say, I understand that you don't understand.

But Ben, the air of arrogance you exhale really is
polluting the *Post*'s reputation. Think about it.

I believe that journalists should be as willing to
admit their own errors as they are to point out mistakes of others. You've done your share (or more) of
the latter; you ought to think about the former.

In the twilight of your career, my friend, you still
have the opportunity to balance your well-deserved
reputation for toughness with some late-blooming fairness. Think about it.

Author to Editor

One of the delights of new business relationships is the
chance to forge understandings through the mail.

The expectations and style of a media CEO aren't necessarily the same as a book editor's or publisher's.

I had a solution: plain talk.

Ms. Harriet Rubin
Executive Editor
Doubleday

Dear Harriet:

Thanks for your note. I was disappointed that you did not meet your self-imposed deadline for some book cover ideas.

I understand. But I hope you realize that if we are going to meet the overall deadlines you have suggested it would be helpful if the same sense of urgency that the author is operating under could rub off on the editor and publisher.

Cheers.

"One Helluva Funeral"

Most of my memos have been designed to improve future operations rather than dwell on the past. After attending Henry Ford's cheerful, well-planned memorial service, I knew that there was one other future event that I didn't want to leave to chance.

To John Curley:

As we discussed yesterday, that was one helluva funeral I attended for Henry Ford in Detroit. The family and the Ford Motor Company cooperated in doing everything the way he wanted it. Bringing in his favorite Preservation Hall Jazz Band from New Orleans was a great way to bring down the curtain.

We should do a little preliminary thinking and planning to see how we at Gannett can properly work with any former (or present) CEOs or their families in case they someday follow the Henry Ford route.

Henry Ford helped because he had written precise instructions about the kind of post mortem services he wanted. Not all people do that. I will.

PLAIN TALK:
Manage with memos and no one forgets.

XI

MARRIAGE AND THE FAMILY

"You never really know a man until you have divorced him."

—ZSA ZSA GABOR
actress

Love. Marriage. Children. All part and parcel of most people's lives. Very precious possessions.

If we're lucky, they last a lifetime. Those are to be cherished, held dear.

If we're not that lucky, the memories of such kinships should be treated sensitively, sympathetically.

I was a two-time winner in marriage, although both ended in divorce.

Twenty-six years with my first wife. A marriage built on a storybook high school romance. From teenage to middle age, it was warm and wonderful. Then it gradually wore thin. Finally it wore out.

But it still holds affection and a great deal of appreciation.

Eight years with my second wife. A mid-life partnership built on both professional power and personal passion. It peaked sooner, exploded more often, wore itself out more quickly.

But it, too, has its marvelous memories. Respect and regard remain.

I rate both my marriages a success. So were the divorces.

Do I wish either had lasted "until death do us part?" Of course. But I count my blessings for half a lifetime of wedlock.

Two of those blessings are a son and a daughter, with whom I have now shared more than half of my sixty-five years. As a parent, I won the daily double.

I was the apple of their eye when they were preschool kids. A nuisance when they were in their early teens. A bore when they turned twenty. Now that they are in their thirties, we're best of friends.

What does it all add up to? What kind of husband was I really? What kind of parent have I been, or am I now?

▷ Ideal? A model? Of course not.

▷ Too demanding, or too detached? Perhaps both, sometimes.

▷ Too much like a corporate CEO in my personal life? Maybe.

Do I have regrets? Sure.

And many more fond memories.

But I am least qualified to evaluate my performance as a husband or as a parent. Others can judge us much more objectively than we ourselves can.

I asked those who know me best—my two ex-spouses and my two children—to write their own report cards on me.

In the chapters that follow, they do so. In their own words. In their own ways. No holds barred. No coaching. No censorship. No back talk from me.

I asked them simply to tell it the way they remember it was, or the way they see it now or feel it now.

I am deeply grateful to them for the way they bared their souls and opened their hearts, to me and to you.

It is my hope that these highly personal retrospections may be helpful to you in your relations with a spouse, ex-spouse, or children.

If they cause you a tear or two as you relate some of these feelings to your own family, that's okay.

I shed my share as I read these report cards on me as a husband and father. Some tears of sadness and sorrow. Some of joy and jubilation.

All of the feelings that family is all about.

"A father has to do everything in his power to keep a tight ship, even though he knows the crew would like to send him away in a dinghy."

—BILL COSBY

EX-SPOUSES' REPORT CARD

He's Loud and in Motion

Loretta Helgeland and Al Neuharth were married June 16, 1946, and divorced July 31, 1972.

She is an artist and advocate of the arts who lives in Rochester, New York, and Naples, Florida.

She has a B.F.A. degree in fine arts from the University of Miami and also studied at Wayne State University in Detroit and at General Beadle State Teachers College in Madison, South Dakota.

By Loretta Neuharth
Wife No. 1, 1946–72

The status quo is something Al Neuharth simply cannot stand.

He gets bored stiff with things as they are and wants to constantly change them.

For twenty-six years, I was married to him and that was my entire life.

But Al was married to his work more than he was married to me, and that was almost his entire life.

I used to think, more in sorrow than in anger, that the wedding ring I gave him should be replaced with some kind of corporate logo.

Now, I can't help smiling when I see him flash the huge diamond-studded *USA TODAY* ring which he wears on his third finger, left hand. That's much more appropriate than the simple little gold wedding band I put on his finger on June 16, 1946.

Being married to Al for twenty-six years was a daily challenge. I happily accepted it and gave it up very reluctantly. When he walked away, I first blamed myself. Then I realized I was not at fault.

He stayed with me much longer than he did with anyone or anything else. In the end I, too, represented the status quo, so I had to go.

In the seventeen years since our divorce, I've taken on my own, new identity. As difficult as it was at times being married to Al, it made me a stronger person. He taught me a sense of reality.

Maybe that helps explain why, after all these years, I am still one of his strongest cheerleaders, even though I've been mostly a silent one.

Cheerleading brought us together when we were sixteen in South Dakota. Al was the first boy cheerleader I had ever seen. Even then, he knew how to draw attention to himself. He was loud and constantly in motion. That hasn't changed much in nearly fifty years.

Although he was cheering for the Alpena Wildcats—bitter rivals of my hometown Woonsocket Redmen—I watched him for two days during a district basketball tournament. My girlfriends and I were captivated by his spirit and good looks.

We giggled about Al, "the cute butcher boy from Alpena." The next Sunday, three friends and I took our family car, a Ford model A coupe with a rumble seat and drove to Alpena—twelve miles away—and "just happened" to find Al. That was easy in a town of five hundred.

We told him it would be great if we could have a picnic. He went to the butcher shop, got hot dogs, then picked up other supplies and drove to a wooded field, started a fire, and we had a picnic. The girls were in a tizzy over Al: One took his scarf, another his little hat, another his gloves. But on the way back to town, Al asked me to ride in the rumble seat with him.

The next Sunday he came to Woonsocket and we had our first date. One by one, my girlfriends gave me the things they had captured from Al.

Though we didn't marry until five years later, I never dated anyone who meant as much to me after that first date. He was unique, very smart, and fun. He was always teasing someone. We grew up in the Dust Bowl depression days. Nearly everyone was so serious and some were pretty sad. But I didn't feel serious or worried when around him. With Al, I felt everything was just fine because he was always so sure that everything was okay. He still is.

When he joined the Army in World War II, I wrote him every day. Al devised this ingenious code of letters and numbers that would tell me where he was in Europe with the 86th Infantry Division. Despite the dangers, he never complained in his letters. I was scared to death.

The day he left for combat, I promised God that I would read one or more chapters of the Bible every day Al was away if God would keep him safe. I never missed a day. By war's end, I knew the New Testament by heart!

Before he was sent to the Pacific in the closing days of the war, he surprised me with an engagement ring. A year later we were married at a candlelight service in the Methodist Church in Woonsocket.

Anything for an Argument

We had lots of dreams but little money. I brought a 1937 Ford V8 to the marriage, from my schoolteacher salary. He bought our first home: an eighteen-foot, secondhand, silver-and-black house trailer with a tiny bedroom, a kerosene heater, and no flush toilet. Al paid $700 for it from his Army poker winnings.

Early in our marriage, our different personalities led to a few squabbles, but nothing serious. He was organized, an achiever, very intelligent, liked to control situations and people. He left little to chance. I was a dreamer, shy and sensitive.

One evening shortly after our marriage, Al talked about the contrast in our styles. He complained that I was too quiet. I surprised myself by flaring back, "It's too bad we can't all be so perfect." He liked that, laughed, and started kidding me. He enjoyed feistiness and playback. But I never liked arguing as much as Al did.

He and Bill Porter, his partner in *SoDak Sports,* argued into the night once about whether God was Protestant or Catholic.

Porter, a devout Catholic, was certain God was Catholic. Al wasn't all that religious but he became a proud Protestant for argument's sake.

When Al was hired by the *Miami Herald,* he drove to Florida, then sent for me to fly down. I was six months pregnant with Jan, and Dan was a year old. We flew out in a blizzard and were fogged in with a change of planes in New Orleans. I was pregnant, with this tiny son, little money, had never been out of the Midwest, and was stuck in the New Orleans airport. Luckily the airline found us a motel room.

The next morning we arrived in Miami in 85 degree sunshine. That night there was a full moon. I never wanted to leave.

We were a happy family in Miami. Our new baby daughter made our lives complete. On Saturdays, the four of us would go grocery shopping. Al took half of the grocery list with Dan; Jan and I took the other half. On the way home we'd sing songs like, "I've Been Working on the Railroad." It was hilarious because Al sang loudly and off-key. I laughed more than I sang and he'd asked why I was laughing. He never realized that he hit every flat note.

After we paid the necessities with his $95-a-week salary, we'd usually end up with a bank balance of less than a dollar. I remember once it was 12 cents; once 79 cents. But somehow we would find enough for special days. On Mother's Day, Al surprised Jan and me with a red carnation each. He proudly pinned them on and then we all went to church and dinner.

I remember a turning point in Al's mind about his career. As a reporter he had covered many Page One stories in the first few months at the *Herald*. One evening he proclaimed: "I'm smarter and have more potential than anyone in the *Herald* newsroom. I don't think there is anything that can stop me."

It seemed like a revelation to him. I had always thought he was smarter than anyone, so it didn't seem so earth-shattering to me. From then on, he was totally confident he could work his way to the very top.

Despite Al's confidence, he and I were still basically naive, country people. That was especially apparent at social functions. Because Al was a rising star at the *Miami Herald* and later in Detroit, we were invited to dinner and social events with the upper crust. This created awkward times for me.

I wore inexpensive dresses and shoes with my Woolworth

costume jewelry—an intimidating contrast with the wealthy women wearing designer dresses and diamonds. In the early years, my role was confined largely to sitting, smiling, and not saying much. Al's outgoing nature covered up his insecurity, if in fact he ever had any, which I doubt.

Trial by Wife

One particular moment in Detroit will live with me forever. At a dinner with all the Knight executives in a beautiful home in Grosse Pointe, Jack Knight gave me a newspaper clipping and said, "You are the youngest, so you can see best. Would you read this for us?" I unknowingly mispronounced a word twice in the article. No one gave me a clue that I had said anything wrong.

During dinner I noticed that I was getting cold, steady stares from Al. No warmth—just penetrating dark, cold eyes. Others in Gannett have felt the sting of those icy stares through the years.

I thought to myself, "What have I done? What is so awful?" The two of us drove home in silence until finally Al said coldly: "How do you say 'constituents'?"

He told me sarcastically that I had mispronounced it twice. I could have died. I believed Al thought his job hung in the balance for my mistake on pronunciation.

When Al was being courted by Gannett in Rochester, the trial of corporate wives continued. I was brought in with great secrecy. Louise Miller, wife of Gannett's president, introduced me as Mrs. Allen over lunch. She showed me Rochester on a rainy day, and I told her that I liked rainy days. It was true, but I had the feeling she thought that strange. Later we met with Mr. Miller and the executives. Thank God no one asked me to read anything!

I later learned that Gannett always looked over the wives with the same care that they did possible future executives. I felt sorry for them. The wife's conversation—and even her table manners—were considered along with her husband's professional abilities. It was so judgmental and unfair. When I was in a position to do something about it, I tried to put the new wives at ease. I tried to end the trial-by-wife.

When we moved to Rochester none of us felt homesick for Detroit. We viewed Rochester as a permanent home.

Family Life: Everything on Schedule

For a time we had a picture-perfect family. All three of us greeted Al at the door when he came home from the office. I had an iced-martini ready, hors d'oeuvres prepared, and the fireplace going.

Because Al worked hard six days a week, he insisted that Sunday be family day. Of course, he still worked in his den part of the day. The kids couldn't go anywhere and they couldn't invite friends to the house. We would play tennis, swim, or play Monopoly. In the winter, we played Fox-n-Geese in the snow and had snow fights.

I took art courses weekday mornings, so I would be home with the smell of cookies baking when the kids came from school. It was important to me to make that kind of home for the family. I felt I was part of a team.

Gradually, Al became eaten up by his concerns that Paul Miller would never relinquish control of Gannett. Even after he became president, Al was at Paul's beck and call. At a Southern Newspaper Publishers Association convention in Boca Raton, Florida, Al had finished a series of morning meetings. He was in his bathing suit and he and I were ready to go out and get some sun when the phone rang.

"If it's Miller, I'm not here," he told me.

It was Miller and he asked if Al was there. I'm a lousy liar and I hesitated: "Well, Paul, he's just leaving."

Paul said, "I'd really like to talk to him."

"Let me see if I can catch him," I said. I opened the door, looked down the hallway, and yelled, "Al, Al!" I came back and told Paul that Al would be right there.

Paul laughed and said, "What's he doing, hanging out the window?"

I guess Paul knew me well enough to know that Al was there all the time. Al took the phone and Paul asked him to drive up to Palm Beach to discuss business matters. I felt disappointed that once again we were being cheated out of some of our little free time.

Al's travel increased with the start-up of *TODAY* in Florida in 1966. He spent less and less time with our family. When he was in Rochester he would play catch-up with the local papers.

At home, he became withdrawn, uptight, more demanding and critical. When I asked him what was wrong, he blamed it on the job.

Bigger, Colder Martinis

More than ever, I handled any situation concerning Jan or Dan or the house in order to give him quality time when he was home. I tried to make our home more pleasant. Even though I knew I had come a long way from the Miami days, I shopped for smarter fashions and tried new hairstyles—anything to make me more attractive in Al's eyes. I even fixed him bigger and colder martinis.

Gradually I began to sense that something at the heart of our marriage was slipping away.

I never understood how Al could be so mercurial. He'd be furious about something, then like a storm cloud blowing over, he would innocently ask "What's wrong?" when he noticed that I was withdrawn and silent.

In the final year of our marriage, Dan was preparing to go away to college and Jan was in her own world with high school friends. I won a Blue Ribbon in a flower arranging show and was interviewed by a reporter. That night I read the newspaper column about me to the three of them: "Loretta Neuharth Loves Family, Gardening and Art." That headline summed it up. It made me feel so special, but Al, Dan, and Jan paid me only ho-hum compliments on my award.

The family cheerleader was finding it hard to get anyone to cheer her.

I knew something was seriously wrong at a publishers' meeting in January of 1972 in Hawaii. Al and I had planned to visit each of the islands after the meetings. I saw it as a chance to relax and enjoy paradise together. But rainy and gloomy weather on each island only heightened Al's preoccupation and silence around me.

We returned home like strangers. The communications gap grew wider. I would ask a question, get a short answer, then silence. One evening, desperate, I finally blurted out: "I don't know what is wrong. You won't tell me. This is no way for two people to live. Maybe the answer is a divorce."

He grabbed me and hugged me and excitedly asked: "Do you really mean it?" His reaction chilled me to the core.

"What else is there to do?" I replied. "I've tried everything to get you to tell me what is wrong. Do you want a divorce?"

"Yes, I want my freedom," he said. "I'll always like and love you but I want to be free and get on with my life."

Hearing his words crushed me. The man I had put on a pedestal when I was sixteen was climbing down and walking away.

A Civilized Divorce

Our divorce proceedings were very civilized. The settlement Al offered was fair, and ended up being generous.

We filed in Florida, because we owned a second home there and because of the "No-Fault" divorce law.

The night before the decree was final, we met in the county seat town of Deland. We had dinner together, shared the same hotel suite as husband and wife, made love sensitively and warmly one last time.

There were no tears that next day—at least not until after we had our final papers and said good-bye.

For the first time in twenty-six years, I was without an identity. The hurt, despair, and anxiety about my future were overpowering. I still have a self-portrait painted in one of my art classes a few months after the divorce. The ghastly, black tone of that self-portrait is still a bit haunting today.

But in the years that followed our divorce, a new, stronger sense of identity emerged—one I might never have achieved had Al and I remained married.

Since our divorce, Al has remained helpful, supportive, and advised me on business matters. He has become very close and caring with Dan and Jan. I sometimes share the "Neuharth family table" at Gannett functions.

Today, Al seems like an old friend. I still enjoy his sense of humor and wit when we talk on the phone or see each other at functions.

Sometimes I feel a twinge of sadness, but mostly I feel thankful for the times we've shared and for all I've gained in the nearly fifty years we've known each other.

He Sneaks and Slithers

Lori Wilson and Al Neuharth were married December 31, 1973, and divorced January 18, 1982. She is a former two-term Florida state senator, former head of the Brevard County Commission and an attorney-at-law in Cocoa Beach, Florida.

She has a B.S. degree in industrial technology/mass communications from Florida International University and a J.D. from Florida State University.

By Lori Wilson
Wife No. 2, 1973–82

Al Neuharth is a snake.

He's cold-blooded. He's sneaky and slithers around and sheds his old skin as he grows and adapts to his newest surroundings.

He outgrew Loretta, his first wife. And he outgrew me. Neither Loretta nor I ever had a chance with Al.

Nobody does.

The world is Al's prey. He's like a stalking animal. Once you're his target, professionally or personally, he'll do whatever it takes to get you. You might as well roll over and enjoy it.

But when he decides he's done with you, look out. There's nothing you can do to change his mind. The road is littered with bodies to prove it—from corporate giants to housekeepers to secretaries.

Give Al this: he doesn't hate. That would require too much emotion and wasted effort.

Instead, Al discards. He forgets you, writes you off as if you don't exist anymore. He never looks back. The past is history. He cares only about the future.

I should know. I live two houses down from him in a town of thirteen thousand. I seldom see him. As far as he is concerned, I could be living in Outer Mongolia.

Perhaps I should have seen this side of him when we first

met. Instead, all I saw was a modern-day Prince Charming on a jet.

I remember the day I met Al Neuharth—April 16, 1972, the day *Apollo 16* took off for the moon.

Emotionally I was a wreck. After nineteen years of marriage to my childhood sweetheart, I had filed for divorce. I was about to become a single parent with two teenage daughters. My only income was $14,000 as chairman of the Brevard County Commission.

Gannett was hosting a prelaunch brunch for Space Coast leaders. As a county official, I felt obligated to go, even though I was in no mood to party.

I arrived very late—most everyone already had eaten—but the party's host, Al Neuharth, was standing at the door. He introduced himself and walked me to the bar. Over Bloody Marys, we talked casually and he asked me if I was going to the launch. I said I was going to drive to a quiet spot on the beach and watch it from there.

Before the brunch ended, he invited me to join him and the local publisher, Jim Jesse, and his wife, Gloria, for dinner at the Surf restaurant that evening. I readily agreed. What politician wouldn't jump at the chance to have dinner with two big shots from the local newspaper?

After dinner Al asked me to drop him off at his hotel suite at the Atlantis Beach Lodge. In the car he told me he had a bottle of champagne chilled. "Would you like a nightcap?" he asked.

Why not? We drank the whole bottle and talked until dawn about everything. It was one of those nights that clicked—instant rapport. But not a hint of any romantic moves.

It turned out Al also was filing for a divorce. But he showed no emotion about it whatsoever.

I Felt Like Cinderella

Two weeks later he called me. "I'm in the neighborhood and wondered if you would like to join me for dinner?"

I agreed. Later I learned that "the neighborhood" he called from was Missouri, where he had been stalking a newspaper deal at Springfield. He flew from there to Cocoa Beach for our dinner date.

After our divorces became final, I began to feel like Cinderella. Champagne, flowers. Since we had met on the sixteenth of the month, Al sent me sixteen yellow roses on every sixteenth during our entire courtship and marriage. How romantic, I thought.

Only later did I learn that it was a chore he delegated to his secretaries.

During the final months of our marriage, I kept all the flowers in my office—the world's largest collection of dried dead yellow roses. A fitting epitaph of our marriage.

But Al was a great person to fall in love with. He was attentive, generous, and fun to be with.

As awestruck as I was, I was skittish about how my private life would affect my political career. As a divorcée, I was uncertain how the public would react to my decision to run for the state senate. It was hard enough to run as a woman. Being a recently divorced woman could have made it even tougher.

At this point Al and I still weren't dating publicly, locally.

Nevertheless Al was offering good advice to me behind the scenes. He suggested that I run as an independent rather than as a Republican. It would mean I could avoid the Republican primary and focus entirely on the general election.

It was a crazy idea. Nobody had ever done that before and won. It also meant I needed to resign as Brevard County Commissioner, which I had won as a Republican.

Al Neuharth was turning my life upside down. I was trying to do something politically that nobody had ever achieved before, plus giving up my only means of support.

On election night I was scared to death. I had gathered my closest friends and volunteers at a small storefront campaign headquarters to sweat out the election returns.

As the results came in and I was winning, Al kept suggesting that we go over to the Atlantis Beach Lodge in Cocoa Beach for a victory drink. Finally I rounded up my closest campaign workers and we headed over there.

When we drove up to the Lodge, the marquee had huge lighted letters: CONGRATULATIONS, SENATOR LORI.

When we walked into the large ballroom that Al had reserved, I was overwhelmed. Throngs of people greeted us. Across one side of the room, a huge wall of yellow roses spelled out, CONGRATULATIONS, SENATOR LORI.

It must have taken thousands of yellow roses and days of preparation, not to mention what it cost. "Al, what if I had lost?" I gasped. "You couldn't lose," he said.

Al doesn't believe in losing. And he believed in me. "You can have it all," he said.

After the election my relationship with Al became more public. He began to take me to conventions and exotic places.

A Wild, Wonderful Week

The tongues really started wagging when Al took me with him to Aruba in January of 1973 for board meetings of the American Newspaper Publishers Association. Most ANPA husbands and wives were straight arrows, establishment types that both Al and I enjoyed shaking up. For appearance sake, we had separate suites. Of course, one of them didn't get used very much.

It was a wild, wonderful, and daring week. We rode motorcycles around the island with Otis and Missy Chandler of the *Los Angeles Times*. Otis also dumped her ten years later.

When a stray dog attacked Al, he wrecked his motorbike, badly scraping his leg. We went back to the hotel, cleaned him up, then limped down the beach and made animated love in an overhanging mangrove tree within eyesight of the hotel.

Now, when I see the tree house Al built overlooking the beach at Pumpkin Center, I still think of that mangrove tree in Aruba!

Al planned our wedding the way he did everything else— with flair and imagination—every detail in place in advance.

We constructed a small rustic open-air chapel on the ocean-front site where we were going to build our home, Pumpkin Center. The wedding was New Year's Eve day, 1973, at sunrise. The cross in the chapel had been built so that the sun would rise exactly over its point as we were saying our vows. God, of course, cooperated with Al and arranged a brilliant sunrise! That chapel still stands today—a monument to a marriage made in heaven. I see it every day when I walk on the beach, and I think something of a love story survives.

The chaplain of the Florida Senate performed the wedding ceremony. Only our four children were invited to attend, because Al wanted it to be small and "private."

Al wouldn't even let my mother and father attend. My mother never forgave him for that. He said if my parents came, then my brothers and sisters would want to be invited, and the next thing you know, there would be a crowd.

I was learning about Al's forceful ways. Once he "suggested" something, it really wasn't a suggestion at all. He'd already decided that's how it shall be done.

I also came to realize that Al always thinks in ink—press and P.R.

Even though my mother didn't make the cut for the wedding, Al thought it was appropriate to have a photographer from *TODAY* there. Al made sure the pictures were available the same day so they could run in the Florida newspapers and on the AP wire nationwide.

Al never missed a trick when it came to controlling events and publicity.

The kids—our only wedding guests—didn't shower us with kindness. Dan showed up in a wild Hawaiian shirt with a scruffy beard and pouted the whole time.

Rhonda, my oldest daughter, was in her flower-child state and wasn't much better.

His daughter, Jan, and my other daughter, Kim, acted fairly normal.

We honeymooned in Acapulco and Barbados. I wanted to go to Barbados and he wanted to go to Acapulco. So we compromised. We went to both places for a week each.

What's in a Name?

I was never Mrs. Al Neuharth. Nor was I Lori Neuharth.

Before we were married, I told Al I had too much invested politically in the name Wilson to give it up.

He agreed, but in his usual arrogant way.

"I wouldn't let you use my name anyway," he said. "Maybe once you're elected to the U.S. Senate or to the White House and I have retired as a journalist, you can use my name. But not before."

That should have been a tip-off that Al was expecting bigger things of me. I realize now that maybe he never really wanted a wife so much as a power partner.

Contrary to popular opinion, I was more involved with

Gannett than Al was involved in my political life. He was very tightly focused on Gannett.

I frequently traveled with Al on his business trips, but I didn't play the role of the traditional Gannett spouse. Rather than sit in a hotel room, I would go to the meetings, which usually were sessions with department heads at newspapers.

I didn't say anything at the meetings, but I began to take notes. A little like Rosalynn Carter, when she sat in on President Carter's cabinet meetings. After several meetings at the newspapers, I began to notice a pattern. All the department heads were white men.

As the prime sponsor of the ERA amendment in the Florida Senate, I realized Gannett needed its own ERA amendment.

Al agreed. He thought the local leadership should reflect the local readership. Al was a color-blind person. He didn't care what color you were or what sex you were, so long as you could get the job done.

I told Al that Gannett's middle-management pool of women and minorities had to be broadened before progress could be made.

He agreed and decided to hire me as a consultant for Gannett to recommend ways to improve opportunities for women.

That raised a lot of eyebrows. But when I talked to publishers and bright women down in the ranks, I got more attention and action than the average consultant. The publishers were a lot more worried about my pillow talk than my consultant's reports.

Al didn't care about the details. He just wanted to be the best in the industry providing equal opportunities for everyone. He figured his wife could cut through the bullshit better than a professional consultant. And he was willing to take the heat for hiring his wife.

Being married to Al was like riding a roller coaster.

We enjoyed life to the fullest. We traveled around the country and the world, staying in the best hotel suites, eating the best food, and drinking the finest champagne.

It was a storybook existence.

But I soon learned that being married to Neuharth was like working for him. He expects his personal life to run as orderly as his professional life. Woe be it to the person who disrupts his disciplined routine.

Al's solution to any problem—at home or at work—was to throw money at it. "Everybody has a price," he would say. He didn't care how much it cost to fix a problem, so long as it was fixed. "Fix it!" was his favorite phrase.

Ultimately that's how he dealt with me.

I realize now that I made a big mistake in following Al's advice not to run for re-election to the state Senate. "You've already done that," he said. "Why run for re-election?" He suggested I run for something bigger, such as governor or the U. S. Senate. I made a brief test of running for the U. S. Senate but didn't pursue it.

Al loved being married to a senator. After I gave up on seeking higher office, Al gave up on me.

No-Fault, No-Emotion

When the end came, Al showed no emotion.

He was interested in other things and other people. I was history.

Under Florida's no-fault divorce laws, we didn't have to establish legal grounds for our splitting up.

The prenuptial agreement spelled out what I would get as a settlement. Al said, "I don't care how you take it. You can have it all in cash or all in stock or all real estate. Or you can have a mix. I have no emotional attachment to any of the stuff. You decide."

I had just finished my first year of law school at forty-four. I knew I couldn't afford to maintain Pumpkin Center. I didn't want to be property rich and cash poor. But Cocoa Beach was my home, and I wasn't about to be run out by Neuharth or anybody else. I lived in Brevard County long before he did. So I took the guest house two doors down the beach and a mix of cash and stock.

When we met with the lawyers to settle on final terms, it seemed so cold. I started crying, really bawling. I threw both lawyers out of the room. "Can't we settle this?" I asked. "I can't handle all this crap. Let's get out of here."

So we had lunch a few blocks away and agreed generally

on the property split. As we were walking back to the lawyer's office, I said, "If you'll throw in 1,500 more shares of Gannett stock, I'll sign the papers right now, and it will be over with."

He thought about it for a second and said, "You're on."

I realize now that I wasn't ready to be married to Al Neuharth, either emotionally or materially. I think I would be now. In fact, I miss him now—we were great partners—professionally. I used to enjoy brainstorming ideas about *USA TODAY* with him. We were a good team.

But it was too big a jump from being a Merritt Island housewife to jetting around the country like celebrities featured on "Lifestyles of the Rich and Famous."

Generous to a Fault

I look back and shake my head at how I spent too much of my energy trying to save Al money. He didn't care about that at all. When we were first married, he wanted to buy me a Mercedes 450 SL. But I refused. He kept offering to buy me a fur coat. I looked a few times when we were in New York but came home empty-handed because I couldn't see spending $20,000 or more on a fur coat while I was living in Florida.

The most expensive gift I ever took from Al was a beautiful gold watch that he had had engraved, "Our time has only just begun."

Even today Al is the most generous man I know. Unsolicited, Al contributed $3,000—the maximum state law allows—to my unsuccessful Senate campaign in 1988.

I think about his generosity now when I see how others react to his gifts. He recently gave one of his current friends, another blonde from Cocoa Beach, Barbara Whitney, a brand-new white Rolls-Royce. She took out a full-page ad in *FLORIDA TODAY* that showed the grill of the Rolls-Royce with a big THANKS.

Al is one of the most eligible bachelors in the United States. He's charming, rich, challenging, and inspiring—a great catch, as long as you don't mind riding a roller coaster with a snake.

GROWN-UP KIDS RATE THEIR DAD

He's Neither Hero Nor Villain

Daniel J Neuharth II was born to Loretta and Al Neuharth in Sioux Falls, South Dakota, November 10, 1953.

Dan is a psychotherapist and president of Dialogues, a San Francisco-based speaking and consulting firm. He is a former newspaper, radio and television journalist, and university journalism professor.

He holds a B.A. degree in political science and sociology from Duke University; an M.S. in journalism from Northwestern; an M.A. in clinical psychology from John F. Kennedy University in San Francisco, and is studying for his doctorate in clinical psychology at the California School of Professional Psychology, in Berkeley.

By Dan Neuharth

Mark Twain's father and mine were a lot alike.

"When I was a boy of fourteen," Twain said, "my father was so ignorant I could hardly stand to have the old man around. But when I got to be twenty-one, I was astonished at how much he had learned in seven years."

As a child I idolized my father. But by age sixteen we were locked in a mental wrestling match that grew ugly as we brawled at the brink of a lost relationship. Since my mid-twenties, Al and I have become the closest of friends.

As chairman and CEO of Gannett, my father was an unqualified success. But how was he as chairman and CEO of our family? What kind of father was he? What was it like to grow up the son of this corporate conquistador?

As an adolescent I saw nothing good about him. He seemed

distant, angry, gruff, confusing, and frightening. At age seventeen, as I packed for college, I concluded that I would never be close to Al. He would die (he was already forty-seven), I would mourn—for a short while—and that would be it. I saw no alternative.

I resented the way our family walked on eggshells around Al, since we never knew what mood he would be in or what would set him off. As Al climbed the corporate ladder, I resented the way my sister and I were paraded to company functions and expected to behave like politicians' perfect kids. I felt I could never be myself around a domineering, harsh father who provided us with material miracles but an emotional desert.

This was quite a change from my kid years. Old photos and my mother's memories offer idyllic snapshots of Al and me:

▷ At age three in my parents' steamy bathroom, intently watching Al shave, and mimicking him by scraping my plastic toy razor across my face.

▷ At age four pushing my toy lawnmower in Al's tracks as he sweated through the Miami sun to cut our grass with his manual push mower.

▷ At age five spending Sundays in the backyard, pounding on my tin toy typewriter as Al sat typing news stories for the *Miami Herald.*

From Idolatry to Hatred

What turned my childhood idolatry to adolescent hatred? It wasn't until my adult years that I saw what lay underneath my anger toward Al: the deep hurt of a young boy whose father chose career ahead of family. Looking back, I saw the toll the rocky, uncertain footing of the corporate climb took on Al and how much he must have wished, in vain, for his family to be at peace. I can see, now, how Al's precarious boyhood without a father left him lacking a blueprint for raising me.

But as an adolescent I knew only that I felt pain. The reasons didn't matter. Some snapshots from my teens:

▷ At age fourteen, when a communications foul-up between me and the neighbor kid who had agreed to deliver my newspaper route during the holidays left my 150 customers without newspapers, I recall Al's wrathful shout: "Damn few people get a second chance in life, and you're damn lucky they didn't fire you."

I had wanted compassion. Instead, I felt a worthless failure. Through tears—and fury—I decided that Al cared nothing about me and was only embarrassed at the gossip that would zip through the office about the boss's son's screwup.

▷ At age fifteen, on a snowy November Sunday, the morning after my first date, I wandered into my father's den, lovestruck, wondering whether 9 A.M. was too early to call for another date. Sunday was supposed to be family day at our house. But my father, deep into his deskwork, looked up and said with disgust, "Boy, you got it bad." I had wanted him to share my joy. Instead, I trudged away, tail between my legs, deciding that males should never get too deeply in love.

Dinner-table rituals tell a lot about a family. Our dinner table was a battlefield. During the Vietnam War, I scorned Al, "I bet you're proud to call yourself an American." I took up with glee a columnist's label of Gannett as "shit-kicker newspapers." In 1968, knowing Al was weighing his presidential choice between Nixon and Humphrey, I preached the praises of Gene McCarthy. When McCarthy dropped out, I assumed the cause of George Wallace. My positions didn't matter, as long as they opposed Al's.

Other times I answered his queries with monosyllabic grunts or a pint-sized John Wayne imitation. ["Wullll, sir, ahm fine."] I made it hard for him after his long days at the office. But I figured he was making life hard for me. I felt we lived in an atmosphere of coldness and distance. Missing was warmth, trust, spontaneity, and acceptance. In my own way, perhaps I was trying to bring some heat to this ice-cold family. Since I didn't know how to bring warmth, I brought the next best thing: friction.

The year I left home for college, my parents divorced after twenty-six years of marriage. Strangely the divorce made me feel both closer to—and even more distant from—my father.

During the divorce I was an intern reporter for the first *TODAY*—the paper Al started in Florida. Al called from New York and said he needed to talk, then flew to see me. I hadn't a clue as to his message.

A Family Falling Apart

The next morning over breakfast Al told me his news. I still remember his heavy, flat tone: "Your Mom and I have agreed to get a divorce. Nobody's fighting, nobody's upset, nobody's throwing pots or pans. We both want to pursue our own interests. But we won't do it if it is a problem for you or Jan."

I responded, without skipping a beat, "It's not a problem. I want you to do whatever is best for you."

We both had lied. Those lies planted seeds for a worsening relationship between Al and me. Our lies were not malevolent. We were doing the best we could to cope with the nightmare. Al lied when he said nobody was upset. My mother was decimated. And he was going to get a divorce no matter what Jan and I wanted.

I lied when I said it was not a problem. It was a *huge* problem; my family was shattering before my eyes. But as I sat there at that motel breakfast table across from the man I had fought with through my teens, I was petrified that if I said the wrong thing, I would lose my father forever. If my parents were separating, I was casting my lot with my father.

The fallout from the divorce lasted for years. On rare occasions when Al and I had dinner, a new fare was served up for argument: Al's treatment of Loretta. I argued that he should give her more alimony. To my surprise, he did.

When my father began openly courting a flamboyant, white-pants-suited state senator named Lori Wilson, I was furious. To commemorate their sunrise marriage on the beach on New Year's Eve day 1973, I showed up unshaven ("I'm starting a beard," I told them), wearing a sport shirt and wild hair. I had wanted to protest even more by not going—but my mother, to her credit, prevailed on me to go.

My dinners with Al and Lori led to inevitable fights. I goaded Lori, much as I had goaded Al, taunting, "All politicians are corrupt." Unlike Al, who had years of debating experience with me, Lori inevitably rose to the bait, then to tears. When they divorced seven years later, I felt vindicated in having my Dad back.

Around my twenty-sixth birthday, Al's and my wrestling match turned again—this time for the better. Al was feeling more confident, firmly in the seat of power as chairman and

CEO of Gannett. I was "finding" myself with a steady diet of psychotherapy, workshops from est to transactional analysis, and self-help books. I found the tools and courage to face my father. Late in 1979 our relationship turned around on two events.

The first was a private father-son dinner in Cocoa Beach, Fla. I rehearsed for days. I was planning to tell Al how much his absence, moods, and quick temper had hurt and embarrassed me. I was also going to tell him how much I loved him and forgave him. I did, and he listened. For the first time since I was a boy, we told each other we loved each other.

The second event came two days later. I came in late at night, locked the house, and took the security keys to my bedroom. Rising the next morning at 11 A.M., I blithely wandered down for breakfast and met a furious Al. He could not find the security keys and hadn't been able to get into the secretary's office to do early morning work. I confessed and he began ranting. For the first time in my life, I simply watched him. I did not counterattack, and I did not run. It surprised me as much as him. He took the keys and left without a word.

Two hours later he approached me and, near tears, chided my lack of consideration. I apologized. Misplaced keys helped us find the keys to getting along. Our relationship has been growing stronger since. The turnaround has given me perspective about Al and those early years.

Al's Soft Side Goes Public

I began recalling memories of Al's love: his tireless coaching of me as a Little Leaguer; his teary breakfast-table prayer when my happy-go-lucky mutt, Smudgie, died.

This soft side of Al gradually became more public as time passed. After 1979, when his mother died at age eighty-six, he could not speak of her for years without getting teary-eyed. In 1982, after *USA TODAY* was launched, Al choked back happy tears as he spoke to my sister and me about the dozens of newspapers copying *USA TODAY.* In 1986 Al's soft side went fully public when he surprised Gannett's annual meeting by announcing his planned retirement and passing of the CEO's title. His face and voice straining with pride and sadness, he could barely get his words out.

When I was fifteen, Al underwent a risky hospital procedure to try to correct a heart fibrillation. Al lost his father when he was two; I was faced with losing mine at age fifteen. Before Al went into the hospital, he wrote me a letter in case he didn't survive. It read:

> You don't know, yet, how much pride a father can have in his son. My pride in you is very great, as great as any father ever had in a son only fifteen. I am proud because you are intelligent, ambitious, honest, and handsome. I am proud because you are already showing that you can be a leader of boys. I know you will be a leader of men. I know you will accomplish more and contribute more to your generation, your country, your world, than I have or will. I hope I will be around many more years to watch you and lead the applause for you. But if I am not there in person, I will be there in spirit.

The letter didn't mean very much to me then. Today, when I think how I might have lost my father when I was only fifteen, I gain perspective on our wrestling match. I never would have known the Al Neuharth who cares so deeply. I might never have gotten over my hate and fury. I might have remained an angry young man forever.

In recent years our snapshots have turned golden:

On Thanksgiving Day, 1986, alone in our Lake Tahoe, Nev., mountainside house, Al and I had a father-son Thanksgiving dinner. Al played chef and in his typical modest style prepared turkey, stuffing, mashed potatoes, baked potatoes, sweet potatoes, peas, corn, squash, green beans, asparagus, brussels sprouts, carrots, salad, and bread—enough to feed twenty people. He wouldn't let me help with any of the cooking.

During dinner he asked about my graduate studies, friends, and career. He was totally interested in my life and willing to talk about his. He talked of how dating was for a sixty-two-year-old CEO, how he hoped to proclaim *USA TODAY* profitable the following year (which he did), and his retirement plans. We were content this timeless evening, a father and son giving thanks for each other's friendship.

After dinner he asked me to show him how the dishwasher worked. Al had washed dishes early in his marriage to my mother, when they were too poor to afford an automatic dishwasher. Since then, wives, children, hotel maids, secretaries, and cleanup crews had done his dishes. He'd never used an automatic dishwasher! This snowy Thanksgiving night, Al washed his first dishes in thirty-five years.

No Fatherly Instincts

It was a hard path that got my father and me to that Thanksgiving. Al's changeable moods—furious one day and acting as if nothing had happened the next—left me feeling like the joke that circulates among the offices where I work as a family therapist: "Roses are red, violets are blue, I'm schizophrenic, and so am I."

As a family therapist, I know that adolescents want only that their parents have it together; they have little concern for their parents' own scars from childhood. In my teens it didn't occur to me that Al never knew his father, never knew firsthand what fathers do to help and hurt.

The advantages of having Al as a father outweigh the disadvantages. He has never been stingy. As he has aged, he has shared his wisdom, time, triumphs, and dilemmas with my sister and myself.

Al never pushed me into journalism. He told me he only wanted me to love what I do. When I became a journalist, he encouraged my love of it. When I left journalism, he accepted it with grace and encouraged my new career loves.

At times I feel like a "poor little rich boy," with no right to complain. I had a father who bought me a Buick Riviera for high school graduation; who got World Series tickets on demand for me and friends. We appeared a model family: successful father, loving mother, smarts, big house, right schools.

But underneath the appearances we were a family full of ache. Growing up in my family taught me about wealth and outward appearances. I learned that money doesn't buy happiness, and rich folk, like anybody, have their personal dragons to slay.

What stands out to me today is not the horrid times between

my father and me, but that we turned around a dying relationship. I reached out and Al reached back. The real confession of this "S.O.B." should be why and how Al turned from a driven, self-absorbed guy into a courageous, loving father who is capable of being gentle toward his family and inspiring to his profession and nation.

Al probably never knew the impact he had on me during my childhood. He seemed oblivious to my hurts. But in recent years he has tried to give of himself to make up for the years when he did not. He has invited me into his heart—and, to my surprise, into this book.

A final snapshot: May 9, 1987. Two hours before my sister Jan was to be married, Al, Jan, my mother, and I took four wooden folding chairs into the billowy, grassy pasture of Jan's Virginia horse farm. The wedding was to be outdoors, under a huge tent overlooking the Blue Ridge Mountains.

We sat, just as we had at our family dinner table—Al and I across from each other, Mom to his right, Jan to his left. We talked of how Al's parents Daniel and Christina, and Loretta's parents Seymour and Anna, all South Dakota farmers, would be proud that we once again had a farm in the family. We talked of Jan's crazy high school boyfriends, and how we never thought she would marry a man of both strength and softness like her Swiss-born husband, Joseph.

We talked of the divorce, that wound that I had thought was the end of our family. As we talked of it, and as I watched my mother and father, the wound healed. We had come full circle, this family that began with a glint in my mother's eye at a South Dakota basketball game in 1941—this family born of love and innocence, ripped apart by alienation.

As I looked at Al, I saw neither a hero nor a villain, but an ordinary man, with extraordinary passion and vision, who loved us the best he knew how.

He's a Tough Teacher

Janet Ann Neuharth was born to Loretta and Al Neuharth on April 22, 1955, in Miami, Florida.

She is president and owner of Paper Chase Farms, a schooling, training, and boarding horse farm in Middleburg, Virginia. She formerly practiced law with the firm of Paul, Hastings, Janofsky, and Walker in Los Angeles.

She has a B.A. in English and political science from the University of Florida and a J.D. from Vanderbilt University.

She is married to Joseph Keusch of Zürich, Switzerland.

By Jan Neuharth

"Is your father really an S.O.B.?"

Since word about this book began spreading, that's the question most of my friends have been asking me.

For years people have wanted to know what it's like to have Al Neuharth as a father. But they have mostly been curious about him as chairman of Gannett or founder of *USA TODAY.* That's easy to talk about.

A much tougher question is whether my Dad is an S.O.B. Since I was a kid, Al has always told me, "If in doubt, tell the truth." So here goes:

Yes, he's an S.O.B., sometimes. But only when he needs to be. He's also honest and direct. Firm but fair. He's loving and supportive.

As my business partner in a horse farm in Middleburg, Va., he's tough. He accepts no excuses. But now that I've learned business from him, I feel sorry for those who try to make it with only an M.B.A. from Harvard or Wharton.

As a media mogul, he was generous. I loved sharing his limos, his corporate jets, some of his meetings with presidents. As a father he's always there when I need him.

My earliest recollection of my father is when we lived in Miami until I was nearly six. While he was a reporter at the *Miami Herald,* he was a normal father by most standards. We didn't have much money, but I didn't know it.

He used to bring us Creamsicles home on payday and we "dined out" on hamburgers at White Castle on some weekends. My brother had a Robot Commando and I had a Chatty Cathy.

He used to work around the house on weekends and had plenty of time to spend with us. But even when we were playing with him, every experience was a lesson in life.

The way he taught us to ride our bikes was pretty indicative of the way he taught us to live our lives. Like most kids, we started with training wheels. But before we had mastered the art, he took the training wheels away, put us on the bikes, gave us a push, and sent us on our way.

That method had its drawbacks. We moved to Detroit right after Christmas in 1960, when I was six and lived in a housing development that was separated from the inner-city slums by a park. My father would push me off on the bike, send me around the park, and stop me by catching the bike when I got back to him.

One day my trip was cut short by a gang of kids who stood in front of me and blocked my path. I ran into them, but of course they didn't catch me. I tumbled hard, got up, and ran across the park to Daddy. When we went back for the bike, it was gone. After that he taught me how to stop by myself.

Learning How to Bluff at Eight

Games were a way for our family to spend time together. I learned to play poker at the age of eight and was taught how to bluff by the best, my father.

Al kept the stakes fair by letting us play with pennies and declaring that no one could lose more than 50 cents, which of course meant that no one could win more than $1.50. But I soon learned that the real thrill wasn't just from winning more money than the others. The real challenge was outsmarting the others. Knowing how to bluff, how to read your opponent. Maybe even more importantly, that's how I learned when to fold and wait for the next opportunity.

He taught us about doing deals with Monopoly. I soon thought I had the strategy all figured out and would let nothing deter me from making deals to buy Boardwalk and Park Place. My father took advantage of that approach. He would buy all the little properties. Every time it was his turn, he'd make a deal for something with someone. It didn't matter what or with whom. Guess who won? I'd end up with Boardwalk and Park Place, heavily mortgaged, and my father owned the rest of the world. Just as he did things at Gannett.

Discipline was big in our house. There was a set of rules and we had to play by them. If we did we were praised, and if we didn't we were punished.

When we were young kids, punishment came in the form of spankings. He never hit us or disciplined us on the spot. If we broke the rules, we were sent to our rooms to await our sentence. He would visit with us individually and discuss the situation calmly and rationally.

He made quite clear what we had done wrong and why we had to be punished for it. We were told the number of whacks we were going to get in advance, and if one of us, usually my brother, got a greater number than the other, we were told why.

One time we both decided to put a book in our pants before our spankings. He was not amused. We both got an extra smack for that one. Somehow, though, I think he respected us for having the spirit to stand up to him and the punishment.

As we got older, punishment came in the form of restrictions on our activities. My brother became a straight A student and never did anything wrong. I played a lot and never did anything that I thought was wrong.

We had a room in our house that we called the den. It was where my father worked. It was also where our family meetings were held when we were going to discuss something serious.

My restrictions mostly revolved around my grades. He would restrict my telephone privileges in an effort to get me to study more. The restrictions were always set forth in writing. I think that's when the lawyer in me was born.

I still have one agreement that he wrote when I was in high school restricting my telephone privileges because of my unsatisfactory grades one semester. The agreement concluded with:

If any question arises on any borderline case, the privileges and/or restrictions may be increased or decreased based on your general attitude in your relationship with your family.

These minor restrictions are being invoked in the hope that they will enable you to arrive at a proper balance between fun, effort, and achievement, so that unlimited privileges may be yours in the future.

It was signed by both my mother and father, and he had prepared a signature line for me preceded by "I understand." I had no choice other than to sign it, but I added the phrase "but I don't agree." Surprisingly, he let me get away with that.

Sharing Dad with a Stranger

I was seventeen years old when my parents got divorced. Al told me one day that he and my mother wanted to have a family meeting with me. I tried to figure out what I had done wrong that they could have found out about.

When he suggested that we meet in the family room rather than the den, I was really thrown off guard. I thought he was going to tell me someone was dying.

He had tears when he told me and talked a lot about how much we all meant to each other and how that would never change. My mother didn't say much. I assumed it was her idea. Of course, it wasn't.

My parents both worked hard to make sure that I did not suffer any more than necessary over the divorce. There was no fighting or visible bitterness. My father still came often for dinner and spent family holidays with us.

It was tough when Al started dating Lori Wilson. She didn't try to act like our mother, but she was very protective of my father. That was hard to deal with. He had been ours first.

When he told me they were going to get married, he really downplayed it and said it would just be a small ceremony and that he would love to have me come if it fit into my schedule. I didn't think it mattered much to him, so I decided not to attend. Fortunately my mother talked me into going.

They weren't married long, but during the course of it I thought Lori and I were on pretty good terms. Until her daughter

Kim told me that Lori had said, "Jan could cut someone's balls off in a dark alley with a rusty knife and never give it a second thought." I never felt very comfortable with Lori after that.

After they divorced, Al declared that he would never marry again. He seems content with that decision. I think he should keep his options open, the way he always tells me to do about everything.

When I used to bring friends home in high school, my father would always make it a point to meet them. He would stride into the room, stick out his hand, and say, "Hi, I'm Al Neuharth." Most of the boys would mumble "Hello," with their hands stuck in their pockets, and the girls would just giggle. Then he'd attempt to make small talk. I was terribly embarrassed, but I appreciated that he cared enough to want to meet my friends.

Even though most of the guys I dated were probably not what he would have dreamed of in a son-in-law, he never criticized them. I dated one guy in college from Plant City, Fla. His friends called him Grit. He had long hair and a goatee. He played foosball (the 1970s equivalent of video game) and wore plaid polyester suits and green platform shoes. Al never could remember his name and called him Scooter.

But my father was great about him. He said he thought Scooter was a nice guy. He always managed to find some merit in any relationship.

That is not to say he is not somewhat protective. He just does it in a caring but unobtrusive way. When my father first met Joseph, the man who is now my husband, we were traveling in Europe. Joseph is a tall, handsome, blond, blue-eyed Swiss riding instructor who had stolen my heart in Los Angeles.

I left Al in Paris to go visit Joseph in Zürich and, if all went well, to bring him with me back to Paris. My father made it quite clear that I should keep my options open, and if things did not go well, I should not feel embarrassed to return to Paris alone. In fact, he said, I should keep in mind that Paris was only a short return flight, and I didn't even need to stay the night if I didn't want to. He would understand.

I was very touched by his concern. It was nice to know that even as an adult I still had my father looking out for me and ready to pick me up and brush me off if I fell down.

Joseph did return to Paris with me, and my father was his

usual charming self. He spoke broken German with Joseph. He even asked me if I wanted our room at the George V changed so we could have a double bed instead of two singles.

That's typical of my father. Although he was obviously leery of my involvement with someone he thought was a Swiss playboy, he also wanted me to know that I had total freedom to let the relationship be however I wanted it to be. Kind of like putting me on the bike and sending me around the park alone. Only by now I had already learned how to stop by myself.

Excuses Don't Count

Being a business partner with Al has taught me more than I could ever learn in the classroom in a million years. He plans carefully, but he's impatient. He's restless, always wanting to move on.

He is tough and sometimes ruthless. He says that's a reality of life. He is usually fair and almost always right. He never lets you give less than 100 percent and he will not accept excuses. He thinks everyone would be much better off if they had an early business failure like he did in *SoDak Sports*.

His theory behind Economics 101 is very simple. You need to take in enough money to pay the rent and still have something left over. Applying the theory is not so simple. You never leave anything to chance, never settle for second best, and never try to save your way to prosperity. Most importantly you never let lawyers tell you how to run your business.

I can still vividly remember a day shortly before we were to have the grand opening at our farm. Our road sign had arrived and had been erected in front of the farm on Highway 50 east of Middleburg. It was beautifully hand-painted and displayed our Paper Chase name and logo. I had made sure the size was in full compliance with the local zoning regulations.

My father arrived at the farm that day, and I ran out, full of enthusiasm to get his opinion of the sign. He hadn't noticed it, he said. We walked up the drive so I could show it to him, and he just stood before it with no comment. I knew I wasn't going to like the answer, but I went ahead and asked what he really thought of it.

"It's a fucking disaster. It will never work. If you don't

replace it, you might as well not have the opening in two days because no one will notice you're here and your business will never succeed." I still didn't get it. I asked why. "It's too damned small. No one will be able to read it." That explained why he had pretended not to see it when he drove in.

I patiently explained to him that the sign could not be any larger and still comply with the zoning regulations. That was a big mistake. I got the "you can't let the fucking lawyers run your business" lecture. "If your stupid lawyer couldn't figure out how to get an okay on a bigger sign, you need a new lawyer."

I burst into tears, and he softened a little and told me I shouldn't take things so personally. I should change the sign if I could and, if not, suffer the consequences and learn from my mistake. The sign stayed.

To this day, whenever we talk about the great response by the public to Paper Chase Farms, he always laughs and says, "Just think how many more would be coming here if you had a bigger sign." I can now laugh about it too.

My father has always supported me fully in whatever I have wanted to do in life. He has never put pressure on me to follow a certain path or, more importantly, not to follow another. He never even missed a beat when I told him I wanted to leave the comfortable practice of corporate law in Los Angeles to go into the horse business.

What I want to do is not as important to him as whether I am happy doing it, go after it 100 percent, and keep my options open to follow other paths in the future.

I have grown up knowing that he thought I could accomplish whatever I want to in life. Having a person like Al Neuharth behind me is pretty inspiring. It's also not always easy. He has high expectations. He makes me demand the most of myself. He also makes me believe that I can do it.

A Father's Love Note

My father is a great believer in putting things on paper and has written me many notes over the years. I have one that he wrote when I was fourteen years old. I often go back and read it when I need a boost. It always makes me cry. I would like to share a portion of it with you:

I love and admire you for so many reasons. You are smart. And kind and helpful. And so pretty. And so excited about life. I am so proud of so many things you have already done, and so many more I know you will do . . . You will be a great woman someday. You have the stuff to accomplish all the things that are important to you and those close to you . . . You are lucky because you are living at a time when girls can be what they want, and accomplish what they want. In person, or in spirit, I will always be applauding you for what you are and for what you are doing . . .

In person or in spirit I will always be applauding Al Neuharth for who he is and what he has accomplished. As a journalist, as a corporate executive, and most importantly, as my father.

XII

A TIME TO LEAD; A TIME TO LEAVE

"Walk off the stage before the sprightlier age comes on and shoves you off."

ALEXANDER POPE
English author

There's a reason for every season in our life.

Each decade can be the right time for the right undertakings and the right achievements.

Of course, the timetable may vary a bit. But here is my strongly recommended agenda for your seasons:

▷ In your teens, play all you can.
▷ In your twenties, take all the risks you can.
▷ In your thirties, learn all you can.
▷ In your forties, earn all you can.
▷ In your fifties, lead everything you can.
▷ In your sixties, leave with all the style you can.
▷ Thereafter, or in the hereafter, enjoy all you can.

That timetable brought me to my retirement at midnight on March 31, 1989, at age sixty-five.

Because I had prepared myself, professionally and personally, I was ready. A full life was behind me. But my sights were set on still more full years ahead.

There were lots of cheers. And, of course, a few tears. Both are leavening facts of life. So should they be in retirement . . . and in death.

"The gradually retiring years are among the sweetest in man's life."

SENECA
Roman philosopher and statesman

RIDING INTO THE SUNRISE

"Neuharth may now be in a position to have his caviar and eat it, too."

BUSINESS MONTH MAGAZINE
February 1989

This was no April Fool's joke. My first day of retirement. Saturday, April 1, 1989.

I started the day as I always do, with my early morning jog.

From Washington's Capital Hilton Hotel, across Lafayette park, past the White House, the Washington Monument, Vietnam War Memorial, Lincoln Memorial, across the Roosevelt Bridge, past the Iwo Jima memorial at Arlington National Cemetery.

It was the same route I had taken hundreds of times. An inspiring way to go to work. But on this morning I had no work to go to.

As I jogged past the White House, I thought of these words of President Ronald Reagan when he left the Oval Office for the last time on his retirement ten weeks earlier.

"I'm riding off into the sunset," said the fortieth president of the United States.

"I'm riding off into the sunrise," I thought to myself and smiled.

Big difference. But both to be enjoyed.

Reagan had had a lifetime of successful sunrises, including a ride to the presidency when he was sixty-nine and eight years of sunrises at the White House. At age seventy-seven, he had followed the sunset west to his home in California.

I, too, have had my share of successful sunrises. But still ready at retirement age of sixty-five for a lot more.

Later on that first retirement day, I shared a round of parties with political, media, and business biggies. They were in town for that evening's Gridiron Dinner, the annual fancy white-tie spoof of politicians by the press.

CEO John Curley and company had arranged another retirement luncheon in my honor at the Gannett Tower overlooking our nation's capital.

Vice President Dan Quayle led the tributes and toasts. My table had a mighty mix of press and politicians: TV's Walter Cronkite. *The Washington Post*'s Kay Graham. The ambassadors from the Soviet Union and from China.

After lunch I joined two hundred others at the White House to play horseshoes with President George Bush as he unveiled his new poolside pitching court.

"Al, tell me. What are you really gonna do in retirement?" the President asked solicitously.

"I'm looking forward to new adventures," I told him, avoiding detail.

That evening at the Gridiron Dinner I rubbed shoulders with Cabinet members, Supreme Court justices, business bigwigs and media stars.

The common commodity in the room: power.

When I woke up early Sunday morning, mine was gone. The power and perks—so easily accessible for years until yesterday—had passed to my successor:

▷ No more private jet.

▷ No more company limousines.

▷ No more aides checking on my every comfort.

I hailed a cab at the hotel's K Street exit to take me to National Airport. I was headed home to Pumpkin Center, to climb into my shorts and my treehouse. And to my typewriter, to tackle this book.

I was about to take my first domestic commercial airplane flight in nineteen years. As I stood in line and fiddled with my ticket in search of my boarding pass for American's Flight 987, I smiled and thought to myself, "All those S.O.B.s who said I would never retire should see me now!"

It didn't have to happen that way. I could have stopped it or delayed it. Any CEO worth his or her salt can control how and when to give up the power and the perks.

Many or most of them hang on too long, some by their fingernails. And most members of boards of directors don't have the balls to tell the boss when the time is up.

Such situations are a shame and often a tragedy. The boss's retirement affects every employee of every company, large or small. How and when retirement comes to pass is important to all.

If it's done right, at the right time and in the right way, the boss, the successor and everyone else benefits. If it comes too soon or too late or too suddenly, everyone's future and fortune can suffer.

Don't Get Sentimental

To try to guarantee that I would do it right, I began planning for my retirement as soon as I was named CEO of Gannett. At age forty-nine.

At my insistence my first employment contract as CEO included this provision: "Neuharth shall retire no later than March 31, 1989." Every contract renewal or change had that clause in it.

In insisting that we establish a career cutoff date before I was fifty, I quipped to the board, "I want the retirement thing settled before I get senile or you get sentimental." I wanted to be sure to leave with my marbles still intact.

With that out of the way, I was able to concentrate fully on my work. That made the decade between age fifty and sixty the most productive of my career and the most successful in Gannett's history.

Every CEO owes it to the company to plan and implement orderly and effective transition to the next generation of leadership.

In turn, the company owes that CEO, if he was a successful one, a financial farewell hug that guarantees a comfort level that won't suffer seriously in retirement.

Actually a CEO's obligation to company leadership should deal not just with a planned transition at retirement. The boss also should always have in the hands of the board recommendations on who should take over if he/she should get hit by a bus.

I made such recommendations once a year from the time I became CEO. Every December I met with the Management Continuity Committee of the board to evaluate the performance that year of our top executives.

I concluded each meeting by saying: "If the bus hits me in the next year, here's what I hope this committee will recommend to the board about a CEO."

I put that recommendation in writing, sealed it, told the chair of the committee to lock it up until or unless needed to share with the board.

Only the other committee members and I knew of the letter's existence and its content. Not the other board members. Not the executives involved.

Since I was able to dodge the bus, and the darts and arrows fired at me, the letters weren't needed. But every CEO owes it to the company to provide for such a contingency.

A planned transition of power is much easier than an accidental one. So simple. You test potential candidates. If they fail an important test, you scratch them. If they pass, you give them a tougher test.

Some will sense they are being tested. Some won't.

John Curley passed all the tests I gave him at Gannett. Reporter. Editor. Publisher. Pulitzer Prize-winning Washington bureau chief. Founding editor of *USA TODAY.* Regional newspaper president.

Of course he had, and still has, some flaws. He grew up in Pennsylvania and New Jersey, so he talks funny. And they didn't teach penmanship in his schools, so you can't read his handwriting. But nobody's perfect, so I overlooked that.

I went public with my plan for an orderly succession at the time of my sixtieth birthday. Curley was named president and chief operating officer.

"If he passes this test, I'll ask you to name him CEO in two or three years, and then I'll coach him as chairman during my last two or three years," I told the Management Continuity Committee members.

They agreed and liked what they heard. But they didn't believe me. Nobody did.

Wes Gallagher, the former Associated Press president, was then chairman of the committee. He told me at my retirement party, "You did exactly what you said you would do. But we didn't believe you. We knew you'd ask us to waive the age when you reached sixty-five, so you could stay on."

One Last Surprise

Would they have done so? Of course. Nearly all boards do, when the CEO or chairman asks them to. Then the S.O.B. of a CEO puts out a press release saying he is staying on at the "request of the board" to complete unfinished business. After that, he works like hell to keep the business unfinished.

I did save one surprise for the board. Never be totally predictable.

Under Gannett's bylaws, directors are elected to three-year terms. I was re-elected in 1988 to a term expiring in 1991. And Gannett bylaws then set seventy as the retirement age for directors who have served as CEO. So everyone expected me to stand for re-election in 1991 and serve until 1994.

On March 22, 1989, the day of my sixty-fifth birthday, I conducted my last board meeting as chairman in a normal and usual way. When we came to the last agenda item, "Other Business," I distributed a letter to the board members, each personalized with handwritten special thanks.

It was my letter of resignation from the board. I had discussed it with only two board members in advance—with Curley a few days before and with McCorkindale a few hours before. I pledged each to secrecy.

The letter read, in part:

> My own experiences and observations convince me that when a retired former CEO remains on the board of directors of a corporation, his/her mere presence is often an inhibiting factor. I do not wish to risk bridling either my successor or the board in any way. Therefore, this is my resignation as a Gannett director.

I moved the resolution to accept my resignation. Several directors raised their hands. Several spoke simultaneously. I cut off all discussion and called for the question, then quickly declared the motion passed and adjourned the meeting.

A shocker, they called it as they gathered around me, some of them in tears. I shed a few, too.

It shouldn't have been a surprise. It was entirely consistent with my sixteen years of planning for an orderly transition. Transition means changeover. The only way for a CEO to do that is to cut the cord completely when it's time to leave.

Most CEOs agree with that in theory. But they lose their objectivity when it comes to applying it to themselves. One savvy outside CEO with whom I discussed my plan in advance not only agreed, but applauded and explained why.

Peter B. Ueberroth, major league baseball commissioner, had become a good friend of mine. He liked what *USA TODAY* had done for baseball and sports in general. I was his guest in his commissioner's box at every World Series game for years.

His retirement date as commissioner coincided with mine as chairman—March 31, 1989. He suggested we celebrate together, in advance.

After the annual spring major league meetings in Fort Lauderdale, he and his wife Ginny came to Pumpkin Center to reminisce and talk about the future.

Over dinner and Cristal champagne on the night of March 9, 1989, at the Mango Tree restaurant in Cocoa Beach, I told him I was not only retiring as chairman but also retiring as a director of Gannett.

He reinforced my decision with this observation, "A former CEO can't win by staying on the board. If you disagree with your successor on issues, it sounds like sour grapes. If you always agree, it sounds condescending. If you stay mute, what are you doing there?"

Amen.

A Hugger and a Huggee

The CEO who loves his company enough to quit at the right time and in the right way deserves the right kind of financial farewell hug.

That may take careful planning or plotting by the CEO, too.

Directors like to look after the future care and feeding of CEOs. Trouble is, they usually reward those who fail more handsomely than those who succeed.

In the merger mania of the eighties, golden parachutes have become the in thing. Generally those call for a CEO and other executives to be paid about three times their annual cash compensation if there is a change in control of the company.

I favor rewarding CEOs in a big way for big jobs well done. I do not believe in heavy payoffs for poor performance or failure.

Parachutes are an incentive to screw up rather than succeed. CEOs who skin the sharks that are after a company usually get just a smile and a thank-you from their boards. Those who get skinned by the sharks get a contract parachute worth millions.

Examples:

When Tom Wyman was tossed out after Larry Tisch took control of CBS, Wyman got a $4.3 million payoff.

If Carl Lindner had skinned me and taken over Gannett, I would have received over $4 million, three times my then cash compensation. When I outfoxed that shark and made him swim away, my reward was a thank-you.

I had been telling Gannett's Executive Compensation Committee chairman, Julian Goodman, and his committee members for years that that was bassackwards.

My retirement gave me a chance to let the committee members practice what I had been preaching.

Over the years my salary, bonuses, and stock options added up to many millions of dollars. But I earned them. No shareholder ever raised any objection to my compensation, as Gannett moved from a $165 million regional company to a $3 billion national media leader.

I thought my performance justified a big financial farewell hug. A gift-wrapped grant of free company stock.

At Gannett, stock grants are made near year-end by the Executive Compensation Committee. In preparation for the committee's meeting at Phoenix in October 1988—five months before my scheduled retirement—I sent Chair Goodman this memo:

> You will recall my feeling is that a farewell hug to a successful CEO should be at least equal to that which a CEO who fails would receive. In my case, failure would have meant $4.5 million—three times my annual cash compensation.
>
> Because I am not good at quick math, I thought it might be helpful if I calculated in advance what the value of stock granted me now would be at various levels (Gannett stock was then trading at $35 a share.)

100,000 shares ... $3,500,000.
130,000 shares ... $4,550,000.
135,000 shares ... $4,725,000.
140,000 shares ... $4,900,000.
150,000 shares ... $5,250,000.

I hope you will consider an award with a value of no less than $4.5 million. I predict that at some time in the future you will take great pride in pointing out that under your enlightened leadership Gannett treated a successful CEO who departed voluntarily at least as well as other companies treat those who fail or are thrown out.

I was giving a multiple-choice test. Most people who face a multiple-choice test, if not sure of the answer, will take the one in the middle. By putting a $3,500,000 grant at the top and a $5,250,000 grant at the bottom, it was easy for Goodman to pick the one in the middle. He did, and the committee and the board approved it.

The 135,000 shares of stock became vested for me on my retirement date. While I held and continue to hold substantial other Gannett shares from earlier purchases or stock options, I wanted to cash this one for sentimental reasons.

I also thought it was a nice way to supplement the crummy retirement watch I expected to get. Actually Curley surprised me with a fancy customized gold watch and ring, with *USA TODAY* insignias.

By the first business day after my retirement, April 3, Gannett stock had risen to $38 a share. I cashed in my farewell hug and picked up $5,130,000.

Not bad for a South Dakota kid whose first job was picking up cow chips on the prairie.

PLAIN TALK:

While you are at the pinnacle of success on the playing field, prepare yourself for the sidelines.

WHEN THEY CALL
YOU THAT, SMILE

You, too, can find happiness as an S.O.B.

And success.

Then you, too, can smile, or have the last laugh, when they call you an S.O.B.

But first you must really prepare yourself for this kind of journey through life. The footsteps you wish to take. The footprints you hope to leave.

Getting ready for this trip is the key to its success—and half the fun of it all.

▷ You must draft your own definition of an S.O.B.

▷ You must define your own dimensions of success.

▷ You must dream your own special dreams.

▷ You must decide to do whatever it takes to make your dreams come true.

Each of us can determine which footsteps we take and what kind of footprints we shall leave.

Henry Wadsworth Longfellow said it in "A Psalm of Life":

> Lives of great men all remind us.
> We can make our lives sublime.
> And, departing leave behind us
> Footprints on the sands of time.

Some favor following in the footsteps of others.

I prefer plowing my own path.

Whether we choose the less-traveled byways or the more crowded highways, every step we take helps shape the footprints we leave behind.

The shape of those footprints will not change. They are in the sands of time to stay—for better or worse.

Others will ultimately measure our footprints. Others can better judge the value of our journey through life than we can.

But we all can always shape our footprints of the future, even—or especially—in retirement.

I step into the sunrise of retirement with all the confidence and comfort of the past. With nothing left to chance, as in the past.

My retirement reach calls for me to work a little less, play a little more, and enjoy it all even more.

All work and no play makes Jack a dull boy. All play and no work makes a bored and boring retiree.

My retirement footsteps into the future are taking this shape:

▷ Doling out money, lots of it, to causes that can make a difference.

▷ Dispensing my style of wit and wisdom to any who will read or listen.

▷ Planning or plotting adventures that might lead to new fame or fortune or farce for me and those who follow me.

As chairman of the Gannett Foundation, I'll help coordinate grants of more than $25 million annually. They go to worthwhile educational, charitable, and other nonprofit organizations across the USA.

If you think you have a cause that qualifies, send me a love letter:

Chairman Al Neuharth
Gannett Foundation
1101 Wilson Boulevard
Arlington, VA 22209

If your cause is worthwhile, I shall see that it is carefully considered.

But con artists, beware. If you try to snooker me, you may end up as one of the S.O.B.s in my next book. Remember, it takes one to know one.

Giving away money is the flip side of me.

My goals as Gannett CEO were to work hard and full-time to build the USA's biggest newspaper company, give the nation its own newspaper, and make a lot of money for my company and myself.

But prosperity without purpose and principle means nothing. Throughout my career, my primary purpose has been to build better newspapers for readers and to open doors of opportunity for others.

Now my goal as Gannett Foundation chairman is to become the USA's champion giveaway artist. I plan to work hard, but part-time, to find out if it really is better to give than to receive.

Treehouse Journalism

When I'm not in the Gannett Foundation offices overlooking Washington, I'll spend a lot of time at my trusty 1926 Royal typewriter in my treehouse at Pumpkin Center in Florida. Or lugging an old portable across the USA or around the world on assignment.

As a journalist, I'm lucky. As long as my mind and my fingers work, I can keep pounding out prose. And I have a former reporter's dream job: I can make my own assignments and then go cover them.

My weekly column called "Plain Talk" will appear in *USA TODAY* and other Gannett newspapers. Combined, they have more than 22 million readers. But I'll write in plain old one-to-one style.

With any kind of encouragement, I might even write another book. Encouragement for me can come only from you, the readers. I only write for readers, á la *USA TODAY.* I don't write for publishers or editors or critics.

Finally, to all of you who stayed with me to the very last page of these confessions: I thank you. I admire you. I invite you into my S.O.B. club. Here are your keys:

PLAIN TALK:

An S.O.B.'s Ten Secrets To Success

▷ Expect others to do unto you what you would do unto them.

▷ Somebody wants something you have. Protect it.

▷ Somebody has something you want. Go for it.

▷ Be as nice as possible, only as nasty as necessary.

▷ Treasure your family and your roots but never turn back.

▷ Explore the byways as well as the highways of life.

▷ Think Big. Big dreams. Big risks. Big rewards.

▷ Scramble to the top and don't tiptoe while you're there.

▷ Bow out while all your marbles are still intact.

▷ Life's a game. Play it to win. And to enjoy.

ACKNOWLEDGEMENTS OF AN S.O.B.

Not even a self-confessed S.O.B. can write a book without help.

In my case I had a lot. Coworkers, family, friends—even a few foes—cooperated to make it possible to prepare and publish these confessions.

They are very special and salutory S.O.B.s and I thank them all sincerely. Some merit special mention.

My three closest colleagues during most of my quarter century at Gannett:

▷ John J. Curley, who succeeded me as CEO.
▷ Douglas H. McCorkindale, chief financial officer.
▷ John C. Quinn, chief news executive.

Curley and Quinn are my kind of S.O.B.s They offered suggestions and support. But they were never subservient, even when I sometimes thought they should have been.

McCorkindale is not my kind of S.O.B. But he is the best of his kind. He was a willing and valuable source on many of the business details.

Three former special assistants of mine helped with the reporting and organization of the book:

▷ Charles Overby, now senior vice president of the Gannett Foundation.
▷ Ken Paulson, editor of *FLORIDA TODAY*.
▷ Peter Prichard, editor of *USA TODAY*.

Each had worked closely with me during the dawn of their Gannett careers. They provided invaluable recollections during the dusk of mine.

Gannett has its own book publishing division, called New Media. Key players:

▷ Nancy Woodhull, president.

▷ Phil Pruitt, reporter and editor.

Their patience, persistence, and pressures helped transform me from a corporate CEO to an aspiring author.

A zealous aide and arranger for me at Gannett was:

▷ Chris Wells, special assistant.

She did most of the fact-checking and fixing in this book, as she had done for me around the world.

Most grown-up authors now compose their prose on computers. I haven't learned that yet. Every word in this book, except for the family chapters, went through my 1926 Royal typewriter. Misspelled words and crossovers were made readable by these secretaries supreme:

▷ Juanie Phinney Fuqua

▷ Suzette Karelis

▷ Marilyn Powell

Books are born in a variety of ways. These confessions were conceived when three top dogs from Doubleday came to court me:

▷ Alberto Vitale, president and CEO of the Bantam Doubleday Dell Publishing Group.

▷ Nancy Evans, president and publisher of Doubleday.

▷ Harriet Rubin, executive editor.

They were looking for something different for Doubleday to do. And they convinced me that *CONFESSIONS OF AN S.O.B.* could make a difference—for Doubleday, for me, and hopefully for you. All three are professional S.O.B.s whose help doubled my delight in delivering this to you.

Family made this more than a single-minded, introspective autobiography:

▷ Walter Neuharth, my brother.

He helped immeasurably with his research about our family roots and recollections of the early days in South Dakota.

For me, the most meaningful personal messages about the ruthless realities of life came from:

▷ First wife, Loretta Neuharth.

▷ Second wife, Lori Wilson.

▷ Son Dan.

▷ Daughter Jan.

Their revealing recitals of our family pleasures and problems made some of this book even more interesting for me to read than it was to write. I love them and thank them.

Finally, a salute to these S.O.B.s everywhere:

▷ All those borderline and bad S.O.B.s who tried to make my life miserable. You failed. You and I know who you are. Thanks for adding spice to my life.

▷ All those lovable S.O.B.s who helped make my life such a joy to live—and write about. You succeeded. You are too numerous to mention, but you shall always be in my memories.

—Al Neuharth

INDEX